What It Is Like to Die and What Comes After

Kay Mielenz

CONTENTS

—

ABOUT THE AUTHOR

Kay is an inquisitive person, open-minded, and questioning by nature. She wants to know how things work and what goes on behind the scenes, which we cannot access. She was four years old when her Uncle Johnny, a police officer, was shot and killed while on duty. Kay watched as her mother especially, but her father as well, cried and mourned the loss of Johnny, a dearly loved and wonderfully compassionate human being. Their family's loss left a strong imprint upon her.

For years as Kay was growing up, as the eldest in a family with six children, she watched over the younger children. Then when she turned sixteen, her parents gave her the responsibility of taking care of the younger children if something should happen to both of them. They instructed her to keep the family together, an obligation, which she took very seriously.

Kay graduated from the University of Colorado and enjoyed careers in computer programming, real estate sales, and as a financial consultant. She was living life as usual when her mother passed and then communicated with Kay from the afterlife the evening of the day that she died. That communication opened a door of receptivity within Kay, enabling her to hear and interact with people who are deceased. She utilizes this gift to assist deceased people who passed from their physical body unable to perceive their best way forward.

Kay's other works include *God Talks to All of Us,* a direct communication from divinity for all of humanity. In this book, God utilized Kay's ability to receive interdimensional communication to educate us in His own words. Creator God explains why you are alive on Earth and leads you to recognize the importance of every person, without exception. He teaches that which is difficult to discern for oneself. His book empowers you to work towards the betterment of yourself, your children, and Planet Earth.

God Talks to All of Us, Thoughts to Keep in Mind is a pocket-sized companion to *God Talks to All of Us*. This second book shines a spotlight on beneficial traits and qualities to expand within ourselves. *Thoughts to Keep in Mind* also provides readers an easy way to reconnect with God's presence on a daily basis.

INTRODUCTION

—————

What It Is Like to Die and What Comes After answers many questions regarding what occurs after a person dies. These answers are not opinions of religious authorities, nor are they conjecture. I became educated as I reached out to support the elevation of newly deceased people after they passed from their physical body. When my mother passed, I reached a turning point in my life. As I was preparing to fly to Denver to attend her funeral, she spoke to me from the afterlife.

This initial contact with my deceased mother thinned the veil within me that separates our physical world from the higher levels of existence. After our first interaction, my mother repeatedly returned to converse with me from the afterlife. During our conversations, she emphasized how happy she was. I could not see her, but I felt her presence and heard her as clearly as if we were physically in the same room. During our exchanges, she told me that our deceased relatives had been visiting her.

Not long after my mother died, a friend of mine passed from her body. I telepathically called to the angelic kingdom to assist her. I trusted that angels heard my request and let it go at that. I did not expect to receive a personal angelic contact confirming that my friend was enjoying herself within the heavens.

For me, the natural next step was to send my angelic partners a telepathic message whenever I heard of a newly deceased person. I ask angels to check on that person and be sure that he or she navigated to their best destination. The angels respond to my requests and assist those who need their support. As time went by, some of the people who received our help returned to converse with me. Those conversations, which are especially insightful, appear in the later chapters.

As I read newspapers, I come face to face with stories of tragic occurrences, which take people's lives. Newspapers report the names of the deceased, which I have chosen not to do. I altered the names of the people in this book, except for my relatives.

CHAPTER ONE

WHAT HAPPENS AFTER DYING

After a person shrugs off their physical body, that person continues to exist in what you might identify as their blueprint. Each person has a spirit body, which acts as a blueprint for their physical body. When the physical body dies, the being-ness of that person continues to exist within their spirit body. One's spirit body feels like one's physical body, but spirit bodies do not have solidity. Solidity only exists within the third dimension. We live our physical lives without realizing that we do not require physicality to continue our experience.

There are different levels of experience, and they overlap. It is similar to being asleep and being awake. When you are sleeping, you are unaware of what the world around you is doing. All you know is your personal experience of being asleep and disconnected from physical life activities. Then when you awaken, your consciousness returns to physical awareness and activity.

After a person completes their physical life, they surrender their physical body but not their memories or ability to think, reason, and navigate. Although they have separated from the physical world, their ability to experience continues. Problems arise when deceased people do not understand the mechanics of successfully transitioning from physicality to a very appealing afterlife.

People regularly think about heaven or hell; after dying, you go up, or you go down. However, it is more accurate to think in terms of you go up, or you stay stuck. You remain affixed between dimensions in a lost and confused state when you have not adequately prepared for the loss of your physical form.

To us, it seems that what we are experiencing during this lifetime is all there is. However, after we die, we realize that we have lived an endless progression of lifetimes and have experienced being both male and female. I have an unusual ability to see, with an inner vision, what happened to me in other lifetimes, and recognize individual people from other lifetimes when our paths cross in the here and now.

One Saturday afternoon, I attended a presentation at a metaphysical center close to where I lived in Sugar Land, Texas. Only a small group of us had come for the talk. Two very tall men were the guests, but only one of them delivered the lecture. The man who was not speaking stood nearby off to the side, and as I looked at him, I saw, transposed over his physical appearance, a black robe and a bishop's hat. My gaze was transfixed. I could not stop staring at this anomaly.

After a while of concentrating on him, I knew without a doubt who he was. He was the bishop in Hawaii when Father Damien ministered to the lepers on Molokai Island in the late 1800s. During that time, authorities took those suffering from leprosy from their homes and isolated them on Molokai to prevent the spread of the dreaded disease for which there was no cure. Officials also took children with leprosy to Molokai, separating them from their families.

The lepers needed food, medical care, and housing but mostly had to fend for themselves. Father Damien volunteered to go to Molokai to care for the lepers. He organized the community helping them to build shelters, grow food and teach the children. The bishop of Hawaii provided very little financial support to Father Damien's colony, so Father Damien, who was from Belgium, wrote to supporters in Europe requesting aid for the lepers.

Father Damien raised a significant amount of money, but very little went to its proper destination. The bishop of Hawaii kept most of the donations, passing on only a fraction of the financial support to sustain the leper colony. There was no doubt in my mind that I was looking at the same man who was the bishop back then. He was the person who took the money donated to aid the leper colony. He was not consciously aware of what his past included.

Each lifetime gives us a fresh start, a new beginning. Without the burden of carrying our past-life failings, we are free to shine brighter than we did before. Our cycle of births, deaths, and rebirths is designed to educate us as we go along, testing ourselves under varying circumstances. The concept of one life to live and then existence ends is an assumption passed along, as if it were fact, by numerous, but not all, spiritual practices.

For the most part, most of us hold as truth that which we learned in childhood. It is common for families to pass down mistaken behaviors and attitudes, along with others that are rational and upstanding, from generation to generation. Almost every person carries a mix of positive and negative family influences, which affect their thinking, attitudes, and perceptions.

In the western world, most people believe that each person has only one life to live. This common belief does not enjoy universal acceptance. Ask yourself a question. Ask yourself how willing you are to uncover evidence that reincarnation is a fact of life and that we all keep coming back to challenge ourselves to evolve to a more advanced level of performance.

As we live our lives, dying is not uppermost in our minds unless we experience a severe health crisis. Anything unexpected that comes up and threatens our confidence that our body will keep functioning poses a tremendous challenge. No one would choose to become weakened, sick, or debilitated, and when those trials arise, we become more pensive about what will happen to us after we die. Whatever your convictions are regarding the potential for a continuation of existence after passing from your physical state, do not assume that your beliefs represent the actual reality.

Each of us can argue our personal theories with one another. However, in this book, you will receive word-for-word accounts from people who are no longer alive in physical form, communicating their personal stories of what happened to them when they crossed the barrier between life and death. Obviously, they are still in existence, or they would not have the ability to communicate.

This book does not preach religious perspectives. It merely reports what happened to a large cross-section of people when they passed from their physical bodies. The delicious part of reading these personal accounts is the crazy situations that develop when newly deceased people become shocked and confused when finding themselves still conscious instead of having their lights turned off.

Most people die with strong convictions about what occurs after passing from the body they identified as themselves. However, some of these people refuse to believe that they are deceased because they still have consciousness. In this confused conscious state, their problems compound. They do not know where they are or what to do next.

You may wonder how religious convictions affect what happens to you after you die. People typically embrace the religious philosophy that their parents espoused. Doing this is like going to a restaurant, and when the server asks what you would like to eat, you reply that you will eat whatever your parents used to eat when they came to this restaurant. Few people investigate spiritual paths other than the one they learned in childhood. In addition, many people are not entirely comfortable with their religion's teachings since some of the teachings seem irrational.

One Sunday, when I was in college, I went to our family church with our sweet, precious mother. As we walked out of the church at the end of the service, I was fuming. Much of what the clergyman said from the pulpit did not sound rational, kind-hearted, or beneficially instructive. My mother, on the other hand, was in a joyful, uplifted state as she said to me, "Wasn't that a wonderful service?" When I asked her how she could say that after what the cleric had said, she sweetly replied, "Oh, Kay, I don't pay any attention to the bad parts. I only pay attention to the good parts." That was our mother's way of keeping herself comfortable within the family's spiritual practice.

Many people feel that practicing a religion is an essential and meaningful part of their lives. Some practice their religion as an insurance policy to guarantee that they will ascend into the heavens after dying. When we arrive in the higher dimensions after passing from our bodies, we do not go through an organizational process that separates people according to their religion, a separate place for those of each faith, and another place for people who did not practice a religion. Within the higher dimensions, everyone mingles together.

It seems that this life, which we are experiencing here on Earth, is all that there is for us. However, after we die, we realize that we have lived an endless progression of lifetimes and have experienced being both male and female. During one of my instances of a past life recall, I experienced myself having my head chopped off by the guillotine in France. Now that was a bizarre experience! I felt like my psyche was smeared over time after I re-experienced that happening to me. I have since met three other people who were with me during that lifetime and had collaborating memories.

It takes courage and open-mindedness to delve into the realm of the metaphysical. Most of the time, we focus on what we are physically experiencing right now, and this is the simplest way to live, but it does not give us a complete and accurate picture of our entirety. All of us are much more than we appear to be. We have been here on Earth before, physically alive and functioning, each time in a completely different set of circumstances. Passing the test of how to become a first-class human being requires that we experience all sides of life, and none of us receives a free pass to the highly advanced levels of existence until we prove ourselves as outstanding men and women here on Earth.

Being open-minded regarding spiritual practices can lead to some surprising discoveries as it did with me. When I was in my late thirties, as I was browsing in a bookstore, a particular book caught my eye. I had never seen this book before and knew nothing about the spiritual practices common in India. On the cover was a picture of Paramahansa Yogananda, a holy man of India, who came to the United States to bring Eastern spirituality to the Western world. Oh, how I loved reading that book. The mysticism of India has a special appeal to me, perhaps because it teaches how to create a direct personal relationship with God.

For years, I read and reread *Autobiography of a Yogi*. Every time I finished reading it, I would go from the last page to the first page and read it again. I always cherished reading about the lives of the saints of Christianity. Until I read *Autobiography of a Yogi*, I did not realize that other religions also had saints. I learned that no one religion or spiritual perspective is the one and only right one.

I like to compare religions to ethnic foods. Our family's ethnicity usually determines the food we ate as a child. For example, our mother was of Italian descent, so as children we enjoyed spaghetti and meatballs, lasagna, ravioli, and other Italian foods. Had our mother been Asian instead of Italian, we would most likely have developed a preference for Asian food.

Broadly, our thinking and our choices as adults are a result of what we experienced as children. We tend to use what we learned in childhood to build a framework to construct our adult lives. Most of us do not come to a turning point where we say, "Now I am going to start a new process and construct my world views based on my personal investigation." Generally, we cling to what we learned as children because it reinforces our current comfort level and does not invite criticism from our families. Yet, open-mindedness brings an opportunity to expand our experience of life, which can be particularly satisfying.

Now that I am in my later years, I realize that my life has been a grand internal adventure. I have not been a mountain climber or a skydiver, yet I have plumbed the depths of my inner self as I began to receive communications from divine beings. You know how it is when you listen to the radio. The first step is to turn the radio on. You will never hear anything from that radio until you turn it on. If you do not know that radio is there within you and you ignore it, there is not much chance it will turn on by itself.

By setting your attention on establishing receptivity to divine communications and then continuing to listen until a breakthrough occurs, you point yourself in the right direction. Your intention is of uppermost importance when you set out to develop interactive connectivity with divine beings. In addition to developing your listening skills, be sure not to give up praying and reaching out to God, saints, and angels. To build inner connectivity with divine beings requires great determination to stay the course until you experience detectable results. Most likely, this will take years of dedicated effort.

With every step you take in your journey of inner spiritual development, blessed divine beings that you draw to yourself by reaching out to them will support you. When you are ready, the breakthrough will occur. You do not have to join an organized religion. Many organized religions have irrational teachings, which are hard for many people to swallow. Some teachings seem to exist to perpetuate the existence of the organization. Whatever your convictions are about religion, you do not have to have that insurance policy to have a glorious after-death experience.

Everyone who passes from their body in a calm, relaxed state makes themselves ready for good things to happen. We do not go into a state of non-existence after we die, and as Franklin D. Roosevelt once said, "There is nothing to fear but fear itself." Remaining calm and rational as we gently release from our connection with physicality is beneficial to practice ahead of time. By familiarizing yourself with the various challenges that deceased people encounter, you will learn how to avoid an after-death reaction that hobbles your forward progress.

Specific causes of death are more likely to hinder a deceased person's smooth transition into the afterlife. Being murdered is one of them, as is sudden accidental death. Accidental deaths are not uncommon, and unfortunately, neither are murders. Not many of us put ourselves through a rehearsal of what we would do if suddenly thrust out of our physical body, still having our wits about us but not automatically transferring anywhere else. Unfortunately, sudden accidental death will happen to a large number of people. If we are wise, we will acknowledge that this may occur to us.

Suddenly thrust out of your physical body, but still being able to navigate in what seems like a shadow world to the physical world from which you were severed, is a nightmare come true. You can try to communicate with people who are dear to you, but you are no longer a part of the physical world. You will see your family and friends mourning your death, and you will have no way to communicate to them that you are still alive.

We can make better use of funerals than mourning the loss of the loved one. Most likely, the deceased person is there enjoying the show. If you think that your attendance at a funeral service does not matter because the person you care about is dead, I advise you to reconsider.

I attended the funeral service for a young man named John. I knew that John suffered from a mental illness, but the illness was not apparent to me. Every time I saw John, he smiled and gave me a warm greeting. The news that John committed suicide hit me hard. I did not know much about his family at that point but later learned that John had two sisters who suffered from mental deficiencies.

As I sat among the group of people who gathered waiting for the service to begin, I debated in my mind whether to walk up to the open casket to view John's body. I kept telling myself, "What is the point. John is not in that deceased body." After a few minutes of my inner debate, something within me compelled me to approach John's casket. As soon as my gaze turned to John's face, I distinctly heard John's voice say, "That's not really me, you know." Telepathically, I responded, "Yes, John. I know."

I took my seat as the service was about to begin. Never in all of the funerals I have attended was the music such an exceptional combination of carefully chosen songs that were particularly appealing. The song that stands out the most in my mind is the song *Something Wonderful* from *The King and I*. The words seemed to describe John to a tee. John was gleeful during his funeral service. I kept hearing him say how much fun he was having.

After returning home from John's funeral, I sat down and contacted the angels that I was working with at that time. I wanted their assurance that John had successfully navigated himself into the higher dimensions and had not become an Earth-bound soul. The term Earth-bound soul refers to a deceased person who has been unable to transfer to the elevated levels of existence after passing from his or her body. When this happens, the person remains trapped in a sort of no man's land, a layer of existence just outside visible physicality in a non-detectable state, usually unable to be seen, heard, or felt within the physical world.

I did not receive a verbal response, but instead, I was shown the answer, which was a surprise. I am used to my interdimensional communications, more often being verbal rather than visual. With my inner vision, I beheld John elegantly dressed in a black tuxedo holding in his arms a radiantly beautiful young woman. She, wearing a light blue ball gown, clung to him as their eyes interlocked. Their deep love for each other was palpable. Then after a while, they began to dance, and they danced, and they danced, and they danced, clinging to each other through time and space. It was clear that I witnessed a reunion of two people who had loved each other dearly throughout time. My heart swelled with joy for John.

My first impulse was to call John's mother to share this vision with her. I wanted to comfort her and allay any fears she may have had about what happened to John after he died. After careful consideration, I decided not to make that phone call. I did not want to stir ill feelings within her if she had a rigid belief system that could not conceive of such an occurrence having validity. It was with a heavy heart that I kept this vision to myself until now.

My interactions with deceased people have given me a broad understanding of the mystery about what happens to us when our physical bodies no longer function. We associate our identity with our physical body. Many of us think that our body is who we are. The reality is that the life essence within our body is what we are. If a truck runs us over and we find our self detached from our physical body, we will still know who we are, and be able to think, reason, and feel emotions with the same capacity that we had before the truck took our physical life.

Only knowing what happens in the physical world is an enormous detriment. You cannot solve a problem unless you have all the pertinent information. How we live our lives, what we choose to do, and what we value are of utmost importance to us after we pass from our bodies.

While we are alive, we are shortsighted. Each of us lives lifetime after lifetime, unaware that we are here to improve ourselves over our last life performance. Many of us judge our success in life by our worldly achievements and pat ourselves on the back for the number of possessions we manage to amass. There is an old saying, "You can't take it with you." This saying applies only to worldly possessions. You do take all of your good character traits with you.

A record is kept of every effort you made to extend yourself to uplift and support those in need, as is every time you put your foot out to trip another person. When one freely gives genuine love, empathy, and support, they earn an A+ on their report card. When you hold back from sharing, preferring to hoard and build a monument to your personal greatness, watch out. It may not come during this lifetime, but in another, you will experience the other side of the coin to teach yourself empathy.

I suggest that all of us have a long way to go to reach our ultimate goal of perfecting ourselves while living here on Earth. While we are here, we are planting the seeds for our next life experience when we return to physical form under different circumstances. Those who excel and reach the epitome of character development while alive on Earth do not have to return. They are the lucky ones. They will have great freedom to explore other universes that are more evolved than ours are. What you see in front of you is not all there is.

Creation is more vast than our human perceptions can ascertain or prove. We exist at a low vibrational level, which prevents us from detecting that which exists in the higher vibrational levels. Physical form is dense. We love our physicality. We like how it feels to hold hands with another person, climb a physical tree, and live in a physical house.

Within the higher planes of existence, solidity does not exist, and people do not miss it. They can get anywhere they want to go by thinking of their intention. There are no cars or buses. There is vastness beyond what we can comprehend. Other worlds to explore are available to those who qualify. Mostly, but not entirely, troublemakers are confined to Earth.

Earth is the training ground. People on Earth are learning to refine their behavior from primitive levels of only seeking their own well-being to becoming love-based. Unfortunately, we cannot turn on a switch within ourselves to make us love-based. We only learn bit by bit, slowly improving over time. This slow process is why we live lifetime after lifetime. A way to describe being love-based is to come from a center of genuinely caring for and accepting all people at all times under all circumstances.

If you are curious and want to know more about the mystery of the ages, what it is like to die and pass from your body, and what happens next, this is your resource. I offer this book for informational purposes only. I am not trying to sway your opinion in any particular way. My intention is only to spread the enlightenment that I received to prevent the needless fear of dying and the confusion that can arise after death when a person does not know how to navigate to the higher levels of existence, the place where everyone ultimately goes.

CHAPTER TWO

MY PATH

—

My unusual path lighted up before me when family dynamics introduced a conundrum. At the age of fifteen, our son Mark began to exhibit mental instability. In a matter of a few months, Mark's world changed from attending the local high school, playing sports, and holding down an after-school job to withdrawing into a fearful state in which he lost his self-confidence. His behavior became irregular, and he could no longer tolerate the pressure of attending high school. He was afraid to eat lunch with the other children, calling me on the phone every day at lunchtime instead of going to the cafeteria with the rest of the students.

These were only some of the warning signs that there was trouble ahead. Ultimately, the doctors diagnosed Mark as having schizophrenia. People who have schizophrenia are unable to stay grounded in the physical world. They are open to intrusions from other dimensions, and as we discovered, there are mischief-makers in different dimensions who enjoy making their presence felt within the physical world.

Some Earth-bound souls entangle themselves within the physical world. These mischief-makers are deceased people who remain near the Earth, attempting to make their presence discerned by people alive on Earth. These unfortunate deceased people passed from their physical form retaining full consciousness without having the wherewithal to ascend into the higher dimensions of existence. Because of Mark's struggle with mental illness, I became educated about the intersection between the physical world and that, which lies beyond physical perception.

By the time Mark was seventeen years old, he had been released from the hospital and was living at home. One day Mark sashayed into the living room, swinging his hips from side to side with a panicked look on his face. With an anxious voice, He said, "Mom, I feel like a girl." I had read that the spirits of deceased people on occasion enter the energy field of a person who is alive and exert some control over them. Fortunately, I also learned that certain therapists knew how to extract these intruders from the person who was their target.

I knew of a highly respected metaphysical church in our area, and my mind went straight to calling the church to ask for guidance with Mark's situation. Surprisingly, the minister did not hang up on me when I asked if she knew of a therapist who could remove the spirit of a deceased person from my son. Much to my relief, the minister gave me the name and phone number of a particular therapist who successfully resolved such situations. Hoping for the best, I made an appointment and took Mark to meet with her.

The session lasted about one hour. When Mark emerged from the therapist's office, he was back to his old self. He was relaxed, and there were no signs of femininity in his movements or gestures. Frankly, I was as shocked as I was delighted that we had determined the cause of Mark's sudden feminine mannerisms and the problem was solved. I was ready to move on to other things, grateful that this episode was behind us.

However, instead of being the end, this was the beginning of what would turn out to be my life's work. As I paid the therapist her fee, I thought to myself, "If this keeps happening, I am going to have to learn to remove those discarnate entities myself." At that point, my only concern was for my son to remain free from having the spirit of a deceased person attached within his physical body.

Not long after this episode, I wandered into a metaphysical bookstore, a completely new experience. As I was browsing through their selection of books, my eyes zeroed in on one book in particular. It jumped out at me. The name of that book is *Prisoners on Earth: Psychic Possession* and *Its Release* by Aloa Starr. In this book, Aloa Starr details the work of a group of older women who met weekly to assist people who were experiencing different forms of psychic interference.

I began reading, and I was intrigued, having no idea if this book was on the up and up. As I read Aloa Starr's description of the techniques they used, I followed her instructions, which with some practice, I was able to duplicate with positive results. At this point, I focused on helping Mark with the disturbances he had been experiencing with no intention of branching out to aid other people.

For years, I sat and meditated every morning and then applied Aloa Starr's methods to clearing Mark of discarnate entities. Clearing Mark became my morning routine. Even when Mark was no longer living at home with us, I continued and then branched out to applying Aloa Starr's methods to aid the other mentally ill people in the string of care homes where Mark lived. I discovered that people who experience mental illness are often susceptible to manipulations by ill-intentioned deceased people who wander around close to the Earth attempting to exert control, usually of a negative sort, upon a mentally ill person.

You would not want to know all the details of the psychic interference that Mark and other susceptible people deal with, sometimes on a day-to-day basis. His natural, pleasant demeanor falls away as he struggles to shrug off the spirits of deceased people who occupy his physical body in an attempt to experience physicality again. I share this private information to inform people of the complexity of what can occur after a person dies.

One of the most dangerous situations you can find yourself in is passing from your physical body without a clear understanding of what comes next. Whether you have been a good person or a disappointing person, you can elevate yourself to a positive placement level in the afterlife. However, this does not mean that all people advance to the same level of the afterlife. Those who acted without morals and ethics when they were alive on Earth are restricted to Re-education centers in the lower area of the heavens, where they will learn to come up to speed with being a decent person.

My objective in writing this book is to prepare you for any eventuality you may encounter after passing from your physical body, whether you are on the younger side of life or advancing into old age. Being unprepared, as many people are, invites after-death confusion, which is precisely what you need to avoid. When you know what to expect and have mapped out a plan for yourself before it is time for you to exit from your body, you give yourself absolute control over your afterlife situation. You can assure your immediate transfer to your most desirable destination.

To be completely prepared for what can happen after dying, one needs to know what happened to people who died under various circumstances and learn what worked and what did not work for them as they passed from their physical bodies. Picture yourself slipping out of your physical body, feeling no different from when you were still in your physical body but without aches or pains. Your body feels terrific, good as new, but you are no longer in your physical body, so no one alive can see or hear you.

You can go wherever you want to go just by thinking about where you want to be. If you think about your family, you will find yourself right there among them as they mourn your death, but you will not have the capacity to communicate with them. Other deceased people will hear you, but people still alive in the physical world will have no indication that you are with them in your spirit form. This situation is very disheartening for the unprepared newly deceased who pass from their physical body, not understanding their best next step.

As an interdimensional communicator, I go beyond the restrictions of the Earth's environment as I coordinate with helpers on the other side of life to ensure that people who lose their spot in the physical world go on to a better place to be. It would take someone like me, someone grounded in the physical world and in the world of the afterlife, to communicate with deceased people. The conversations that I present in this book are exactly what each deceased person said when we communicated. I learned what happens after we die from deceased people themselves.

Every person's after-death experience has something to offer each of us who wants to have a clear picture of what to expect after separating from our physical body. By reading these conversations with deceased people, one thing becomes certain. We are not our bodies. We occupy our body while we are alive, but we pass from our body with our consciousness intact when we can no longer sustain physical existence. Ultimately, we return, coming back repeatedly, living lifetime after lifetime until we reach a state of perfected self-expression.

I did not look into a crystal ball to come up with these assertions. As I traveled my son Mark's path alongside him, another world opened up to me. It is the world of what happens after we die.

Since the onset of his schizophrenia, Mark and I have teamed together, two partners with different roles to play. Mark's role has been to attract discarnate entities into his physical body's energy field, which he does naturally. He senses and often sees the deceased people in their spirit forms. He is open about his intention to help them. The external signs of entities occupying Mark's energy field are apparent. He goes from being calm, relaxed, and agreeable to being hard to deal with and stressed. When discarnate entities occupy a living person's energy field, the hostile intrusion disturbs that person's typical self-expression.

Some deceased people wandering in their spirit forms deliberately interfere with people who are still living. This activity is invisible to those of us in the physical world, and some of you may doubt that what I am describing is possible. Had I not read Aloa Starr's book, I would never have been able to understand what was happening to Mark. Armed with that book and Aloa Starr's techniques, I set out to protect Mark from interference by deceased people who attempt to use him as a target for their harassment.

Protecting Mark has become a lifetime commitment for me. Through my partnership with certain angelic beings, we extract the troublemakers from Mark's energy field, and then angels deliver those deceased people to their proper destination within the heavens. I am convinced that Mark and I came into this incarnation for the dual purpose of assisting lost souls and informing others about the afterlife progression that awaits all of us.

The more thoroughly you understand what will happen after you die, the more prepared you will be when it is your time to transfer from Earth's atmosphere into another type of existence. It benefits every person to know what to expect after his or her death occurs. We all go back into the elevated dimensions where we will receive a gracious reception regardless of our performance while we were alive on Earth. This inclusivity may be hard to believe for those of us who accept the premise of heaven, hell, and purgatory. Many common spiritual teachings conflict with the information that I received from those who contacted me from the afterlife to tell me what it is like where they are now.

Reading about various situations that deceased people encountered is highly entertaining and is the best way to prepare yourself for your separation from physicality. The time to prepare yourself is now. News reports are full of harrowing stories of people losing their lives unexpectedly. None of us should assume that we would leave this Earth only after living life to its fullest and growing old. Familiarizing yourself with the pitfalls that commonly occur when people die unexpectedly is bound to be especially advantageous for those of us destined to separate from our physical body prematurely. Sometimes death bangs at the front door, and we know we are leaving. Other times, death sneaks in the back door, and we do not see it coming.

I recommend that you read this book more than one time. One pass through the contents is not enough to ensure that you will be able to reign in instinctive actions contrary to your well-being, especially if your death comes about because of frightening circumstances. Knowing how our lives will end is a big question with which we all live. We may live to be an old-timer or run into a dangerous situation and be dead tomorrow. Eventually, we will all transition out of our physical form. Then what? Experience does not end when our physical bodies can no longer sustain activity within the physical world.

Keep your mind open to learning from the experiences of others. Who wants to fall into the same ditch that other people have fallen into when you can hop right over it? Would you rather know what to expect after you pass from your physical body than take a chance that everything will work out all right without any form of preparation? Suppose you pull the wool over your eyes by not being realistic about the potential of running into occurrences such as a sudden fatal traffic accident. Anyone who dies suddenly is at risk of experiencing afterlife disorientation due to the unanticipated separation from their physical body.

I received an education about the activity that goes on beyond the boundaries of physicality. We assume that what we see, hear and feel defines existence, but that is not the whole story. That is only the physical side of life and not the entirety of one's personal experience. You will receive an expanded view of creation by studying, not just reading, but also processing the information passed on by people, who are now deceased to the physical world, but who are very much alive and active within the higher dimensions of existence.

When I was in my forties, I yearned for clarity regarding the reason for our being alive. To me, this was a puzzle, which I could not solve. I still would not have the answer to this question if my mother had not communicated with me from the afterlife the same day that she died. Her consoling words spoke of how happy she was to return to the heavens. That conversation with my deceased mother opened a door within me. From that time on, I have had the capability of communicating with disembodied people.

CHAPTER THREE
VIBRATIONS

—⁓

When I began communicating with deceased people, they told me their intriguing stories. Angels brought a deceased man named Peter to me, but it was hard to convince him that he deserved to go to heaven. Peter seemed like a gentle soul, but he could not forgive himself for something he had done to his brother when he was physically alive. Peter was too ashamed to tell me what he did. He would only say that it happened a long time ago.

Peter was a person who did not make a smooth after-life transfer to his best destination because he would not forgive himself. When I first approached him, he adamantly declined to consider moving on to a higher level of existence. It only was after he reversed course and agreed to try to forgive himself that the sweet consoling angels who were surrounding him became apparent within his perception. He could not have been more surprised that they were willing to take him with them.

Peter was not the only one. Another person who judged herself harshly was a woman who was secretly married to another man before her enduring marriage to her second husband. She kept her guilty secret for the rest of her life. After she died, angels came to take her with them, but initially, she turned them away because she assumed that her transgression disqualified her from receiving their assistance. Both Peter and this woman made their after-death existence a punishment for themselves.

When we are overly tough on ourselves, our thinking distorts, and we do not like ourselves very much. Some of us have this self-defeating tendency in spades, which is a sure ticket to losing one's accurate self-perception. Honest self-evaluation accompanied by compassionate self-forgiveness clears the road ahead, helping us reach a state of tranquility. When we are tranquil and make it a point to be positive and upbeat, we automatically create elevated vibrations within ourselves.

What we think and feel, and how we choose to act and react ultimately determines how successful our lives are. Most of us tend to live our lives more instinctively than deliberately, leaving the trend of our life to chance. Few people awaken in the morning and say to themselves, "I will be the best person that I can be." This statement may sound simplistic, and it is. However, after making a habit of repeating this intention, it puts us on course to elevate our energetic vibrations at the beginning of each day.

Our energetic vibrations usually vary within specific ranges that are typical of people living on Earth. Our thoughts and actions either raise or lower our vibrational rates. Those who are engaged in bringing harm to other people or those who have difficulty with self-loathing are examples of people whose vibrations are on the lowest end of the earthly spectrum.

The mid-range is where most peoples' vibrations primarily reside. The middle range is common within those of us who tend to live day to day, allowing our emotions, desires, and moods to dictate how we engage in life that day. Those within the higher earthly vibrational ranges live life deliberately. They are determined to do the best they can to control their negative impulses and desires, preferring to follow a higher standard of beneficial behavior, which protects and honors their well-being and the well-being of others.

When we carry a highly elevated vibration, the world is our oyster. We are happy, enthusiastic and we look for ways to have a positive impact on other people. Our positivity brings smiles and warm acceptance from others. Positivity is an ideal state to maintain throughout our lives. If we were to die in this elevated vibrational state, we would enjoy a most graceful and desirable exit from this life and an immediate arrival into the joyful realms of the afterlife. Although maintaining a highly elevated vibration would eliminate any potential problems when we die, realistically, not many of us can guarantee that we will successfully create and sustain this advanced state throughout our lives.

Life brings joys and disappointments, and our emotions tend to bob along with the positives and negatives of everyday occurrences. As our emotions change, so do our vibrational rates. When we are depressed or feeling miserable, our vibrations drop to the low side of the spectrum. When we are joyful and in love with life, our vibrations sail into the higher ranges of the spectrum. The most elevated vibrations appear within the highest dimensions, which exist well above our third-dimensional Earth. We cannot comprehend what all the other dimensions are like from being here on Earth, but it is helpful to know that they exist because this will help us understand our after-death progression.

Having a low vibration when we die invites trouble. Even when we have lived most of our lives in the middle or high ranges of thinking, feeling, and acting, if we die when we are frightened, angry, or vindictive, our vibrational rates are likely to be dangerously low. We do not want the last thought of our life to be on anything other than something uplifting. Thoughts of loving gratitude for the adventure that has been our life will create peaceful vibrations and focus us on where we are going with a conviction that we will be well cared for and safe.

After we die, there is only one way that we would ever want to go, but if our vibrations are not high enough, difficulty looms. Angels have very high vibrational rates, and so do our loved ones who come from the elevated dimensions to assist us. When our energetic frequencies are too low, we are unable to detect their presence. They could be speaking to us, and we would not hear what they are saying. Our vibrations must be high enough to connect with them, and we can assure that they will be if we direct our intentions to ascend into the most desirable place to be.

While we are alive, we can monitor ourselves for signs of our vibrations being at a high level. If we are relaxed, feeling uplifted, and joyful, these are signs that we may be experiencing elevated vibrations. When we disengage our minds from life's difficulties, live peacefully in the moment, and feel sublime happiness coming over us, we experience high vibrations. The energy field surrounding us is light and airy, and we feel that we are immune from the intrusions that usually swirl around us. This state is ideal to maintain throughout our lives whenever possible, but especially when we are about to pass from this life.

If we had the ability to adjust our vibrational rate as we do our thermostats, depression would no longer exist, neither would sadness or despair. Unfortunately, changing our vibrational rate to higher levels takes concentrated effort and a willingness to let go of what bothers us. Our minds tend to agitate on our problems, disappointments, and failures, which pull us down. Then our negative emotions can become overwhelming and hard to manage. Almost all of us have spent time in the cellar of emotional despair. To die in this state invites trouble, and that is why many people experience after-life difficulties.

When people die, dedicated angels are present to ensure that the deceased person returns to the higher dimensions. The angels are there, Johnny on the spot, and do not miss a single person. However, if a person's vibrations are too low to see or hear the angels, they will be unable to detect the angels' presence or respond to their offer of assistance. Eventually, the angels reluctantly withdraw but only after a prolonged effort. They stay with their assigned person until any reasonable hope of establishing an interactive connection with them has been exhausted.

I did not intentionally try to collaborate with rescue angels. This would never have occurred to me. The angels may have been looking for a solution to their inability to connect with some of the people they were trying to assist, people whose vibrations were too low to detect the angels' presence and respond to the angelic offers of assistance. Without trying to develop these skills myself or even knowing that they could exist, they appeared within me.

The angels must have recognized that either I inherently had this capability, and they knew how to activate it, or they had some other method of instilling this capacity within me. Fortunately, we team together very effectively.

Over the years, we have become quite efficient at extending a helping hand to many deceased people. Without our assistance, these deceased people would have continued to endure the hardship and confusion caused by not transferring into the higher dimensions after they died. The after-death experience is challenging when the deceased person remains unaware of the mechanics involved in creating a smooth and enjoyable transfer into an appealing afterlife.

When a deceased person does not have a high enough vibration to perceive the angels, they have unsatisfying experiences, which I characterize as a detour. These detours create nothing but confusion. Fortunately, helper angels are aware of the after-death pitfalls that commonly occur and are determined to do their best to aid people who become lost and confused after dying.

I enjoy working with these rescue angels, who I sometimes refer to as my guidance. It has been fascinating to navigate behind the scenes of the reality that we are familiar with while we are alive. I have appreciated the opportunity to help people in challenging situations. I do not want to give the impression that I knew what I was doing from the start. I was as bewildered as anyone else would have been when I began interacting with dead people in their spirit forms. As disquieting as this was for me initially, I soon adjusted, becoming grateful for the ability to communicate between dimensions as I came to know and hold dear the deceased people that the angels and I combined our efforts to assist.

Living and dying are interrelated. You make choices every day of your life. You decide how you will spend your time, what you are going to accomplish, and the ethical standards you will employ. After you arrive within the heavens, you will evaluate your performance from this lifetime. If you deviated from good sound behavior, you are going to be greatly disappointed. Imagine looking back over your life, realizing that what you thought was valuable and important while leading your physical lifetime was what set you back in your evolutionary progress. As a result, you lost ground instead of advancing yourself.

Everyone who works to extend their list of positive attributes, and shrink their list of regrettable thoughts, feelings, and actions, will enhance their well-being. No one should construct a barrier that makes it more challenging to establish elevated vibrational frequencies within oneself. You will not receive the advantage of flipping a high vibrational switch within yourself right before you die to assure your safe and speedy arrival at the best destination for you after you pass from your body. We all need to prepare in advance and establish our own insurance policy by raising our standards and behaviors.

As you read about individual people's circumstances, you will learn that all of us, regardless of our behavior while living on Earth, belong in the higher dimensions after we die. Moving into the higher dimensions is our natural progression. However, if you lived a destructive life or underwent a difficult death circumstance, you may not detect your preferred path. When this happens, deceased people wander around in a state of existence that the angels refer to as the In-between.

As the name implies, the In-between exists between the physical world, which the deceased no longer inhabit, and the elevated spheres, which they cannot perceive. They cannot detect the elevated spheres because of the limitation of carrying an energetic vibration that is too low to discern any higher vibrational activity. Because of their low vibratory rate, they are unable to perceive the angelic assistance extended to everyone.

The In-between is complex with many levels of experience, and none of these is preferable to being in the heavenly realms. People in the In-between are doing the best they can under various circumstances, but they all share a sort of stalemate existence. None of them would choose to remain there if they knew that they had the choice of being there or in the higher dimensions. The people in the In-between do not understand where they are or how they got there. They find themselves there after dying and do not know what else to do.

People in the In-between are no different from you or me except that they dissociated from their physical body, not knowing where to go next. The In-between is not a place of paying the penalty for past behavior, although some residents must feel that way. I say this because when I have offered to assist people in the In-between, some of them have refused my offer, citing that they do not deserve to go to an ideal place to reside.

At one point, I participated in a massive intervention intended to uplift all the people stranded in the In-between into the higher dimensions. Uplifting the people in the In-between was a complex undertaking. In one of the later chapters, I will describe this carefully planned orchestration, and then you will understand why you do not want to take a side trip to the In-between. It is far preferable to go directly to your most desirable destination.

Dying is a simple release from bodily attachment. This detachment does not have to be difficult once the pre-death phase has been completed. The prior-to-death period can be challenging, and it usually sets the stage for what happens after dying. When the person accepts that their life has drawn to its conclusion and nothing remains for them that they have to do or that they can do, they are more likely to relax and calmly let go. This gentle release sets the stage for a smooth and pleasurable transition into a far better reality. When the dying person carries along with them their resentments, the injustices they endured, their self-pity, self-loathing, or other objectionable mind disturbances, they create a potentially bumpy road for themselves after dying.

If the last impulse of our lives is to be angry or feel vindictive, we must fight against it with all our might. We do not want to damage our progression into the higher spheres of existence, so we need to use good judgment, self-control and focus on getting to the best destination. The last moments of our lives are critically important in another way, as well. These moments present our final opportunity to ask forgiveness for the harm we did to other people, intentionally or unintentionally, and to declare our love.

As we know, living on Earth comes with limitations and challenges. We do not remember being here before, and we did not receive an instruction manual when we arrived. Most of us assume that this is a one-time experience. When we think that this is a one-time-only opportunity, it is tempting to focus single-mindedly on satisfying our urges and enjoying ourselves as much as we can. While doing this may be the road to personal delight in the short term, it will not hold up over time. People who focus only on themselves and satisfying their desires develop feelings of emptiness inside. Living a very self-absorbed life is not satisfying and ultimately leads to feelings of worthlessness when one takes stock of their life.

You will know that you are on the path to becoming a better person when you evolve your perceptions and behaviors, instilling high-level ethical standards within yourself. Your worldview will expand, and you will consider every person in the world as a member of your family. As you will have demonstrated when you read the accounts of what it is like to be in the higher dimensions, people in those dimensions care about one another and treat everyone with respect and consideration. They give us a model of what we could be constructing here on Earth right now.

As we live our lives, we are typically unaware that we carry long-term responsibility for what we create while we are alive on Earth. As a result, many of us hurt ourselves and other people without regard to what this will bring us down the road. Our unacceptable behavior will most certainly lead to regret when we return to the higher dimensions and view what we did, clearly understanding the effects of our negative actions.

Within that elevated atmosphere, we have clarity that we were missing when we were alive on Earth, and we cringe when we acknowledge all that we did, which was indecent. It is a good idea to give yourself a life-so-far review after reading these chapters, with a better understanding of how to evaluate how you are doing. Any enlightenment that may come from such an exercise will undoubtedly be beneficial and may save heartache later.

When people deliberately harm other people, they set themselves up to endure the same pain and suffering they imposed upon other people. Unless there is heartfelt repentance while they are still alive, they will carry karmic indebtedness, which will bring them the same or similar harsh experiences that they created for others. Be aware that if we deliberately harm other people, we are shooting ourselves in the foot.

We came into this life not knowing that we set an agenda for ourselves before we arrived and that we will be disappointed later if we do not accomplish our custom-designed agenda. Most of us are familiar with the common religious perspective that after we die, God judges us. You will confirm by reading the accounts in this book that God does not judge our performance. We evaluate ourselves, and with this in mind, we might prefer to live our lives more thoughtfully and constructively, not only to benefit others but to benefit ourselves as well.

Although it may seem premature to think about the end of your life, it is not too soon to think about what will happen when the last day of your life arrives. Instead of waiting to see what happens, you can create your path to the most desirable circumstances. Begin now by forgiving yourself for the harm you may have done in the past and take a clear view of what you need to do to improve yourself. You can overcome repeating your past missteps by focusing on regulating your behavior and becoming more observant about your impact on other people. Assume that you are here to learn through your personal experiences and incorporate a higher level of self-expression. Determine to value yourself and every other person as well.

We have come here to work on ourselves, so let us not shirk from these challenges but rise to meet them head-on. Let us determine to support and assist one another, lessening others' burdens whenever the opportunity arises. Working supportively always produces better outcomes than butting heads with each other, and loving produces better outcomes than hating. Acting collectively to make our world a model of compatibility and compassion will elevate everyone's lives. Instilling higher vibrations within ourselves will ensure our easy transfer into the higher dimensions when it is time for us to return to our resting place between lifetimes.

From this framework, let us think about our death. If it arrives tomorrow or fifty years from today, we will be ready. We will have earned our first-class airfare home. We will easily adapt to the higher vibrations, which the angels have. It will be natural for us to see them and communicate with them. We will smoothly pass from our physical body, understanding that we are in our spirit form, and ascend with our angelic escort.

CHAPTER FOUR
SUICIDES

—

Suicide is a perplexing problem within society. You cannot pass a law against it, and you cannot impose a penalty for engaging in it. Suicide is an all too frequently used option to extract oneself from severe psychological discomfort. Committing suicide is an over-employed way to sidestep one's difficulties that seem to be unbearable at the time. Without a clear path of resolution and an urgent impulse to free oneself from the stranglehold of their problems, taking one's life is an overused option that usually backfires and causes unforeseen complications.

Read this chapter carefully, not as entertainment, but as a preview of interdimensional consequences that arise from a person acting on an impulse to free themself from an uncomfortable life situation. At some time or another, many of us have had the thought of committing suicide flash through our minds. When pressed by life circumstances without feeling capable of working our way through them, we are more likely to turn to thoughts of committing suicide to escape from our feelings of desolation.

As shown by these communications with people who have committed suicide, not everyone experiences adverse effects from their decision to end their earthly experience. Those who feel complete with their life and have no worthwhile future to create by remaining physically alive may not regret their choice. Typically, people who commit suicide to escape an impermanent situation exchange one set of difficulties for another.

People who commit suicide are trying to escape from having to deal with their life challenges. Expecting freedom from their problems after dying is a mistake made by many people who commit suicide. After taking one's own life, the relief experienced by ending the prior too-hard-to-handle life situation gets replaced by the confusion of new reality. Being fully conscious but outside of one's physical body with no way to reenter it is a frightening, disorienting experience when the person had been anticipating nothingness.

People who commit suicide face the problem of changing their minds while being isolated outside of their physical body without the ability to reenter it. How many times do we make snap decisions that we later regret? Committing suicide is not a snap decision that any one of us should ever consider. Not being able to reenter one's physical body is a horrifying experience, especially when the newly deceased person has instantaneous regret over taking the action they did. Filled with despair, they often find they have created more problems than they had before.

Being emotionally overwhelmed is not a sound condition to be in when considering something as serious as suicide. If there are valid reasons, evaluate them from every angle. Taking one's life is a monumental decision to make, and often it is made in the spur of the moment when under psychological distress. Rarely do people who are so distraught that they are considering suicide give enough consideration to the effect their action will have on those who are close to them.

The suicide of a loved one is especially difficult for the family and friends of the person who died. They go through a period of desperate soul searching to perceive if they could have done something to prevent their suicide. Although the responsibility is not theirs, they may place an unjustified burden of guilt upon themselves for not noticing warning signs ahead of time. The suicide of someone we love almost always undermines our psychological well-being.

As I communicated with people who had committed suicide, rarely were they happy with their decision. Mostly they were befuddled. They were right about escaping from their life's problems, but they did not look far enough ahead to know that they were introducing another quandary. Being without a physical body and cut off from communicating with their grief-stricken family and friends, they bear a burden of guilt for having caused their loved one's enormous pain and have no way to apologize. The sorrow and heart-wrenching suffering of their loved ones is the new calamity that has no resolution.

As you read the conversations in this chapter, pay attention to what caused these people to end their lives so, if you face a similar challenge, you will remain levelheaded and make sound decisions for yourself. Also, keep in mind how some who committed suicide managed to find the way to their beneficial destination by attracting the assistance they needed. You may want to pay special attention to this chapter. Sometimes we think that we would never do what other people have done; however, with overwhelming psychological distress we may lose our ability to make rational choices and succumb to emotional impulses.

Ken Durant

Ken faced a serious life challenge. As he was living his day-to-day life, he assumed that his marriage was intact, and when Ken found out otherwise, he became enraged. In his extreme distress, Ken decided to strike back at his wife. Ken wanted to make her pay for the pain he was feeling, so he exposed her transgression over social media and then killed himself. Ken intended to humiliate his wife and end his misery. But instead, in the depths of despair, he made everything worse.

When I heard about this sad situation, I asked the angels that I collaborate with to find Ken and bring him to me so we could assist him.

Angels: Ken knows who you are. He has some things to say. Please record what he says to you.

Ken: I was so angry with her that I lost my mind. All I could think about was causing her pain. I really did not want to die. I just did not know how to handle my anger. I acted impulsively, and I regret what I did. I still love my wife. I felt so deceived. All I could think about was making her pay dearly. I took extreme measures that made everything worse. I sure made a mess of things. Now I do not know what to do. I do not know where I am. Do you know where I am?

Kay: Yes, Ken. You are between worlds. You have given up your physical body, so you are deceased. Luckily, as you can tell, you still feel alive.

Ken: Please continue. You are right. I feel alive.

Kay: You are having the experience of living in your spirit body. You have lost your physical body, but you will always have your spirit body. Your spirit body enlivens the physical body but does not need the physical body to experience awareness, thought, and communication. Do you agree? You are experiencing our conversation, are you not?

Ken: Yes, but I am still confused. If I am still alive, why can you hear me, but other people cannot. How can I get around if my body is dead? What takes me from place to place?

Kay: Your mind. You go where your thoughts take you. If you think about your parents, you will be there with them. Haven't you been thinking about how your death is affecting different people only to find yourself watching their reaction?

Ken: How did you know this? Can you see me?

Kay: No, Ken, I cannot see you, but I feel your presence, your energy field, and I hear you surprisingly well. You must have found me through our mutual friend, Kyle. I am sure you know how distraught he is about what happened. He called me to see if I could help you in any way. I suspect you may have followed the connection between Kyle and me. I should be asking you. How did you find me? What made you come to me and start talking to me?

Ken: I do not know.

Kay: Any ideas?

Ken: I just wanted to talk to someone to say that I regret my anger that led me to kill myself. I am sorry for the pain I caused so many people but especially my wife. I could not handle my life, so I took the cowardly way out. I guess you are the only one I could talk to, and I do not even know you.

Kay: I know about you because Kyle told me about your situation and asked if I might be able to help. I am able to communicate with people who died. In addition, I work with certain angels who help people get to heaven when they are having trouble finding the way by themselves.

Ken: Like me?

Kay: It looks like it, doesn't it? You have had angels with you continuously since you left your body. You probably have not noticed them because you were absorbed in your feelings about what happened. What do you want, Ken? Do you want to stay where you are and monitor what happens to those you left behind, or do you want to move on to the spiritual plane of existence? If you are ready to go to a higher level of existence, angels will take you, but you must let go of your attachment to those you left behind. If you release them to go on with their lives without you, the angels will take you up.

Ken: Will I know what happens to them? I am especially worried about my wife. I do not want her to suffer because of what I did. What I did was juvenile and underhanded. I wanted to humiliate her, to strike back because I was hurt. Now I cannot say that I am sorry. It is too late to undo the harm I caused her.

Kay: If you stay where you are, feeling your pain and regret, you will not be helping her or yourself. I am offering you assistance to reach the higher dimensions. Are you ready to accept angelic help?

Ken: I do not want to be foolish and miss this opportunity, but I do not want to abandon her either. I am responsible for causing her this pain, and I do not want to duck out on her. If I stay around, maybe there is something I can do to help her. I do not know what, really, but I do not want to abandon her.

Kay: I understand your concern, Ken, but the sad fact is that you cannot help her if you stay where you are. Your choice is not between helping her or not. The choice is whether to remain separated from both the physical and the spiritual worlds, in a position where you are not living in either. It would be like wandering in a kind of no man's land. It is your option. What do you say?

Ken: Are you sure I cannot make her life better by staying around even though she does not know I am there?

Kay: Realize that you are no longer a part of her life. If you hang around, you will be punishing yourself and not benefiting her.

Ken: You make a good case. I have already made a wrong decision, and I do not want to make another. You sure are nice to help me. I feel so confused and unable to think straight, but while I have you, I had better decide. I may not be able to find you again if I wait. Where are the angels?

Kay: When you are ready to turn your attention to being with them and going to the world of spirit, they will appear to you. They are just waiting for you to decide. Once you make your decision, you will see them.

Ken: Are you sure?

Kay: Works every time.

Ken: I wish I could tell my wife goodbye and that I still love her. I also want to tell her that I am sorry for what I did.

Kay: I wish that were possible, Ken.

Ken: I have decided to go with the angels if they will have me. (Long pause.) I guess I am an okay person because I see several angels. They are walking towards me with their arms reaching for me. I was afraid they would not want me, but it looks like they do. I think this is the best decision for me to make. They could not be nicer. Now they have their arms around me, and I feel like crying for joy. I am going to be all right. I know I am.

Guidance: He has gone with the angels.

The next day my guidance returned with this report. Ken is adjusting to his new surroundings. He learned a lot about himself by going through his suicide and its aftermath. His main lesson was not to take destructive action against someone else or himself when he feels emotionally vulnerable. He could not handle his life circumstances without losing control of his good judgment. He gave in to his desire to rage against his wife to make her pay for his inability to remain calm under adverse circumstances. Now he sees his actions as a reflection of his own character deficiency.

He is at peace, although he deeply regrets his actions. Ken will come back into physical incarnation again soon. He will keep coming back until he learns to control his emotionalism with reason.

The Escaped Prisoner

One morning, on the Houston newspaper's front page, was a notice about an escaped convict. Evidentially he saw an opportunity to dash for freedom, and off he went. He was an African American, and I felt sorry for him.

The next day the front page of the paper reported that the prisoner drowned. Authorities who were searching for him brought in trained dogs to follow his scent. The prisoner took to a bayou swollen from heavy rains to avoid the dogs, where he quickly died. As soon as I read this report, I asked my angels to see if he needed help to elevate into the higher realms. The angels found him and came to his rescue.

In the following day's newspaper, there was an interview with the prisoner's grandmother. She said that she raised him from the time he was a small boy and that he had been a good boy and that she had been praying for him constantly ever since the report that he escaped. Her following comment startled me. She said that he could not swim. Evidentially, he decided to risk drowning rather than return to prison.

With a heavy heart, I thought about this man and all of the other imprisoned people. The prisons fill with people convicted of committing crimes. But, this does not mean that they should be mistreated. In most cases, they are no different from the rest of us except for a difficult life situation that caused them to deviate off a wholesome path. Difficult situations often come from factors that they had no control over, such as growing up in an abusive household. Many prisoners lost respect for authority when those that had authority over them did not honor them.

Instead of scorning them, we might want to ask ourselves what would have happened to us had we encountered the same challenges that they did. We may well have made the same mistakes as them if we had to lead the life they faced. Whether we make terrible mistakes or not, we are precious people who are here to learn our lessons as we go along. We all require compassion, fair treatment, and respect even when coming back from dark past behaviors. If we genuinely believe we should treat others as we would like to be treated, we may need to reevaluate our perspective on those suffering the misfortune of imprisonment.

Joe Armstrong

Word passed quickly amongst his former business associates after Joe committed suicide. He had been very successful throughout his business career. Joe made a lot of money and he spent a lot of money. He was a multimillionaire who had a reputation for spending lavishly. In his early 60's Joe committed suicide by jumping off a California bridge. When I heard about his situation, I asked my angels to find him. After they located him, they gave me their report. "Joe was sobbing when we found him. He did not know where to go or what to do. As we gently took him into our arms, he relaxed and smiled. We took him into the light."

I did not expect to hear from Joe, but not long after the angels scooped him up into their arms, my guidance announced that Joe would like to speak with me.

Joe: Do you mind if I get a few things off my chest?

Kay: Of course not, Joe. May I record what you say if this might help someone else?

Joe: I am hoping that what I say will help other people be different than I was. I was proud and arrogant. I thought I was one of the most successful people on Earth. I had all the extras – lots of money, more than I could ever use, and a big name. Everybody knew me and that I was one of the lucky ones who had it all. In my mind, I did have it all. I thought that spending money, being a big shot, and throwing my weight around made me better than other people.

I did not realize that I was shallow and pretty darn stupid. Yeah, I killed myself because, with all my money, the cars, the flashy stuff, I felt like nothing I did or accomplished amounted to anything. The parties did not do it for me anymore. Neither did the phoniness, the pretentiousness that went along with them. Everyone bragging about what they did or what they owned – all trying to be impressive, finally got to me.

I felt like nothing inside, as if I really did not matter. I gave up on life. I felt miserable, so I took the only way out. I could not pull myself together, so I jumped off that bridge, feeling like a total failure.

Those blessed angels carried me to heaven, and I felt better the instant they lifted me into their arms. I had never felt so peaceful and calm. I did not want them to let go of me, ever.

After I saw the movie of my life, I felt ashamed of myself. I had my priorities all mixed up, and I used the wrong scorecard. I gave myself credit for all the money I made, but I spent it foolishly instead of wisely. I squandered my money on insignificant whims of mine. I had the opportunity to use a vast sum of money on projects that would have made me feel good about myself in the end, but I decided to worship my money for its own sake. It never occurred to me to share my fortune with other people in a meaningful way.

Now I will learn firsthand how I could have used my money. I will experience what it is like to not have enough money and be in desperate need of someone else's charity. I will have firsthand experience of what it is like to be poor and not have a fair chance in life. I will experience what a small amount of money from a rich person's kindness can mean to someone stuck on the low rung of the prosperity ladder. I deserve to learn this lesson the hard way.

My next life experience will not be easy, but I am hoping to make up for my excesses of this last experience. I want to be a better person than I was before. I am not eager to go back, but I have to do this for myself. It never occurred to me until it was too late that I was not a successful person just because I had a lot of money.

Kay: Joe, I am sorry this happened to you. I would like to ask you a question, if I may. If you were to start out living your last lifetime again, what would you do differently with what you now know?

Joe: That is something I have thought about, and here is what I have decided. I would choose to be born with some kind of personal disability, so I would be sensitive to people living with life challenges. I would learn to overcome or compensate for my disability enough to earn a lot of money. My heart would be sensitized to the plight of others who had to struggle as I did, so I would dedicate my efforts and my fortune to finding ways to help people. I would especially like to help handicapped people get the support they need, whether it be financial like finding jobs, or getting job training, housing, and community support. I would like to build self-sufficiency and support for people with handicaps.

Kay: Wow, Joe, that sounds like a better life plan than being impoverished and struggling. I vote that you set up the second scenario for yourself rather than the first one.

Joe: I am hoping to do that, but I must decide which plan better suits my purpose of teaching myself the value that can come to oneself and others through the wise distribution of financial excess.

Kay: Thank you, Joe, for sharing your background with me. I wish you the best of success for your next lifetime.

From what angels have told me, Joe's situation is not unusual. People with financial excess often put it all in their own oversized pockets and ignore better uses for some of it. After we die, the winner of the prize is the person who has done the most to benefit other people, and you do not have to have a large bank account to do this. Even if we have little to give monetarily, there are innumerable ways to advance the well-being of others. If we have this goal and have deep pockets, the sky is the limit to what we can do to help others in need. We all need to remember to look for opportunities to support the well-being of others.

Fred Lynch

Fred was a rancher who, over time, felt the effects of old age and other challenges that he was dealing with and began considering his options. He was not interested in trying to get every last mile out of his broken-down body. Fred made a reasoned and well-thought-out decision to end his life. Fred was fortunate because he managed to make the connections he needed to make after he died, giving him an unobstructed passage into the desirable afterlife. In answer to my request to see if Fred was okay, my angels brought him to me so he could tell me for himself what happened.

Kay: Hello, Fred. Are you here with me?

Fred: I am happy to speak with you. I want to clear up something.

Kay: What is that, Fred?

Fred: Yes, I committed suicide, but it did not hurt me one bit.

Kay: What do you mean?

Fred: Well, no one damned me to hell. I was taught that we were damned to spend eternity in hell if we committed suicide. I would not have done it under ordinary circumstances, but I could see that my body was done for, and I did not want to hang on with false hope that it would improve enough to give me a half-decent life. This was not going to happen.

Kay: Tell me what it was like after you committed suicide.

Fred: Well, I looked around. By then, I was in perfect shape again. I was looking for someone to direct me. I knew which way to go, up to God and the angels. I was not afraid. I was confident that I was not going to be punished. I do not believe in that hell stuff. I was not sure, though. I thought I would take my chances. I did not see how God could care if I saved myself misery and suffering. After all, I was 75 years old, and I lived a good life. I was not perfect by any means, but I can honestly say that I was a good person, as far as I could tell.

So maybe I got off track here. You asked me what it was like. I will give it to you straight. It was stupendous. That is right. That is the only way to describe what happened.

There were angels galore blowing me kisses. I never thought I would see so many angels having such a good time. They were laughing, probably at the startled look on my face. I thought angels would be serious, but not these. They were devilish – I probably should not use that word – and playful. They were making me laugh. I was expecting a solemn occasion. I would never have guessed in a million years that such a thing could happen to me.

Well, that is about it. The next thing I knew, I was zipping along at lightning speed to where I am now. When I got here, those same angels were already here. I do not know how they could get there before me; I was moving so fast. I have said enough.

Kay: Oh, do not go, Fred. This is interesting.

Fred: Well, then, I will tell you what happened after that. Jesus and Mother Mary came to say hello. They told me that I was going to like it here and that I deserved to be here. They were very nice. They did not say that they were disappointed in me. I really expected them to say I should not have done it, but they could not have been nicer. I felt so welcome.

Do you want to hear more?

Kay: Sure, Fred, I am all ears.

Fred: Since then, I have been thinking about my life: what I did right and where I made mistakes. Oh, I made plenty of them. It does not seem to matter, though. I was told that what matters is what we learn from our mistakes. No one here is proud of their poor behavior when they were still alive. Not that I am not still alive now, but you know what I mean, when I was on Earth. We are all figuring out ways to cue ourselves into doing better next time.

That is another thing. I did not know that there would be more than one lifetime. I thought we got one shot at it, and that was it. Now I find out that I have already had enough shots at it that I ought to be perfect by now. Sorry, that is not the case. I would love to stay here and not have to go back. I wonder if I will ever get it right so I do not have to go back again. Oh, well, I am enjoying myself while I am here. I am digging in my heels, and I intend to stay as long as I can.

I feel that I have talked your ear off. Do you have any questions to ask me?

Kay: What is the one thing you wish you had done better, which is more important than all the rest?

Fred: That is an easy question to answer, Miss Kay. I was levelheaded, but I was stubborn. I was not easy to live with. I wish I had been gentle and considerate. I really was not a considerate person. Too tough. Too gruff. I am determined to change the next time they pry me loose from the good spot where I am now.

Kay: Fred, you have been wonderful to talk with me. I appreciate your insight. Do you mind if I share what you have told me with other people, so maybe they can learn some lessons from what you had to say?

Fred: Go ahead, that will not bother me. Up here, we own up to our mistakes.

Kay: Fred, you sound like a terrific person. I will look for you when I get up there. If you see me, come and introduce yourself.

Fred: You have my word on that.

Fred had what he felt were legitimate reasons to take the action he did, and he did it with a plan of what to do afterward. You cannot mask invalid reasons. They will become apparent after the fact and may cause great heartache when our foolishness takes its toll. We do not come into our lives to take a quick ticket out when things get tough. It is in dealing with life's challenges that we refine ourselves and build strong character.

Heidi Baldwin

Heidi was a delightful young woman who brought sunshine into the lives of others. She was twenty-eight years old when, for some unknown reason, she took her life. All who knew Heidi were stunned and deeply saddened. When I heard about what occurred, I called upon my angels to assist her. They quickly reported that she was all right, that she did not need their assistance. Later they returned to give me this description of what happened to her.

Immediately after Heidi lost connection to her physical body, she panicked. She wanted to change her mind, but it was too late. Being back in her physical body was not an option. Heidi was disappointed that she had not been strong enough to fight the despair that had come over her. She cried and cried what felt like physical tears.

Heidi had been devoted to angels when she was a child. She felt close to them and would tell them all her problems and ask them what she should do. Heidi did not realize that she was drawing angels to her by talking to them and asking them for advice. When Heidi grew up, she stopped talking to the angels and did not think about them much anymore. However, after she died, Heidi needed the angels more than ever.

After Heidi's crying stopped, she felt exhausted and sincerely remorseful for not choosing to solve her problems without hurting herself and ending her life. She thought about when she was a child and how she would ask the angels what she should do. Heidi reached out to the angels by asking a simple question, "Angels, what should I do now?" Before she had time to wait for an answer, several angels appeared before her with their hands outstretched. Heidi gasped with joy and dove into their midst, where the angels warmly embraced her.

Heidi's frightening predicament resolved instantly because of her childhood reliance on angels to assist her in times of difficulty. Angels play a special role in the protection of children. Once a child establishes a closeness with angels, the connection remains. The hearts of angels are sensitive to children's love in particular, and angels are ever alert to children's cries for help. When children become adults, they may lose their childhood attraction to thinking about and trying to talk to angels. Still, once children establish those childhood connections, they endure forever within the angels.

Sara

One morning my dear friend, Amy, called to tell me about her friend Sara who had just committed suicide. Amy said that this was shocking to her since Sara was a lovely person who showed no signs of severe depression. I promised Amy that I would ask the angels to find Sara and help her if she needed it. When I asked my guidance to check on Sara, they had a quick response.

Guidance: We have Sara Morrison here to talk with you.

Kay: Did she get into the heavens?

Guidance: Let her tell you.

Kay: Hello, Sara. Are you here?

Sara: I am pleased to have this opportunity to say a few things. I regret my action. I killed myself because I became emotionally out of control. Had I been wiser, I would not have given up my desire to continue living. I was so self-absorbed. If I would have given myself more time and reached out to others for support, the urge I acted on to end my life would have passed, and I could have finished living what really was not a tough life.

Kay: Did you have any trouble going into the heavens?

Sara: Thank you for asking. Immediately after I committed suicide, I felt terrible. I knew I acted on an overwhelming impulse. I also knew that what I did would cause crushing pain to the people that loved and depended on me. As I extended myself to God, asking for forgiveness, I became enveloped in sparkling white light, which caressed me and took away the shock and horror I felt. I swirled around as the light seemed to move in a gentle circular motion. It was not disturbing or frightening. I knew that I was being welcomed.

Soon I could see two angels holding out their arms and motioning me to follow them. Ever since then, I remain engulfed in the same light. It glows all around me as I travel around between dimensions. Most of the time, I counsel people who are contemplating suicide. I try to persuade them through inspiring dreams and uplifting vibrations.

In the beginning, I would talk to them, but not many were aware of my words. Another person that does the same work suggested that I send uplifting energy. Sometimes, uplifting energy is enough to pull a suicidal person up out of the morose state of mind that leads to taking one's life. I am proud of myself. I have had quite a few saves.

I know that life can be sorrowful and seem futile in the moment, but I also know that it is a great gift to live upon the Earth and within a human body. In dark moments, people may give up this precious gift and then regret it. Almost everyone I have met that has committed suicide regretted their action and felt that life was not as difficult as they thought it was.

Usually, people that commit suicide suffer from a distorted view of reality and a sense of hopelessness. That certainly was true of me. It has given me enormous satisfaction to help people who are contemplating suicide. Every time I am successful in changing minds and saving lives, it eases my sorrow over my decision to cut my life short.

Tell Amy (a special friend of mine) that I still care about her. I could tell when she was young that she was different from the other children, and I loved her as my own. Amy is a bright light. Of all the people I check on, she is the easiest to find because she shines the brightest. Our hearts are still connected, and I continue to love her very much.

Both Sara's story and Heidi's story demonstrate how easily one can elevate one's self from being in the lost and disconnected state that typically envelops people who commit suicide. Sara and Heidi found their way into the higher dimensions, and so can others who call out to divine beings. People such as Sara and Heidi demonstrate what can happen to those who had developed a spiritual side earlier in their lives, which they automatically tapped into in their moment of desperation. It appears that spiritual connectedness, which is no longer front and center, can still come to the forefront to aid us in our time of need.

Calling on angels and other divine beings may be all we need to do to attract heavenly support after dying. If a person does not believe in the work of angels or the existence of a divine benefactor, it may be somewhat difficult for them to take this step. If this is the case, I suggest that they call out within their minds to God and the angels while holding an attitude of open receptivity, which allows for their existence. There is no penalty for being uncertain of their existence. The destination for all of us is the same, and we all receive a warm welcome. Do not think that you do not deserve to receive that which you may have denied was possible.

Jay Taylor

When Jay Taylor died, we lost someone we admired and would have liked to know personally. We who relished his humor and his joyful delight in life were stunned that he committed suicide. After Jay died, news reports referred to health problems that were not common knowledge, and there seemed to be other life challenges, of which we were unaware. Whatever they were, he had his reasons, and his choice was to terminate his life.

What follows is the record of the two conversations that I had with Jay after he died. Some angelic pals of his who were keeping watch over him arranged the first one. He did not know they were there. He could not see them or hear them.

I was cooking breakfast the day after Jay died when I felt angels around me jumping with delight. These angels were all atwitter with excitement in a way that I had not experienced before. As they told me that they brought Jay Taylor to me for us to assist, I looked down at the eggs I just cracked into the frying pan and decided that Jay could wait the few minutes it would take to finish cooking them and for me to have a quick bite to eat.

I gulped down my food as the angels kept repeating, "Jay Taylor needs your help. Jay Taylor needs your help" several times. As soon as I finished my meal, I mentally asked, "Is Jay Taylor with me?" His answer was immediate.

Jay: Yes, ma'am, here I am. I'm in a fix and don't know what to do about it.

Kay: Jay, how did you find me?

Jay: I was wishing for someone to give me directions, and then I saw you cooking eggs.

Kay: That's all?

Jay: Yes, and those eggs looked mighty fine.

Kay: Jay, I can help you go on to heaven. Would you like that?

Jay: That's what I was wishing for, but I'm not sure where it is. First of all, are we sure there is such a place? I know I'm dead now, but I don't see arrows pointing the way.

Kay: Yes, there is a heaven, Jay, and you are very close.

Jay: If you tell me which way, I'll head off in that direction. I don't want to be late. They might be looking for me, or maybe not.

I wanted to get out of there. I'd had enough. I know we shouldn't kill ourselves but living as me was tough. It wasn't easy.

Kay: I'm sorry that things were…

Jay: Are you writing this down? You aren't going to make a spectacle out of me, are you?

Kay: No. I do not intend to make a spectacle out of you.

Jay: I don't want anyone to know about this part of what happened to me. I'm relieved but ashamed that I couldn't handle things better. That is all. (After a pause) I guess I've already made a spectacle out of myself, so why should I care? Hey, lady, what is your name? I'm starting to see angels. Did you call them to help me?

Kay: Not really, Jay. They were already with you when you came to me as I was cooking breakfast.

Jay: Well, then, why didn't I see them? Explain that, if you can.

Kay: Jay, do you feel better since we have been talking? Possibly more relaxed? Maybe even a little happy?

Jay: More than a little. I feel downright jovial now. I think this feeling came over me when I saw the angels.

Kay: Are they still there?

Jay: More than before. It looks like they are planning something. I'm going to go over and listen to what they are talking about.

Kay: Will you come back and tell me what it is?

Jay: (After he left and then returned) They are unraveling a banner that says, "Welcome to Heaven, Jay." I still don't see heaven. Oh, there is something else written on the banner. I can see it as they extend the banner. It says, "Tell us a joke, and we'll laugh our way to heaven with you."

Kay: I suppose you know plenty of jokes to tell them?

Jay: I'll have them laughing all the way there.

After that last statement, the angels whisked Jay away. I did not expect to hear from him again, but about a week later, he returned.

Jay: Hey, lady, it's me. I'm back again.

Kay: Jay, is that you? My guidance just told me that you wanted to come back to talk to me.

Jay: After I got up there – there weren't any pearly gates, by the way – I had the time of my life. I've never laughed so hard in my life. I thought I was funny but not as funny as these characters that I met when I first arrived.

Kay: Who were they? Friends of yours or people you didn't know?

Jay: Both. My friend Johnny got it all started. He always did crack me up. Everyone had something funny to say. People I didn't know had good ones for me. What a good time! Of course, I dusted off a few.

Kay: I cannot hear you now.

Jay: I see you are writing down what I say again. Why are you doing this?

Kay: I am glad you brought this up. I did not have time to explain the last time we talked. I have been helping people like you who are disoriented after dying and do not know what to do next.

Jay: You sure helped me. Those angels didn't show up until I found you.

Kay: Actually, they were with you all along, but you just could not see them. I am recording what you say because I decided to write a book of instruction so when people die, they will not be confused like you were. This book will not sensationalize. It is a book of education to help people. If you do not mind, I would like to use our conversations to assist people.

Jay: I'm all for that. I guess we should get better acquainted then. How do you do and what is your name?

Kay: My given name is Carolyn and Kay is my nickname. Nearly all my relatives and friends call me Kay.

Jay: Then Kay it is for me too.

Kay: Jay, I would love to know what happened after those angels with the banner took you to the higher dimensions.

Jay: That's why I came back to talk to you. I wanted you to know how lucky I am that I ran into you because now I have the time of my life all of the time. Even when I had to see the mistakes I made and where I flubbed up and the health issues and such – you get to see it all, you know – I couldn't believe what a charmed life I led. Of course, I didn't do everything right. I had major, regrettable poor behavior at times. Sometimes I was an idiot and not the funny kind.

Kay: Jay, what helpful advice do you wish you had when you were alive that you think might benefit the readers of this book?

Jay: I'd like to sit down with them and say, "Hey, look at what you are doing to yourselves. You want this and that, and that's all you think about. What am I gonna get next? Then you're happy if you get it and sad if you don't. And you know what? All those this's, and that's don't add up to a hill of beans."

All that adds up, all that counts when it is all over like it is for me now, is the laughs, the joy, loving other people, and feeling their love coming back at'cha. That's what counts. That's what matters.

A new Mercedes? Who needs it? Wouldn't you rather have the joy in your heart that would come from using that money to help disadvantaged children get a break in life? If the whole world turned their attention to helping other people instead of focusing on what they could get for themselves and just letting their numbers add up, everyone would be walking around with smiles on their faces.

Kay: Wow! What an answer. Is there anything else you would like to say?

Jay: Oh, you know me, when I get started talking, sometimes I don't know when to shut up. Yeah. I've got more advice if you're interested.

Kay: Thank you. I am very interested.

Jay: Get along with each other. That's another good one. Would you like me to expand on that topic for a while?

Kay: Yes, please do.

Jay: People go looking for things they don't like about other people. This puts distance between them. If people only thought about how great other people are and let the rest slide, we'd all think the other is wonderful. There are many more reasons to like someone than there usually are to dislike them. If the person is despicable, then don't think about them at all. Put them out of your mind instead of parking them smack dab in the middle of it. Think positively, not negatively, or don't think at all.

Kay: Is there anything else?

Jay: This isn't advice. I've done enough of that. I want to thank all the people who loved me and put up with me. I wasn't easy to be with at times, and I could be insensitive. I wasn't perfect – far from it – but I tried to make everyone happy. Deep down, although I didn't show it all the time, I really love people and didn't want to hurt anyone. What I'm getting at is I want to ask forgiveness from the people in my life that I disappointed – all of them.

I didn't understand the impact of some of my actions until I got up here and saw myself in action. We see a live-action movie of our lives when we get here, and some of it is hard to watch. Not only do we see what we did, but how it affected other people. Oh, the pain I caused, and I had no idea at the time. I won't go into details, but I'd like to be forgiven for my hurtfulness. I want a clean slate, no leftover buggers.

Kay: Anything else?

Jay: That does it for me, Miss Carolyn Kay. Nice talking wit'cha. I'll stop by and say hello when the news flashes over the hot wire when you get up here. I appreciate what you did for me. Thanks again.

My conversation with Jay demonstrates that Jay could see angels after we began our conversation when he could not see them before. These angels were with him from the moment he died and led him to where I was. Had Jay been in a relaxed and joyful state of mind after he separated from his body, he would have immediately spotted those angels. After committing suicide, it is not generally typical for a person to have positive, uplifting feelings and a clearly defined idea of what to do next.

By now, I hope it is clear that no matter what we did when we were alive, we all receive an escort to aid us after we die. After dying, our primary goal is to connect with our escort, and the sooner we start to see and hear them, the better it will be for us. Had Jay not received the special help from his angelic escort who delivered him into my vicinity, he could still be trying to figure out where to go since he was not sure of his destination.

The same destination awaits us all. Usually, those who die from an act of suicide are in a very low vibrational state, so they rarely detect their angelic assistance. Fortunately, Jay's vibrations were high enough to respond to the angels who were guiding him into my presence.

In this chapter, I highlighted several suicide situations to give you enough information to navigate to safety if, in a moment of desperation or premeditation, you conclude that your life is no longer worth living. I suggest that this chapter merits going over a few times as a protective measure. If you decide to give up on this life, know that you will most likely be creating heartache for yourself and those who love you in the aftermath of an impulsive act. As we have seen, there are valid reasons, but deep emotional despondency may also influence a person to take their life.

People who are deceased feel like and look like they did when they were physically alive on Earth. They maintain the same appearance they wore during their lifetime and retain the same consciousness within their spirit bodies. We do not die and instantly become brilliant, knowing all the mysteries of the universe. We are the same self that we were before we surrendered our lifeless body.

As you read along, expect to uncover problems that deceased people commonly run into after passing from their physical bodies and how they overcame their challenges. Remaining calm and rational is of utmost importance. The angels who come to assist are only apparent to those who are calm enough to detect their presence.

These angelic teams transport deceased people to a more refined area of creation. Instead of Earth, heaven, and hell being the places for humans to reside, there is a limitless Creation, devoid of hell, that human beings have access to experiencing after they pass from their physical body. However, only the most evolved people have free reign to go into certain areas. Strict qualifications are required to have access to the uppermost levels of Creation.

A bit of advice to convey is to come clean with yourself regarding your less than admirable traits and actions right now. Erase them from your repertoire while you have the opportunity. When a divine being calls you on the carpet for trying to mask unevolved intentions, there is no denying that which they are forcing you to face within yourself.

CHAPTER FIVE

ACCIDENTS

Suddenly becoming detached from one's physical body due to a fatal accident is a punch in the gut that sends us reeling. Losing our grounding within the physical world without time to prepare throws us into a disoriented state. Being severed from family, friends, and the physical world mars our sense of stability and wellbeing. As heartbreaking as this type of experience is, the resolution will be glorious when we navigate to the higher dimensions.

Do not dismiss the possibility of a fatal accident happening to you, nor be frightened that it will. It is far better to be primed for an event that does not happen than to be caught off guard and unprepared if it does. Pay attention to this chapter and think about coaching yourself into becoming levelheaded and taking the right steps if such an upending experience should occur to you.

As you read this chapter and the next, do not flee to a point of safety in your mind. People tend to put distance between themselves and the unfortunate occurrences that happen to others. Rarely do we personalize or internalize another person's situation to the extent of making a plan of what we would do if we were facing the same challenge. News reports notify us of accidental fatalities, and we cannot always count on it being someone else who is affected.

Two California Boys

This brief story carries an important lesson. One morning a friend of mine, who lived in California, called and told me about a car crash that took two teenage boys' lives. The night of the accident, these boys were out late driving on one of the California highways. The two boys were speeding and crashed into a concrete barrier. They were very inexperienced drivers. The boys had their driver's licenses for only a short time and did not fully understand the hazards of speeding. As you can imagine, everyone who heard about this tragedy was heartsick over what happened to these young men.

Angels: We have both boys. They are still together. They are ready to go with us.

Kay: Stewart and Reed, can you hear me?

Both boys: Yes, Ma'am.

Kay: The mother of a friend of yours called and told me what happened to you.

One of the boys: It was terrible. So much crying. We could hardly take it.

Kay: I am sorry about the accident.

The same boy: So are we. We did not think that could happen to us. We were not careful.

Kay: Who has been talking?

Reed: Stewart was talking. He has not blamed me for what I did. He has been cool about it.

Kay: Would you boys like to meet some angels and go to heaven?

Reed: Yes, Ma'am. We could sure use something different than watching people cry.

Kay: Okay. Look around you. What do you see?

Both boys: Wow! Lots of angels are walking toward us from every direction.

Kay: What do they look like?

Reed: They are taller than Stewart. They kind of glow. They look serious. They are saying it was too soon. We were not supposed to die like that. We will be missing all that was planned for us. They are not angry. They are sorry it happened because of what we will miss.

Stewart: Now they are telling us to go with them. They have a shortcut to heaven, and it is not against the speed limit.

Kay: Goodbye, boys. Have a good time in heaven.

Reed: Goodbye, Ma'am. Thank you for helping us. I wish we could tell our families that it is okay here and it is going to get better.

Hearts break when needless deaths occur, especially to children. Teenagers often tend to have euphoric feelings of invincibility, which can lead to dangerous situations. Many of us, if we are honest with ourselves, will recognize that we were the same way when we were teenagers and, if it were not for the grace of God, or good luck, we could have had the same early ending to our lives that Stewart and Reed did. As this story illustrates, people who drive cars need to value their safety and the safety of others over creating an exhilarating experience for themselves.

The Man, the Woman, and the Truck Driver

One weekend when the Shell Houston Open Golf Tournament was being held, a tragic accident occurred. My husband, Mike, was watching television coverage of the tournament when there was an interruption in the program to make an announcement. Two married couples were driving on their way to attend the golf tournament when a young man driving a pickup truck jumped the medium strip and lost control of his vehicle. The truck catapulted into oncoming traffic, hitting their car broadside and killing one of the men and one of the women. Each of the couples lost a spouse. The seventeen-year-old driver of the truck also died.

My husband worked for the same company as the man who died, and my husband was very upset about what happened. Upon hearing the news report, Mike asked me to contact the angels to see if those who lost their lives needed assistance. I requested help from the angels right away, but two days later, I received their report.

The angels explained that they had no difficulty locating the deceased man and women. They were wandering together in the In-between in a state of shock, trying, without success, to communicate with their spouses who were still alive. Since the deceased man and woman were good friends, it was natural for them to remain together.

The man and woman were delighted when angels approached and offered to escort them to the heavenly realms. They quickly agreed to go, but as they started to leave with the angels, the woman halted their progression and insisted that they could not go yet. The rest of the group puzzled over her change of mind until she declared that it would not be right for them to leave without the young man that hit them. She put her foot down and refused to proceed. The angels promised her that after they escorted the two of them to their new accommodations in the higher levels of existence, they would return and search for the young man who had been driving the truck.

The man was ready to leave immediately. He agreed with the angels' proposal, but neither he nor the angels could talk the woman into changing her mind. She stubbornly refused to budge. She was adamant that she was not going anywhere until they found the young man who was driving the truck. No amount of persuading could make her change her mind, and the man had difficulty accepting her resolve. They were at a stalemate. He would not leave without her, and she would not leave without the young truck driver.

The attending angels offered another solution. They agreed to delay the couple's immediate transfer while they searched for the young man. The angels left and promised to return with the other accident victim. Sure enough, when the angels returned a while later, they had the remorseful young man with them. Tears were streaming down his face, and his chest was heaving with loud sobs. He held his head down as he continued crying and reluctantly walked over to where the man and the woman were standing. An angel walked next to him for support, but he still could not raise his head and look at the man and woman whose deaths he caused. He was ashamed and overcome with remorse.

Without a moment of hesitation, the woman walked over to the young man, put her arms around him, and gave him a wholehearted embrace. She held him close to her until he stopped sobbing. Then she gently put her hand under his chin and pulled his head up so she could look directly into his eyes and he would be able to see her smiling at him. After that, she took him by the hand, and together they walked over to where the man was standing. As they approached, the man locked eyes with the boy. Instantly the man's face lighted up in a warm smile as he stepped forward and embraced the young man. The three of them joined hands while the woman announced to the angels, "Now we are all ready to go."

The woman in this story had a compassionate heart filled with love. Her actions are a fine example of unconditional love that dissolved the young man's deep heartache. Considering the good of all, such as this woman did, is an example for every one of us. Especially in times of crisis, we think of our loved ones and ourselves. However, the most caring and compassionate among us are also concerned for the well-being of everyone, including misguided individuals who disrupted other people's lives.

People who create problems for other people may be acting deliberately or making avoidable mistakes. Even people who intentionally harm others require humane treatment and the opportunity to make amends. In this instance, the young man had no intention to harm. He made an avoidable mistake. We all know how it feels to be disappointed in ourselves and how a heavy burden lifts from our shoulders when forgiven for our errors. It does not hurt any one of us to be kind and forgiving. No matter our situation, if we see a person who needs comforting, we will feel better ourselves if we do whatever we can to help them.

Charles Gill

As I glanced at the Sunday newspaper, my eyes noticed a short article about a man shot and killed by two police officers. The article aroused my interest because it reported that the dead man's mother called the police to check on her son, who had been isolating himself in his bedroom for days. The article did not mention why the mother felt she needed to call the police. I thought there was a possibility that the deceased man may have had a mental illness. I am especially concerned about those who have the burden of mental illness to manage. I immediately called for angelic assistance, which came swiftly.

Angels to me: Charles Gill wants to talk to you.

Charles: Will you tell me what happened? I do not know what happened.

Kay: I read in the newspaper that your mother called the police to investigate because you had been isolating in your room for several days. She was concerned about you. The paper said that two police officers entered your bedroom while you were sitting on the bed. You reached for something behind you, and then the police fired two shots.

Charles: Why did they do that? What right did they have to come into my bedroom?

Kay: I cannot answer your questions. I am sorry that happened to you, Charles. I can do something for you, though. Would you like me to help you feel better?

Charles: What can you do? Put me back in my bedroom before the police officers came in?

Kay: I would if I could, Charles, but I can offer you something else, even better than that. Do you mind if I ask some friends of mine to pay you a visit?

Charles: They are not police officers, are they?

Kay: I would not send police officers. I am sending angels. Tell me when you see them, Charles.

Charles: Those pretty ladies over there. Are they angels?

Kay: I suggest you go over and talk to them. Ask them who they are.

Charles: I do not have to ask them. They are walking toward me, and I see the glow around them. They are telling me they love me and are going to take care of me. They make me feel happy. I love my mother. I will miss her. (Silence)

Angels: He is with us now. Calm, peaceful, and happy.

I felt sorry for Charles' mother. She acted out of concern for his well-being and inadvertently set up a situation that caused his death. I also felt sorry for the police officers who misread the situation and acted defensively, which turned out to be an inappropriate response. It is hard to believe that a person could be sitting in their bed and be intruded upon by two police officers.

Life can place us in a dangerous situation without realizing that this is happening, emphasizing the need to be prepared should this occur. If we were suddenly to become ejected from our physical body as Charles was, the best thing for us to do is stay calm and levelheaded and set out to contact angels. We must call to them with confidence that, at any moment, we will begin to see and hear them. Angels will undoubtedly answer our call. Panicking in situations such as these creates obstacles to detecting when angels are present, so remaining calm is of paramount importance.

Two Alaskan Fishermen

My brother, Steve, called from Alaska asking me to have the angels investigate what happened to two fishermen whose boat had capsized. Steve was listening to the radio when he heard a report that two fishermen were feared lost when an unexpected storm came up earlier in the day. Fragments of a boat had washed ashore, but it was uncertain if they were part of the fishermen's boat. The men were missing and feared to be dead.

As soon as I made contact, the angels told me that they were aware of the fishermen's plight and had already sent a boat to pick up the men. The angels gave me this account of what happened. "The rain was pounding, and huge waves were crashing against the fishermen's boat. As their boat was about to break apart and the men had given up all hope of surviving, something incredible happened. A sturdy rescue boat pulled up alongside theirs and took the men aboard. Angels were operating the rescue boat and spared the men from having to undergo the experience of dying. These men did not immediately comprehend that they had passed from their bodies and were dead. The reality that they experienced was of being rescued, and they were whisked off to the hereafter feeling exuberant."

I did not expect to have any personal contact with the fishermen, so I was especially delighted when one of the fishermen later found his way to me.

Fisherman: Hi, lady. You do not know me, but I know all about you.

Kay: Who am I speaking with? I do not recognize you.

Fisherman: Oh, we never met personally. I am one of the people whose boat capsized when that storm came in and caught us by surprise.

Kay: Are you from Alaska?

Fisherman: I lived there all my life. You ever been there?

Kay: No, but I wanted to go fishing up there where you fly into a remote area with a guide and supplies and then stay several days. I would have loved that experience. I never had the opportunity.

Fisherman: We took some risks that day when our boat capsized. We knew there might be storms coming in, but the forecast was for them to arrive later. We thought we had enough time. That squall was violent. Visibility was near zero. Then that rescue boat pulled up next to us. They had five men onboard a well-supplied, large, sturdy boat.

They hustled to hoist us into their boat, and once me and my fishing buddy were onboard, the singing began. What a great time we had with our rescuers! We never knew their names, but I will never forget their faces. They were radiantly joyful. Not like they won the lottery. More like the nicest thing in the world just happened to them. Like looking at the newborn Christ child on Christmas Eve. These guys were literally glowing.

Their glow was puzzling to my buddy and me. These guys almost did not look real. Then I saw an angel wing hanging below one guy's jacket. My mind was in a state of pure bewilderment. I poked my buddy's arm and pointed to the angel wing. We both stood there with our mouths wide open, totally speechless!

Before we knew it, the whole boat disappeared, and so did the water. Things happened so fast, but everything was calm. We did not feel upset in any way. Actually, we each became very calm, peaceful, and extremely happy. There wasn't any reason. That is just what happened.

The angel fishermen, who in time did not appear to be fishermen anymore, delivered us to where we've been ever since. Some people, who we both knew, warmly greeted us, but they had been dead a long time. That is when we knew that we must be dead, too. Nothing hurt. We were the same two fishermen that we were before, but everything changed. We were not sure where we were, but we liked being here and still do. Nothing goes wrong over here. There aren't any problems. You never run out of money because there isn't any to run out of. No one needs it. No one has to work a job to survive. I am living in the most wonderful place, and everything is freely available to everybody.

My buddy and I still spend a lot of time together. We like to go back to Earth to see how our friends and families are doing. Our families are still missing us. It hurts us to see them when they are sad because we are not there anymore. They would rather be with us if they had a choice. I do not know why my buddy and I were the lucky ones. We talked about this and could not think of anything we did that warrants our good fortune. Neither one of us had ever been particularly lucky until our boat went down in that storm.

Angelic rescues may seem impossible, but some of my interactions with deceased people document instances when angels arrived moments before the impact of a catastrophe, sparing the trauma of an unpleasant death. Angelic interventions may occur even in terrifying circumstances, such as mountain climbing accidents or airplane crashes. It may be that the more connected a person is to divine resources when they are alive, the more likely they are to be spared the experience of the death blow. If you find yourself facing imminent danger, instead of panicking, keep your wits about you and summon help. Whenever you need divine assistance, make a forceful command such as, "Angels, help me!"

Doing this worked for me. One Sunday morning, as I was driving home from church on one of Houston's busy highways, a light rain began to fall. Traffic was moving a little slower than usual because of the rain. I was alert and driving carefully, but my car must have gone over a rain-moistened oil slick on the highway as I was driving along. Suddenly my car started spinning out of control in a circular pattern.

The steering wheel did not respond and seemed disconnected from the car. I was horrified as the vehicle began to careen straight toward the concrete divider. Instinctively, I shouted within my mind, "God, help me!" As I braced for the impact, my car behaved as if it had spun into giant soft pillows. Then the car made a quarter turn and rolled to a slow stop facing sideways in the middle of the three-lane highway.

My heart was racing as I glanced at the cars that were behind me. I could not believe my eyes. Gasping, I saw that there were hundreds of vehicles on the highway. Cars filled every lane. They all came to an abrupt stop when the drivers saw my car spinning out of control. Most of these stopped cars were bumper to bumper, and some were sideways in their lanes. There was no space between any cars and the cars in front and behind. None of this even seemed possible.

It looked like the hand of God had lifted some of these cars and set them down sideways in their lanes to keep them from crushing. The vehicles were wedged between each other as closely as pieces in a puzzle. Not one car hit another, although they had all been traveling at highway speeds.

Shaken to my core, I could hardly comprehend that just as I was about to smash into a concrete divider, my car gently rolled back into the middle of the highway, and I was uninjured. I got out of my car and walked around in a dazed condition for a few minutes. Then I bent over and looked underneath my car, expecting to see that the motor had fallen out, and was shocked that it had not.

The people within the stopped cars were beginning to get restless, so I gathered my courage and tentatively turned the ignition key and was surprised when my car started up. I maneuvered it so it pointed in the right direction and slowly began to drive home. As I drove away, I glanced in the rearview mirror and saw the lines of traffic behind me gradually start moving forward again.

To me, it was utterly astonishing that no one was injured, and none of the other cars hit another during this dangerous incident. I felt divine protection very profoundly when my car contacted those giant soft pillows that gently cushioned my car and me. I kept thinking, "God, you heard me. You really heard me!" In addition, I loved that God not only protected me but He also protected every other car and its passengers.

Jamal Malouf

While bicycling on a busy downtown street, a car struck and killed Jamal Malouf. When I asked about him, this is what the angels reported. "As far as Jamal was concerned, he did not get hit by a car. Jamal experienced going right into the light from his upright bicycle. A group of angels came to retrieve him and spared him the experience of being hit by a car. He could not have had a more pleasant return to the light."

If Jamal's family and friends thought that Jamal suffered terribly, they were mistaken. He did not experience fear or pain, which seems impossible. Evidently, the angels have some latitude when it comes to assisting people that need their help. The dividing line between what is possible and impossible is not as clearly defined within the angelic realm as it seems to be to us here on Earth.

The Pilot

News reports were distressing. An airplane piloted by an inexperienced pilot had been flying with two passengers in turbulent weather when the plane disappeared from radar screens. There had been no contact with the pilot since the aircraft dropped off the monitoring devices. Those who heard the news kept hoping that the occupants may have made a safe landing and just not have been able to communicate their position. I asked my guidance to find them and see if they needed angelic help.

I did not want to hear what the angels said. A short time after I asked the question, my guidance reported that their airplane had gone down in the storm. All three died. My guidance informed me that one of the women went straight into the light without any difficulty but that the pilot and the other woman aboard needed angelic assistance.

At 11 p.m. that same night, angels maneuvered the pilot to me. He was very polite. He spoke in a well-measured way, very serious, very clear. I explained how I could connect him with angels who would take him to the higher dimensions. He did not seem interested. The pilot focused on one thing only. He was distressed that he could not find his wife, who was one of the passengers, and the pilot bluntly stated that he was not going anywhere until he found her. Then I repeated to him what the angels had reported to me earlier, that his wife had already gone on to the higher dimensions, and that is why he could not find her. As soon as he heard that his wife was safe, he visibly relaxed and asked, "How do I get there?"

The pilot listened to and accepted my explanation about the helper angels who transport people to the light when they miss their natural connection. He was not going to delay any longer. He was cooperative, business-like, emotionally strong, and ready to go. When the angels became apparent within his vision, he spoke with them and verified that his wife had gone straight into the heavens. Then the pilot and the angels began an animated conversation. I sat there listening to them talking with each other for at least fifteen minutes.

After that, the pilot and the angels began to drift upward together. Suddenly, the pilot paused, reversed direction, and came back to where I was. He stood right in front of me, looked directly into my eyes, and with heartfelt gratitude said, "Thank you for helping me." I was in awe of his stately presence and intently watched as he rejoined the angels, and they floated upward out of my vision.

The other person was still unaccounted for, but not for long. After the pilot left with his angelic escort, I asked my guidance for information about her.

Angels: She is having difficulty. She does not want to leave her family. She is crying.

After saying this, angels guided her over to where I was, and she spoke with me.

Second lady: I'm having a hard time.

Kay: Are you interested in going to heaven?

Second lady: If there is no other choice.

Kay: There is no other reasonable choice. Would you like to see some angels, my dear?

Second lady: That would help. (The angels arrive.) Oh! They are beautiful. The angels are beautiful, but it is hard to decide.

Kay: Talk to them for a few minutes. They can answer questions.

Second lady: They said I could come back to visit. I think I will go.

Angels: She's gone.

Sunday Morning I read the newspaper. The plane was still missing. I checked with my guidance to see if there was any more information but received no answer.

2:50 p.m.

Angels: The man is in his heavenly home. He found his wife, and both of his parents are there. He is experiencing great happiness.

Then I received a gift. My guidance showed me the pilot and both of his already deceased parents sitting in comfortable outdoor chairs on a porch overlooking a densely wooded area, smiling broadly and animatedly catching up with each other. They each had a lot to say, but especially the pilot. His mother had a joyful look on her face as she watched her husband's reunion with their son. Her husband was engrossed in every word that their son was speaking and listened with rapt attention. They had a beautiful family reunion that I was allowed to glimpse.

I then asked the angels how the younger sister was doing.

Angels: She underwent a tough time. She is still adjusting; however, she is tranquil, relaxed, and pleased to be with her older sister.

Kay: How about the woman who went directly into the heavens?

Angels: She is ecstatic. She had the strongest pull of the three of them. She found it easy to pull herself home. She felt the strong attraction to return home to the higher dimensions, did not put up any obstacles, and found herself instantly transported into the elevated realms.

Admittedly, this was easy and natural for her, more than it would be for many other people in similar circumstances. If you unexpectedly disconnect from your physical body, remember that your route to the higher dimensions is innate within you. If you do not become overwhelmed with fear and confusion, you are most likely to access it automatically.

Many people who die unexpectedly have the same experience that the pilot's wife had. Going home to the higher dimensions is like diving into a welcoming body of water. We set our course, let go of our fears and release into the exuberance of freedom from everything else.

Dr. Daniel Mills

Dr. Daniel Mills was a well-known veterinarian in California. One day he was swimming in the ocean when a Great White Shark attacked him. The shark shredded his legs and took his life. My sister Stephanie, who lived in California, heard the news reports and asked me to check on him. The angels I worked with reported that he needed our help and had a story to tell, but I had to call him a few times before he answered.

Daniel: Hello, did somebody call my name?

Kay: Yes, I did. I was calling you to come and visit with me. I might be able to help you.

Daniel: Would you like to hear what happened to me?

Kay: Sure.

Daniel: The day that the shark took my legs, I felt better than I had felt for a long time. All my training had paid off, and I felt totally alive and exuberant. I did not know that this was the day I would die.

After the shark took my legs, I bled to death. I hardly knew what happened until I floated out of my body and was above the water, looking down at the bloody scene below. I was so angry that the shark did that to me. I have led my life caring for animals, and one comes up from the depths and attacks me.

I wanted to tell you about what I could see when I was above the water looking down into it.

Kay: What did you see, Daniel?

Daniel: I saw the whole panorama below me. There was no difference between above the water and below the water. I saw the people trying to help me, and at the same time, I saw fish swimming in the ocean. My vision went right through the surface of the water, and I could see everything above and below.

When I got over the shock of being dead and watching the whole scene, I realized that I am still alive. You might not believe me, but I got my legs back, and I am ready to go again. I do not know how I did it or what to do next. So far, you have been the only one with whom I have been able to talk. You hear me, don't you?

Kay: Yes, Daniel, I hear you. I am recording your words as you speak. Please continue.

Daniel: I am ready to go back, but I cannot figure out how to be real again to my friends, and of course, to my family. There must be some way, or I would not have my legs back. A miracle happened to me. Now I just have to get myself recognized, seen, and heard by everyone that knows me.

Kay: Daniel, you will be disappointed that the miracle you are experiencing does not mean that you get to go back to your former life and pick up where you left off. When we die, we retain our consciousness and what feels like our physical body. Daniel, after we die, we exist in our spirit body, which feels physical. We do not feel any different than we did when we were alive, but we are limited to continuing our existence within the higher dimensions instead of going back to Earth. Everyone feels alive after dying. Our physical body seems repaired, but we are not in our physical body anymore. We are in our spirit form.

Daniel: So, I do not get to go back?

Kay: No, Daniel. There is only one great place for you to go.

Daniel: Do you mean heaven?

Kay: Yes, Daniel.

Daniel: I am not really interested in going there. I want to go back to my life in California. I will have to think about this. Do I have a choice? Are there any other options?

Kay: The only other option that I know of is for you to remain as you are, kind of caught between the Earth and the higher realms but not being in either.

Daniel: I see. Kind of sobering, isn't it?

Kay: It might be unsettling for you because you had your heart set on going back to your physical life, but actually, you have an excellent option. Going to the higher realms is appealing because it is so vast with so much to do. You may continue studying animals, play music, or do whatever else interests you. In addition, you will see your friends and family that preceded you. People in heaven have a wonderful time. Are you interested in checking it out?

Daniel: How do I get there?

Kay: I am asking some angels to take you up with them and show you around. I expect that you will remember being there before.

Daniel: Really? Hmm. Interesting. Are you sure I cannot go back?

Kay: Your next step is forward. You cannot go back to Earth to live as you did before the accident. Daniel, some angels are gathering around you now. Are you aware of them?

Daniel: Do you mean those people in the wet suits and snorkels? Are they angels?

Kay: Oh, Daniel, you are going to have fun with these angels. You are going to like them a lot.

Daniel: I think you are right. I can relate to them. I am feeling better. What you say makes sense. I guess I have to let go of wanting to go back home. Thanks for setting me straight. There is a boat here now, and my snorkeling friends are climbing into it. They are motioning to me to go with them. It is the best offer I have so I am leaving with them. Thanks for talking to me. I do not suggest you ever swim in the ocean. You never know where you will end up next.

Daniel's experience confirms that our spirit bodies are indestructible, always with us, and we can count on being conscious within them after we die. Regardless of what kills our physical body, whether it be old age, an illness, or a bullet, our spirit bodies remain vibrant and sound. When we abandon our physical body, we may be much better off as we experience ourselves wholly restored within our spirit bodies, youthful and healthy.

As Daniel's account points out, the angels have a delightful way of coaxing people to go with them. They are experts at relating to people and understand how to gain their confidence. Angels are creative and playful. They seem to delight in disguising themselves to appeal to recalcitrant people that need their help but may not be open to interacting with them in their true form. They want everyone to be comfortable and unafraid, and they do their best to be appealing to whomever they are trying to assist.

If you should experience an abrupt and unanticipated end to your life, you will continue with your existence. Your best bet is to remain calm and be on the alert for already deceased relatives or friends, angelic beings, or disguised divine assistance that may appear to be other than who they really are. Angels are delightfully creative and like to please those who they have come to assist. Donning disguises to make the deceased people they are aiding comfortable and relaxed is one of their innovative techniques.

CHAPTER SIX

BEING MURDERED

———

When a murderous act steals a person's physical life, that person immediately catapults into a state of confusion and disorientation. Confronted with the loss of their ability to navigate inside the body they identified as themselves, they must come to terms with losing their place in the physical world. Understandably, fury rages within them, as does the desire to get back at whoever caused this to happen. Sudden deaths from being murdered are among the most difficult to navigate.

The psychological impact of someone ejecting us right out of the life we have known is devastating and extraordinarily difficult to overcome. Sometimes murdered people were in a relationship with the person whose violent act took their life. Knowing the person who committed this heinous invasion typically inflames one's agitation and may create a crazed desire for revenge.

Not infrequently, murdered people place their singular focus on devising ways to expose the person who caused them to lose their physical body. Their fixation creates a distraction, diverting them from concentrating on solving their immediate challenge. If this jarring experience happened to you, you would be wise to exercise strong personal discipline to control your desire to expose the perpetrator of the crime. Instead, set your sight on the more important goal of making visual and auditory contact with angelic beings, who will be present and trying to gain your attention.

Andrew

This situation uncovers an evil plot to murder for pleasure. In a Florida coastal community, two men deliberately set out to entrap single young men new to the area, enticing them with friendship, only to murder them in slow motion. These two torturers met their match for evilness in each other. Andrew accepted their invitation to join the two of them for a drink when he was alone in a bar. What seemed to be a harmless encounter was the beginning of a most horrific experience.

After receiving my request to check on Andrew, angels brought him to me.

Kay: Andrew, a friend of your brother, called my brother, Steve, and told him that you died of a drug overdose under suspicious circumstances. Steve let me know that you might need assistance. I work with angels to help people who die in a confused state, unaware of what they can do to help themselves.

Andrew: You just described me.

Kay: What happened to you, Andrew?

Andrew: I met some guys who seemed nice. There were two of them. We had some drinks and talked. They seemed like really nice guys. There were no warning signs. I think I was targeted.

Kay: Targeted for what?

Andrew: They had a plan all along. They have done this before. I think I was the third one.

Kay: What exactly are you talking about, Andrew?

Andrew: Listen to me carefully because you are not going to believe what I am telling you. Those two guys were looking for someone to kill.

Kay: What? Why would they do that?

Andrew: They think that it is fun.

Kay: They do it for pleasure?

Andrew: Exactly. They told me that they had done this before, three times.

Kay: Three times?

Andrew: Then they chose me and did it again. They need to be stopped! It is too late for me. I am with two of the other guys that they killed. They have been following the killers around.

Kay: Why?

Andrew: To see what else they are going to do and to help whomever they kill next. They are on a kind of rescue mission. One of the guys said he hated being alone after he was killed, and that is when he decided to track down the two killers. Then when they killed the next guy, the two men teamed up to stop the killers from murdering other people. Where we are now, all we can do is watch what goes on where I used to be in my body. I still feel like I am in my body, but I know I am not. At least it helps a lot for me to be with these other two guys, so I am not alone.

Kay: Is there anything you can tell me about the murderers to help the police find them?

Andrew: They live right across the street from where I met them. They told me they did. I do not do drugs. They injected me with drugs, and then they talked to me until I died. They enjoyed telling me that I was going to die. There was nothing that I could do. It did not take long. I felt myself separate from my body, but I still feel like I am in it, but only it is different now.

Kay: How is it different, Andrew?

Andrew: I float. I do not need to walk to get somewhere. And, I can move faster than airplanes.

Kay: Is there anything else you want to say?

Andrew: I am so sorry this happened to me. I did not do anything to hurt myself. I never would.

Kay: Andrew, I have some good news for you and the other two people who are with you.

Andrew: We could use some good news right now. What is it?

Kay: If you look around in a gentle, relaxed manner, you are going to see some welcoming angelic beings who are going to take the three of you to your new home.

Andrew: We have a place to go? Is it heaven? (Then there was silence.)

Angels: We have them now.

When we were young, our parents warned us not to talk to strangers. When you grow up, you assume that you can size up the people who come into your orbit and some you choose to avoid. The worst snake in the grass is the one who does not look like one or initially act like one. Andrew experienced a unique situation when being friendly, outgoing, and accepting had a tragic ending.

Melissa

Someone that knew about Melissa brought this young woman to my attention; she appeared to have died from committing suicide. This sad occurrence was disturbing on two levels. Melissa was a joyful person who had a large circle of supportive friends, and she did not seem to be unhappy or moody that night before she died. She was with a group of her friends, and none of them saw any shadow of discontent in her demeanor. There seemed to be undisclosed questionable circumstances surrounding her death, and her friends were suspicious about what happened.

As soon as I contacted my angels, they replied that they were bringing Melissa to me. Then without my asking any questions, Melissa started talking and told me what occurred.

Melissa: I will tell you what happened. I did not kill myself. I want my family to know that someone killed me. I did not trust him when he said he loved me, but part of me wanted to accept what he said.

Kay: Is this Melissa?

Melissa: (Impatiently) Yes. I think you already know that.

Kay: Okay. What happened?

Melissa: He manipulated me. I think he meant to kill me the whole time. I did not like something about him.

Kay: What did you not like?

Melissa: Creepy. There was something creepy about him. I could feel that there was something wrong.

Kay: What was wrong?

Melissa: The way he followed me around. The way he interfered with what I wanted to do. The way he had such strong opinions about what he thought I was doing wrong. I did not like that about him. I was stupid to keep seeing him. I should have called the police. If I had, I would still be alive. Nobody knows this about him. They think he is a nice person as I did in the beginning. I want him to pay for what he did to me. Moreover, I do not want to see him killing anyone else.

Kay: What do you want me to do?

Melissa: I will give you his name, and then you tell my parents and the police.

Kay: What is his name?

Melissa: His name sounds like he would be a nice guy. Anthony.

Kay: How can the police prove that he killed you?

Melissa: I do not know if they can. I want my parents to know that I did not kill myself. I would not do that to my parents. I do not want Anthony, the slime ball, to walk, so I will tell you what happened.

He was angry, and I was scared. I had never seen him this angry before. There was no justifiable reason, just small stuff, mostly things that would not have bothered anyone else. He slapped me hard. I fell back, and then he put a stranglehold on me, took a knife, put it in my hand, pushed down on it, and forced me to slit my wrist. I started bleeding, and he pushed his hand down stronger so the knife would cut my wrist in a big gash, and the blood poured out of me then. I do not know anything else that happened after that. Do you think this is enough information for the police to make him pay for what he did to me?

Kay: I do not know, Melissa. We can see what happens. If the details you gave me, certain ones, are corroborated, I will consider sharing the rest of the details with your family. If not, I will not cause them more pain by giving this to them. This is a delicate situation. I want to help you, but I also want to protect your family from additional pain.

Melissa, are you ready to go to the place where people go who are no longer in their physical bodies?

Melissa: Yes, if you will give this information to my parents and the police.

Kay: If I can verify certain details, I will pass your message to your father and mother. They can share this with the police.

Melissa: Then I am satisfied. Do you know where I am supposed to go?

Kay: I know some angels that understand where you are supposed to go. Do you believe in angels?

Melissa: I love angels!

Kay: Then you are in for a real treat. Look around you, Melissa. Tell me what you see.

Melissa: I am speechless! I am stunned! Let me count them. There are too many to count. They are smiling and laughing. Now they are extending their hands to me. Thank you, dear lady. I do not know how I came here to where you are sitting at your table and writing what I say to you. I do not understand.

I had no way of verifying any of the details that Melissa gave me. Although I anguished over whether to pursue this further, the decision was clear in my mind. I decided to stay with my established working relationship with my angels, which does not include murder investigations. Our objective is to aid those who have gotten off course on their way up to the higher dimensions. It bothered me that I could not follow through with Melissa's request, but I relaxed and felt satisfied that Melissa got to where she needed to be.

Melissa's story carries a warning about being in a relationship with a demeaning, critical, and abusive person. Artificial pleasantness often camouflages their evilness at the beginning of the relationship. An abusive person can put on a persona of being likable and caring, but after a while, the mask crumbles, and the abuser reveals their true nature. By the time the abuser discloses their true nature as a destructive manipulator, the victim has often lost the ability to think clearly and act decisively to protect themselves. As a result, the abuser takes the upper hand over the victim targeted for abuse. What may have appeared to be a healthy relationship, in the beginning, may disintegrate into a dangerous situation such as the one that Melissa described.

In my conversation with Melissa, she details some of the traits of abusers, and there are others, which are typical and easily identifiable when people become informed. We tend to think of men abusing women, but women can also abuse men, and abusers can exist between children of young ages and between parents and children. We owe it to ourselves to ensure that our relationships are healthy and that we do not tolerate abuse to ourselves or other people.

Isaac Helms

Sometimes, terrible acts of violence take our precious children's lives, and we cannot bear to think of what they had to endure. A sex offender murdered Isaac Helms when he was 11 years old. Police apprehended and arrested the offender. Although it does not seem possible, Isaac did not experience the violence inflicted upon him.

I received this report about Isaac. "Angels protected Isaac Helms. He did not feel the pain inflicted by his murderer. The angels gently removed him from his body and did not let him see what was happening to it. He went straight into the arms of angels."

Years ago, I read about an instance in which a group of children somewhere in China had lost their lives. I do not remember the specific details, but I remember being disturbed because I wanted to help them and did not feel that I could. I asked my angels, "What will happen to the Chinese children who have lost their lives? I do not know their names, so I cannot ask that you find these specific children."

The angels had a comforting answer. They said, "We pay special attention to children. When children die, angel mothers fly to them. The angels comfort the children while holding them in their arms. Children receive special attention. Angels take the children into the light with loving tenderness."

The following story, about a little girl who needed and received angelic assistance, illustrates how angels care for children. I did not know about her ahead of time, so I did not ask angels to bring her to me. She appeared during my morning meditation, and I could see her as clearly as if she were physically present. I had no idea how she lost her life or what her name was. The angels did not volunteer any background information.

Mommy Angels

The angels did not say a word to me, but there she was, a picture of a little angel herself. She was wearing a pink dress, and she had long blonde curly hair tied back with matching pink ribbons. A bright angelic beam of light surrounded her and the whole area around her. She was standing in the center crying and rubbing her eyes with her hands. She appeared to be about four or five years old. I began to speak with her.

Kay: I have come to help you. Can you hear me okay?

Little Girl: I do not know you.

Kay: Do you know what angels are?

Little Girl: (sniffling): Yes, I do.

Kay: I am going to send angels to help you.

Little Girl: (Sobbing and demanding) I do not want angels. I want my mommy! I want my mommy!

A group of angels appeared and spoke to her, but she ignored them and continued crying. The angels kept trying to get her to focus on them and what they were saying, but she was not the least bit interested. After several attempts to connect with her failed, I started to get worried. I asked the angels, "What do we do now?" They did not respond, but these angels left, and a short time later, five sweet motherly angels appeared, each holding a cherub in her arms.

One by one, each angel bent over and gently placed her cherub next to the little girl. The girl stopped crying, and her eyes sparkled with delight. Immediately the little girl and the cherubs began to play together. The mother angels stood aside and lovingly watched the children playing. Then suddenly, the elated little girl looked up at the angels and crooned, "Oh! Mommy angels!" At this point, one of the angels gently picked up the little girl and held her close. The little girl, who by then was completely relaxed, smiled with delight as she nestled into the Mommy angel's arms.

The scene before me was reassuring. These wise angels knew what to do to comfort the little girl so she would go with them to the higher dimensions. They gave her exactly what she needed to feel safe, cared for, and loved. My heart filled with joy as I watched the beaming little girl, her new cherub friends, and the Mommy angels gradually disappear from my view as they lifted into the heavens.

The assisting angels are wonderfully inventive as they relate to deceased people with patience, kindness, and sensitivity. They do whatever they can to make those they are helping feel comfortable and safe. Some of us require a lot of special attention before we are willing to trust, which does not deter these angels. It especially warms my heart to witness the special loving care the angels give to children, the dearest of the dear.

Susan Sherman

One day while eating breakfast, I kept hearing the name Susan floating in my brain. I recognized this as a prompt from my angelic partners, who were answering my request. The previous day a friend of mine asked me to check on a woman named Susan

Sherman. She had been murdered a year earlier. So, the following morning, when I heard angels whispering Susan's name, I knew that Susan had not been able to maneuver herself into the higher dimensions. My partner angels found her and brought her to me. After breakfast, I sat down with paper and pencil and began to record my conversation with Susan.

Kay: Susan Sherman, are you here?

Susan: Who are you, and what do you know about me?

Kay: Yesterday, a friend who knows Joseph and is concerned about his battle with depression asked me to check to see if you need help getting into the light. My friend said that you raised Joseph and treated him like a son. Unfortunately, last year you were murdered. Joseph recently told my friend that he has been depressed ever since you died.

Susan: Well, you know a lot about me. I will tell you who killed me.

Kay: Is it somebody you knew?

Susan: Very well.

Kay: If you want to tell me, you can, but you do not have to.

Susan: I am thinking about what I am going to say. I do not want this to be misconstrued.

Kay: Take your time, Susan.

Susan: I was involved in something dishonest, and my son found out. He was very angry with me, disgusted. We quarreled, and he insisted that I tell the police about my activities and reveal the names of the two individuals that got me hooked on drugs and were also doing this to other women.

Kay: What were these individuals doing?

Susan: I am ashamed to tell you, but I will. I was addicted to cocaine. When my son found out, he wanted to know how this could have happened. I told him that I had known one of the men for about two years and liked him because he was funny. He introduced me to a friend of his who I did not particularly like. I should have known better, but I went out with them to this restaurant not far from where I used to bowl. It was not far from the bowling alley.

Anyway, they cajoled me into using drugs for the first time. I should not have, I know, but I thought they were my friends, and I thought it was a one-time-only experience. Now I realize that I was a patsy. They targeted other women and me in particular that they thought they could get hooked. Then they used us to deliver drugs to some of their paying customers. They gave us drugs to feed our habits. That is how they controlled us.

By the time my son discovered what I was involved in, they had me, so I could not break free. They threatened to kill me if I went to the police. I had my son pushing me to go to the police, and I did not know what to do. Unfortunately, I told the drug dealers that I was through doing their dirty work and, if they did not leave me alone, I would go to the police. I gave them an ultimatum in a moment of sheer stupidity.

My son knows who the people are that killed me. He does not want the same thing to happen to him, so he did not tell the police what he knew. He is trying to live with this secret, but it is too much for him to bear. He has become angry, sad, and very insecure about his safety.

Kay: What about Joseph? Does he know about all this?

Susan: Joseph has reason to be depressed. It was because of Joseph that I met the first person, the funny one. Joseph was not using drugs that I know of, but he knew and liked this person. That is how I met the first drug dealer. He was a friend of Joseph's. That is how he introduced himself.

Of course, Joseph had no reason to know that his drug dealer friend was looking for women, particularly women who were too naïve to catch on to their operation. If Joseph had not befriended him, I never would have gotten involved. I have known other women they did this to. I guess we were somewhat the same – too naïve, too trusting, and not smart enough to say no to that first hit.

Kay: Do you have more to say, Susan?

Susan: I do not fault Joseph or my son for what happened. I blame myself for allowing this situation to develop. I do not want them to hurt themselves or their relationship because of what happened. However, I do want something from both of them, and it will take courage. I want to expose those two drug dealers, not to get revenge for what they did to me, but to keep them from underhandedly recruiting unsuspecting women into their drug trafficking.

Here is my plan. I have seen how these people operate, and their weakness is that they think they can get away with anything. My son knows who they are, and Joseph can identify the funny one. They can send a letter to the police, preferably to a specific person familiar with my case. The letter can tell the story of what happened to other women and me. First, they targeted us and gave us drugs as a way to get us addicted. Then they forced us to deliver their drugs to paying customers. These guys deserve jail time. They should be locked up for that alone.

I do not think anyone could prove that they murdered me, so I do not think that should be the objective. If the police know what these men are up to, they can gather evidence to convict them of drug dealing. Some of the women they have been using would testify against them if they had immunity from prosecution. I hope that by revealing my story, the police will put these murdering drug dealers in jail.

Kay: Susan, this is quite a story. May I ask you a question?

Susan: Sure, go ahead.

Kay: Are you suggesting that Joseph and your son should write an anonymous letter to the police? Should it be unsigned? If so, should they use your name or make the, I am not sure what word to use, revelation or accusation generalized? If they use your name, the police will undoubtedly go to them to ask questions. That could alert the drug dealers if they are keeping an eye on your son and Joseph.

Susan: I have thought about these things. If the letter does not have a signature but mentions what happened to me, the police will think that it was written by someone who they got hooked on drugs and is afraid to step forward. If the boys do not get too specific about my murder but use it as an example of what has been going on, the police will consider it a chance to uncover a drug ring that preys upon unwary women. This approach will actually evoke more interest from the police.

I do not want the boys to put themselves at risk, but I also do not want those hoodlums to keep hurting innocent people. If the boys do not want to do this, I certainly understand. However, if there is any way they can give the police this information without the drug dealers finding out, I think they could be stopped.

At least I got my story out, and I hope this clears the air between my son and Joseph. I love both of them dearly and do not want either one to blame themselves or each other. I think I am ready to leave this whole episode behind me.

Do you mind contacting Mother Mary to see if she would mind coming to get me? When I saw her talking to you, I could not believe my eyes. I would love to go with her to see God. Is that how it works? First, you die, then you wander around being invisible for a long time, and then you finally find someone you can talk to that hears what you are saying?

Kay: In your case, Susan, this is exactly how it worked, but you had other options all along.

Susan: Where does the God part come in? I have not been in heaven, and I have not been in hell. I did not know what to expect when I died, but I would never have expected this.

Kay: Susan, when you died, angels or loved ones were there to greet you and escort you into the heavens. Some people go straight into the tunnel of light themselves, but most have escorts. Sometimes when people die in a fearful state of mind, which you probably did, they fail to notice that they are not by themselves.

As they dwell on what happened to them, they fail to discern that they are not alone. Angels and other greeters come from heaven, where the vibrational frequencies are much higher than they are on Earth. These higher vibrations make it more difficult to detect their presence, and especially if you are not looking for them, you might not see them.

Susan: Oh, I get it. I thought I saw some other people when I died, but I was so shocked that those lousy drug dealers did that to me that I did not pay attention to what must have been the people you are talking about. I did not notice them again.

Kay: Susan, I would not be surprised if some of them are still with you. How did you find me today? Yesterday I asked some angel friends to check on you to see if you needed help to get to heaven, and here you are today. I will bet that angels, who have been with you all along, brought you to me. I will ask Mother Mary to come over to you, and while I am doing this, I suggest that you look around and see if you have any angels around you.

Susan: I see four angels standing off to one side. I think they are waiting for something. Oh, she is back! Mother Mary came, and now the angels are moving forward alongside Mother Mary. They are floating over to where I am. I cannot believe how lucky I am. I feel very wonderful.

Kay: Susan, I am happy for you. Are you ready to go with Mother Mary and the angels to heaven?

Susan: First, I want to tell you something. I never thought I would tell my story to someone who would actually hear what I had to say. I feel relieved that I could unburden myself, and there is a chance that my son and Joseph will know what happened to me. Even if they do not contact the police, I hope they use this information to become close again.

Kay: Are you ready to go with Mother Mary and the angels?
Susan: Sure am!

When people such as Susan ask that I become involved acting on their behalf in the physical world, I am torn between wanting to help them with their request and limiting my involvement. What may seem like a simple request would take a lot of detective work on my part. Only sometimes do I know where the crime occurred, and rarely do the deceased mention last names. The details are insufficient to make a credible statement to authorities without full names, dates, and places.

Joanna

The newspapers had another report of a child's abduction. Most of us feel revulsed by those who injure children, and we carry extreme sadness for the child and their family. Nearly all of us have a special place in our hearts for children and cannot imagine anyone deliberately hurting a child. Children are precious and require our protection. We all carry the responsibility to safeguard children and to treat them with loving respect.

Joanna was a teenage girl lured into the car of someone she barely knew. She was trusting and had no idea that this person would take her life. Often teenagers are especially vulnerable to trusting people that are not what they seem to be. Joanna's life ended after she made this one critical mistake. On her way to school one morning, she was kidnapped, and then her abductor killed her. My angels found her immediately when I asked them to look for her. I could feel her presence, so I started to call her name.

Kay: Hello, Joanna. Hello, Joanna.

Joanna: Yes, ma'am.

Kay: Are you here with me?

Joanna: I can see you sitting on your chair writing something down.

Kay: I am sorry, Joanna, about what happened to you.

Joanna: I do not understand what happened. I had seen this guy. He had a car. I knew who he was, and he offered me a ride. I should not have gotten into his car. He grabbed me and held me down. I could not get away. Then he did terrible things to me. I could see my mother in the kitchen. She did not hear me telling her what was happening. She could not hear me. Then he killed me, and I went back to my mother. None of my family can see me or hear that I am talking to them. I am okay now. I want to get back to my family. I want to go to school again. Where am I? What is going to happen?

Kay: That man killed your physical body, and now you are living in your spirit body, which cannot be hurt. It is time for you to go to heaven, Joanna. Wonderful angels have been with you since that happened. These angels will take you to heaven and stay with you. They will show you wondrous things and take you to your grandmother who is already living there. In addition to your grandmother, other people are eager to welcome you and care for you in heaven.

Joanna: How am I going to get there? I do not know what to do.

Kay: Look around and tell me what you see.

Joanna: One, two, three. Oh my. There are angels everywhere. Some are my age. They are taking me by the hand, and I am happy. This makes me feel wonderful. They say they will take care of me, and there is a lot for me to do that is fun in heaven. I am going with them. They tell me I can come back and visit my family any time I want. I almost forgot to say thank you. You helped me. Now I know what to do. You are a nice person. Thank you for helping me.

Kay: You are most welcome, Joanna. Have a great time in heaven.

I had a heavy heart knowing what happened to Joanna, and from time to time, I thought about her and wondered what life was like for her since she went with the angels. Two years or so had gone by when, much to my delight, Joanna returned to pay me a visit

Joanna: Are you the lady who found angels to come and take me to heaven?

Kay: Yes, Joanna.

Joanna: I wanted to come back and tell you how it worked out for me. I am doing very well. I do not think I am carrying any damage from what that guy did to me. I forgave him and let go of everything that he did. I do not think about any of it usually, and if I do, it seems like a made-up story and not something that happened to me.

Kay: I am happy to hear this, Joanna. I think about you from time to time and wonder what it is like for you now.

Joanna: I do not go to a real school, but I am receiving a great education. When I first got here, I met a group of kids about my age. They were teenagers, and we hung out together and talked a lot. Now I know them well, and we are still together. We are maturing into adulthood together as if we were sisters and brothers from the same playful family. They all arrived up here prematurely as I did. Most of them died at a young age because they had illnesses that took their lives. We are all happy being together.

Kay: Do you attend high school or college?

Joanna: We have informal lessons about cultures on Earth. Some of my friends are from countries that I never even heard of before. When offered different subjects to become knowledgeable about, we decided to study each other's cultures. What we are learning helps us to broaden our view of what life is like on Earth. We have become knowledgeable on different cultures, many of which we are considering being born into when we return for another life on Earth.

We all want to come back close to each other so we can continue our friendships in the culture we all choose as our top pick. We do not have a unanimous vote yet, but we are close. Almost all of us want to experience living in India.

Kay: What attracts most of you to India, Joanna?

Joanna: None of us, not even one, has experienced living in or even visiting India. Some of the people here, who have come to teach us about the culture they were from, came from India. They seem to have strong family ties there, which is important to us. We like their gentleness and their spirituality. Unless we change our minds, it looks like we will be reborn in India.

We are all hoping to be born into successful, loving families. In addition, we would like to be related to each other. There are fourteen of us so it could work out that we would be brothers, sisters, and cousins. Wouldn't that be fun? We want to continue being best friends even when we are there.

Kay: Joanna, that sounds like a wonderful idea. I hope you all stay very close to each other when you come back. I just thought of something. What about timing? That is a large group of newcomers to enter a family, even an extended family.

Joanna: (laughing) We all had thoughts about coming in as triplets to get us all back together. I do not know if our plan will be accepted. We may have to compromise. Maybe we should just shoot for coming back in the same village if we cannot be in the same extended family.

Kay: May you and your friends receive your hearts' desire to come back together, Joanna. Meanwhile, continue having a good time where you are. I wish your parents could know how happy and fulfilled you are now. If they could see how joyful you are now, whatever pain they still feel over losing you would be greatly soothed.

When I reflected on how Joanna initially explained what was happening to her during the abuse, I remembered reading that sometimes when people suffer abuse, they disassociate from their bodies. Their minds go off, away from the abuse, and focus on something else. Disassociation is one way to lessen the impact of abuse.

When the violence began, Joanna's consciousness focused solely on her spirit body, which had disassociated from her physical body. In her spirit body, she effectively fled from the crime scene. Her mother could not know her daughter's spirit was present with her.

Joanna knew what happened to her body, but she had physically and mentally detached from what occurred. She was not present in her body to feel it. Our ultimate consciousness and sense of self come from our spirit body, not our physical body as we typically think. Since our spirit body contains our consciousness, whatever happens to our physical body after our spirit has left does not physically hurt us.

The Couple from Houston

One bright sunny morning after a great night's sleep, I walked into the kitchen and glanced at the morning paper. The report on the front page was distressing. Someone had murdered an employee of a Houston oil company, and his wife, at the residence where they lived while working in Saudi Arabia. At that time, it was common for the major oil companies to send representatives to Saudi Arabia to work there to develop a closer relationship between the Saudi's and the U. S. oil companies.

The article said that there were no suspects, but an investigation was underway. Immediately I summoned my guidance to check on the couple who died. Within three minutes, the deceased husband and wife were right there in front of me. They were surprised and bewildered that they were instantly transported from Saudi Arabia to some woman's kitchen in Sugar Land, Texas.

They had shocked looks on their faces, and they wanted to know how I knew of their situation and how they came to be with me in my home in Texas. I explained that I read what happened to them in the newspaper, and as soon as I finished speaking, they both piped up. Simultaneously they both blurted out that the gardener killed them. They explained that they were living in the compound that housed foreign workers and their families. The couple told me they barely knew the gardener since he had been hired before they arrived.

The couple's main objective was to disclose that the gardener was the one who killed them. They did not seem focused on anything else, and they were tremendously relieved when finally they were able to communicate with someone to identify their assailant. They did not notice angels standing right next to them. When I asked who was standing near them, their surprised faces lighted up with joy. Only after they had unloaded what they were concerned about did they observe the angelic presence and comprehend what was about to happen to them next. They could not have been more pleased.

My reason for mentioning this particular occurrence is to demonstrate that once a person detaches from their physical body, they no longer experience the limitations of time and space. Within their spirit body, they can navigate halfway around the world if that is their intention. Once we throw off the constraints of physicality, our mental processes direct our spirit body to go where we want it to go. We are free of the limitations that we experience while we are physically present on Earth.

Islamic State Hostages

In 2014, the horrific crimes committed by the Islamic State, also known as ISIL or ISIS, hijacked the worldwide news reports. The Islamic State took non-combatant hostages, tortured them, and bragged to the world that they would execute the hostages, which they did in a series of beheadings. These people captured three hostages. One by one, the terrorists beheaded them. The Islamic State posted graphic videos of their deaths and threatened to continue beheading others.

When I asked angels to check on Joseph Franklin, they reported that Joseph immediately went into the higher dimensions. He had no difficulty whatsoever after he passed from his body. The same was true for David Harrison. Of David, the angels said, "He was a very spiritual person, and he prepared himself. He forgave his butchers and set himself free from the trauma they inflicted upon him." Samuel Sutter underwent a more problematic transition and needed assistance. The angels brought Samuel to me and began our contact.

Angels: We have Samuel Sutter.

Kay: Hello, Samuel. I am sorry about what happened to you.

Samuel: They were terrible to us; they kept threatening us all the time. They treated us abusively. They got me to say things I did not mean. I was afraid. Actually, it was a relief to die to get away from them. They are terrible people. They enjoy torturing and killing people.

Kay: Did you happen to see any angels after you died?

Samuel: No. Was I supposed to?

Kay: You had the opportunity to see them. They were there with you. You must have been too afraid. The good news, Samuel, is that they are still with you.

Samuel: They are? Where? I do not see them.

Kay: Keep looking, Samuel. I assure you that they are right there with you.

Samuel: I am starting to see images – like shadows.

Kay: That is all? You should see more than shadows. Are you afraid to see the angels?

Samuel: Maybe I am. I hated those people that captured us and tormented us. I would have killed them if I could. I did not start out having these feelings, but they were boastful and cruel. I could not stand being there with them. Do you think I will be forgiven for having thoughts about wanting to kill them?

Kay: Samuel, I think you have to forgive yourself and not hold it against yourself for having those feelings. If you can be kind to yourself and forgive your thoughts about wanting to do to them what they did to you, it will help you see your angels.

Samuel: Did you say, my angels?

Kay: Yes, Samuel, your special angels are with you and ready to take you with them as soon as you can see and hear them.

Samuel: I forgive myself. I know, with all my heart, I would not have had such feelings if I had not been tortured. I am only human, and I was reacting to their cruelty. I do forgive myself. (Short pause) Wow, that was quick! They must have already been here. There are several beautiful lady angels and one big, strong-looking male angel.

Kay: Ask him what his name is.

Samuel: I did what you asked. He said to tell you that he is the one who protects you from harm.

Kay: Then that is Archangel Michael.

Samuel: He is smiling and nodding his head. I feel like he is going to protect me, too. I am going with him and the beautiful lady angels. Now I do not mind what happened to me. Look at me now. I am safe with heavenly angels safeguarding me. I am okay now, no more problems for me.

About a week later, angels announced that Samuel came back to speak with me, and I strongly felt his presence.

Kay: Hello, Samuel.

Samuel: Are you available now? I see you busily doing one thing after another. Do you have time for me?

Kay: Yes, Samuel. I definitely have time to be with you and hear what you have to say. Go ahead.

Samuel: You are a remarkable person.

Kay: Why do you say that?

Samuel: I know what you are like. If one of those militants died and needed help, you would help them too, wouldn't you?

Kay: Yes, Samuel, you are right. I try not to differentiate between good guys and bad guys.

Samuel: How can you do that?

Kay: Maybe because I have not had to face their direct blows as you did. I am more removed, and I try to look at the greater picture.

Samuel: What greater picture? Bad guys are bad guys, aren't they?

Kay: Samuel, you have not been up in the higher realms for very long. You just got there.

Samuel: I feel better since I got here, and you are right. I do not understand how everything works yet. Archangel Michael took me directly to the place where I am now. It is a kind of rehabilitation center for people like me. Many people here suffered gruesome deaths.

Kay: Is it like a hospital?

Samuel: No, not at all. It is more like - I do not know how to describe it – a beautiful area with acres upon acres of wooded land, lakes, sweet animals that come right up to us to say hello, gentle breezes blowing, and the sounds of birds singing. We love it here. We have not mixed yet with the general population, so there is a lot I do not know.

Everyone is friendly and very interested in this new place. None of us wants to think about what happened before we came here. We wish we could forget. We were told that we would become peaceful, accepting, and even forgiving towards those who brutalized us. We have also been told not to rush this process, that we must feel it within our hearts for the forgiveness to be valid.

You are right, I have not been here long, but I am not inclined to dismiss what was done to me.

Kay: This is hard to hear. I feel very sorry for you and the other people who are where you are. I cannot imagine how tough it must have been for you.

Samuel: I do not like to bare my feelings usually, but I am comfortable speaking with you. I think it helps me. Do you mind?

Kay: Not at all. What else would you like to bring up?

Samuel: My family. I miss them. I wish I had not gone on that last adventure. I did not think that such cruelty existed or, if it did, that I would become its target. Don't people know that it destroys part of themselves when they kill another person? Maybe the people who killed me killed so many other people that their hearts are gone. They have no love or respect for other people, especially when they are different. They will eventually end up hating themselves. They will feel like filth inside.

You know what happens after you die, don't you?

Kay: Do you mean seeing the movie of your life?

Samuel: Yes. Wouldn't you hate watching yourself torturing and killing people? Those terrorists think they are getting away with their barbarism, but there is no escape from evil actions. They will have to atone for all of them. Then they will understand the full impact of what they did to me when they feel how I felt when they tortured me and slaughtered me. I do not take any joy in them having to go through experiencing what they forced me to experience. I pity them.

Kay: Samuel, would you like to say anything else?

Samuel: Warn people that cruelty imposed upon other people will come back and hit you hard. When you get over here where I am, it is too late to erase the slate, and you are on the hook to suffer what you imposed on other people. You actually feel what they were feeling when you were hurting them. You risk your own well-being when you destroy someone else's in deliberately hurtful ways. In the end, none of it is worth it. Whatever satisfaction you gain by hurting someone else is not enough to put yourself through the same thing.

I am going to be all right. I am still processing what happened to me. I keep going over it, and each time I do, the impact decreases. I am desensitizing myself to what occurred. Already it seems like, in a way, it did not really happen. Almost as if it was a nightmare, and now I am awake.

I will remain here in this serene environment until I put all that happened to me while I was in captivity behind me.

Kay: Samuel, may I use what you have told me to alert other people?

Samuel: If I can help someone else in any way, I would like to. Be my guest.

After a few weeks went by, the same terrorist group beheaded another aid worker, Albert Harrison. My heart dropped as I read the report of what occurred in the newspaper. Again, I sent my angels, this time, to see if Albert needed assistance. After hearing about the lingering problems that Samuel was still wrestling with, I was relieved to receive the angelic report that Albert had prepared himself and had no after-death difficulty. He went straight up into the heavens despite the brutality he experienced.

Samuel's and Albert's experiences demonstrate that, in the end, we determine what happens to us after we die. It is our state of mind and our ability to let go of what happened, even though it may have been excruciatingly horrible to endure, that sets up a superb resolution for ourselves. We are not our physical bodies, although while we are physically alive, we tend to feel that we are. Our ability to experience continues after we shed our physical body, as demonstrated in Samuel's and all these other people's communications. If something as horrible as what happened to Samuel should also happen to us, we know that the terrible part is over once our physical life has ended, and all we need to do then is reach for the angels who will have their arms extended, ready to receive us.

CHAPTER SEVEN
MURDERERS

The other side of the coin from being murdered is being the person who committed murder. Rarely do we receive enough insight into murderers' backgrounds and their psychological states to begin to understand what led them to take such an inhumane course of action. Often, murderers lose their lives while killing other people, which obscures public knowledge of their motivations. The big mystery of why they did what they did leaves an ache in our hearts that does not easily release. This chapter presents four conversations with deceased people who committed murder and two conversations between Muhammad and people who committed terrorist acts.

The Las Vegas Shooter

After someone goes on a killing spree, the big mystery is what motivated the killer to take such action. The Las Vegas Shooter chose his time and place well. He was determined to kill as many people as possible, so he stockpiled guns and ammunition in his hotel room. His room overlooked the site of a country music performance. On October 1, 2017, he began his mass execution of fifty-eight people and the wounding of hundreds more in a planned and systematic way. His act was deliberate. He thought he was making a valiant effort to defend his country as he unleashed a barrage of bullets upon people who were relaxing and enjoying themselves.

Angels were busy that day soothing and transporting deceased people into the higher dimensions. The mass killing horrified the whole country, and the big question in everyone's mind was why would a person deliberately set out to slaughter as many people as he could and then give up his own life? For nearly a year and a half, investigators searched for answers to that question. In January of 2019, the FBI issued a final behavioral report saying, "The shooter wanted mass destruction but was not motivated by a grievance against anyone killed or injured in the attack."

In October of 2017, as I monitored the unfolding news reports about the shooting in Las Vegas, I remained in constant contact with the rescue angels with whom I collaborate. I thanked them for helping the people who died. I also requested angelic assistance for those wounded by the mass attack and for all of the people present who were experiencing extreme psychological distress. Two days after the attack, my helper angels brought the very remorseful shooter to me for an interview.

Kay: Hello, can you hear me?

Shooter: I don't know why I did it. I don't know why I did it.

Kay: Tell me what happened.

Shooter: You know what happened. I saw you reading that newspaper. Your husband said something to you about it.

Kay: I am asking you what happened from your perspective. What led you to think of killing so many people? Have you had an ongoing desire to hurt people or even kill them?

Shooter: Oh, I see what you are getting at. Lady, this is going to... (Pause) I am not sure I really want to talk to you. I am not sure how I arrived where you are. You seem nice enough, but I do not even know you. I feel that I have a lot to get off my chest. (Long pause).

Kay: I feel your reluctance. It seems that you want to talk about what happened, but you are not comfortable talking to me.

Shooter: Lady, I have no other choice. You are the only person I can access. For some reason, I find myself talking to you, a total stranger, and you do not seem to be infuriated at me for what I did. The rest of the world hates me, and I hate myself.

Kay: I am motivated by a desire to assist you. You would not be talking to me now if you had been able to navigate your way into the higher dimensions of existence.

Shooter: You mean heaven? If there is such a place, that certainly is not an option for me. I ought to be burning in hell for what I did.

Kay: May I ask why you stockpiled machine guns and then used them to massacre as many people as possible?

Shooter: You do not understand. I was on a rescue mission.

Kay: What kind of a rescue mission?

Shooter: I was convinced that I alone could stop the mass annihilation of humanity. That it was all up to me because I knew ...

Kay: Knew what?

Shooter: Now I am not so sure.

Kay: Sure of what?

Shooter: I had been convinced that ... Oh, this is going to sound stupid. I had been thinking for quite a time that there was going to be a sneak attack on the United States. I was sure that it would happen the next day, and the concert was where the plotters of the attack were going to arm themselves for the takeover. I knew the time was getting close for the attack, so I was accumulating defense weapons.

Kay: How did you learn about what you thought was an imminent attack on this country?

Shooter: Some people told me. I was asleep one night when five FBI agents talked to me. They said they knew I was trustworthy, and they said there was something I could do to help them protect this country.

Kay: This sounds crazy.

Shooter: I know it does. Now it sounds crazy to me, too. I was awake while sleeping. I was fully conscious while I was asleep, but I did not think I was sleeping. I believed them when they said it was up to me to save our country. They told me not to tell the police because the bad people who were going to take over our country had infiltrated the police. I had to pledge secrecy and work alone to defend our country.

Kay: Do you mind if I ask you if you take drugs?

Shooter: I used to but not for a long time.

Kay: So you were not under the influence of drugs or alcohol.

Shooter: Having a few drinks is more my style. When I heard the concert start, I knew it was time to take action against the plotters. I did my best to safeguard this country from Communist plotters.

Kay: Why did you kill yourself?

Shooter: I became frightened because it was so evident that people were dying. I panicked and started to think that I was not really saving my country, and I could not undo the mistake I made.

Kay: This is quite a story. Have you seen any of the people you killed?

Shooter: No, and I do not want to, either.

Kay: Have you ever had hallucinations?

Shooter: I did drugs for a while but not lately. Sometimes my thinking becomes confused, and I tend to be a little neurotic. I have been concerned about Communist elements within our government. This idea of a Communist takeover of our country is something fairly new. The more I thought about it, the more real it became.

Kay: I think there is a chance that dead people of evil intent manipulated your thinking and decision-making. I do not know for sure. Give me a minute. I am going to ask some angels if they will reveal what happened behind the scenes.

Angels: Your suspicions are accurate. Evil deceased people duped this man. They placed their thoughts into his mind and manipulated him to take action to prevent Communist interference in this country. His mind was open to the power of unconscious suggestions, so evil deceased people led him on a feigned heroic quest to save his country.

Kay: Sir, were you able to hear what these angels said?

Shooter: Yes. I cannot stop looking at them. They have the kindest, most peaceful looks on their faces. I feel their love flowing into me. They say they are taking me to a certain part of heaven, especially for people like me. They are telling me that I need to learn to lead a more contributing life. They also said that I have a problem with being emotionally stopped up. I think they are right and I am going to go with them.

Before I leave you, I want to ask forgiveness from all the people that I caused to suffer because of my idiotic quest to protect our country from my illusion of an imminent Communist takeover.

This man was not the only person that evildoers manipulated into massacring other people.

Joseph

A school shooting occurred in the western part of the United States. An outgoing, very well-liked student, who had great potential for a bright future, acted against his nature and became involved in a scheme that would cost some of the other students their lives. Evil-intentioned deceased people manipulated Joseph by implanting their thoughts into his mind.

Joseph acted out what they had convinced him was a joke and then watched in horror as his actions took the lives of his best friends and ultimately cost him his life as well. His horrific act caused significant pain and sorrow to the entire community, especially those who knew and loved the children wounded or killed. Actions such as these are incomprehensible, and the community was left baffled as to why this seemingly well-adjusted young man performed this dreadful act of terror.

I felt horror-struck, as did the rest of us who read the account of what happened. My mind searched for possible reasons that could have motivated this young man to act so entirely out of character for him. In similar situations, the aggressors seemed to be on the outskirts of society because of psychological problems or ideological fixations. This situation seemed different from the others and was alarming because of the inability to attach a reason to the madness.

As is typical for me, I contacted my angelic partners when I heard what happened and asked them to ensure that those students who died transitioned into the heavens. My angels' report was as I anticipated. The murdered students, who were all good friends, remained together after passing out of their bodies. They moved around from place to place, within the ethers nearest the Earth, in a state of confusion, wondering what to do.

The angels promptly brought them close enough to me that I could detect a conversation going on, but I could not discern what they were saying. I did not know until later that angels tried to convince all of the teenagers to go with them. After a brief time, the angels told me that those who were shot and killed went with some other angels. However, the shooter refused to go with the rest of them. He was not receptive to the angels' offer of assistance and stayed behind. The angels directed me to speak with him.

Kay: Joseph, can you hear me?

Joseph: I do not want to talk.

Kay: Joseph, I read about what happened at the school that day. Angels told me that the other students who died already went to heaven. Did the angels offer to take you to heaven?

Joseph: There were not any angels. The rest of them made it up, and then they all left.

Kay: Joseph, I communicate with angels, and they told me that the other students went with them. The others are in heaven, and you could be, too.

Joseph: I would not be accepted there.

Kay: Change your thinking, Joseph. Whatever happened before is not going to keep you out of heaven.

Joseph: (Incredibly) It won't?

Kay: Joseph, the angels are as determined for you to go to heaven as the others who died during that sad day. If you are willing to go, they will immediately be at your side to take you.

Joseph: But what about what I did? I acted out a fantasy I had. That thought kept playing through my mind. I felt like I was in a movie. It did not seem real. Even as I was shooting my best friends, I did not feel that it was really me. It could not really have been me. I loved them. I would not want to hurt them.

Kay: Joseph, that shooting may not have been entirely your fault. There are people like yourself, as you are now, that have died but have not gone up to heaven. Some of these people are particularly evil, and sometimes they can take over the mind of someone who is still alive and try to get that person to do something to hurt themselves or other people. That may be what happened to you. Those evildoers could have been controlling your mind and feeding you this fantasy, thereby exerting control over you.

Joseph: So maybe I am not completely at fault?

Kay: If what I suspect is true, you were not completely at fault. You are ultimately responsible, but in these situations, it can be nearly impossible to differentiate your thoughts from the intruders' overriding power to imprint their evil intentions into your brain.

Joseph: (Crying) I did not want to hurt my friends or anybody.

Kay: Joseph, would you consider going with the angels?

Joseph: If you think you can get some angels to take me to heaven, I will go. I do not know what else to do, and besides, I think what you just told me is what happened. How can I know for sure?

Kay: When you go to heaven, you will see exactly what happened that day when you view the movie of your life. You will know what compelled you to act as you did. Your friends will forgive you, and you will be able to forgive yourself.

Joseph: I really need to understand what happened to me that gave me that fantasy to start with. Do you think I could be mentally ill?

Kay: That is also a possibility, Joseph. Once you get to heaven, you will find out the true cause. Are you ready to meet some compassionate angels?

Joseph: Yes, ma'am. (Pause) Oh, look! My friends are with them. They all look radiant. One of my friends just said, "We forgive you. We miss you. Come with us." I am going with them, but before I leave, I want to thank you for caring about me. I do not despise myself anymore, and I am going to find out the truth. I will know for sure what it was that made me do what I did.

Kay: I am happy for you, Joseph.

I could not stop wondering what it was that compelled Joseph to go in such an unlikely direction. When I spoke with him, he seemed very rational, contrite, and hard on himself. Joseph did not seem like he had a chip on his shoulder or any resentment. He took full responsibility for what had occurred. Not long after Joseph went with the angels, he returned to give a more detailed picture of what happened on that regrettable day.

Angels: Joseph is eager to discuss what he learned when he saw the movie of himself.

Joseph: It was awful. What I created was awful. I cannot believe I did that. Heartless. Cruel. Disgusting.

Kay: Joseph, were you able to identify why you went on that shooting rampage?

Joseph: I saw it all, everything that happened leading up to my big blow-up. The movie I saw of my life was clear and accurate. Nothing in that movie was different from what actually happened to me growing up. It was all the same. That part was fun for me to see. I wish there could have been a different ending. That part was not fun for me. It was horrible, but now I know what happened. It was just as you thought it might be.

Kay: It was?

Joseph: You said that dead people might have been putting thoughts in my mind.

Kay: Yes. I thought that was a possibility.

Joseph: It seemed like I was thinking those things: that it was my fantasy. Now I know that I would never have done what I did. I would never have had that fantasy if those three dead people had not manipulated me. They took over my mind. They gave me what I thought was a fantasy. They were placing their evil thoughts into my mind.

They started slowly, and then the fantasy got stronger and stronger. Finally, I could not stop thinking about putting on a play with my best friends, and we would all act out the fantasy that was in my mind. It would be kind of a joke. Then, when it was over, all of us would laugh at the other kids' reactions.

However, when I started shooting, there was real blood and screaming. I saw myself massacring my classmates, my dearest friends. It was me doing this but not me doing this at the same time. It felt like I was living in a nightmare that I was asleep and dreaming a frightening dream. The next thing was me shooting myself because my hand was pushed upward. It is a good thing that happened. It stopped me from hurting more people.

After I died, I felt better. I could not stop crying, but I was not hurting anyone anymore.

Kay: Joseph, after you died, did you see those three dead people? How do you know there were three of them? Did you know at that time, or did you find out from watching the movie of your life?

Joseph: The movie showed more details than I was aware of as it all happened. After I died, my brain was scrambled. I was shocked at what I did. I could not make sense of anything. Then I saw them out of the corner of my eye. They were like three shadows fading away from me. As they disappeared, I heard them cry out, "We got ya, kid." I did not know what they were talking about.

When I saw the movie of my life, I understood. I saw how they manipulated me to do what they wanted me to do and made me think it was my own idea. I told myself that it was a fantasy. That is the only way I could be comfortable with the crazy thoughts in my head. I told myself that these thoughts were not what I was thinking or what I would do. I knew I would never hurt anyone, so I thought I was safe. I do not know what I could have done to get me out from being under their influence. Do you know?

Kay: No, but let us see if we can get some angels to answer your question. Dear angels, we would like to know how to protect ourselves from evil thinking, whether it be our evil thinking or evil thoughts fed into us by other people, either living or dead people.

Angels: There is one best way to clear minds from evil thought processes, and it comes in three separate steps. The first step is to keep repeating, either in your mind or aloud, "I am a good person. I will not bring harm to myself or any other person." Repeating this will largely help dissipate evil thinking, especially when the person utilizes strong will and determination while saying this.

Deliberately erasing evil thinking is the next step. Whenever evil or even troublesome thoughts arise in your mind, tell yourself to delete them. Hit a mental delete button and be done with them. Then do not allow them back. Feel free to practice this procedure daily to keep your mind tuned to only the most positive thoughts.

The third step is only for use when the first two steps combined do not entirely eradicate evil thoughts. If the problem still exists, understand that you may not be willing to give these up, that you are hanging onto these thoughts to punish yourself or other people. If this is the case, search for, identify and resolve the cause of one's need to punish someone. Seek assistance from people who are sensitive, caring, thoughtful, rational, and trustworthy. Sometimes turning to others can help accomplish what we cannot do by ourselves.

Kay: That is all?

Angels: Yes. Following these steps would have booted Joseph right out of evil thinking and out from under the control of those miserable, evil-intentioned dead people. He could have avoided the heartache brought about by interference deliberately put upon him by forces outside of himself.

Kay: Thank you for explaining this. What happened to the three deceased people who set Joseph up?

Angels: There are angelic forces always on the lookout for evil-acting deceased people who interfere with the well-being of people on Earth. Angels apprehended those three troublemakers who took over Joseph's rational mind and placed them in a reeducation center.

Kay: This is good news. Joseph, do you have any questions to ask these angels?

Joseph: Their advice would have stopped me from doing what I did. I wish I had it before all that happened. I would have had a way to overcome those thoughts they put in my mind.

Kay: Joseph, I am in the process of collecting people's stories about their death experiences to help other people. Do you mind if I include what happened to you in this book of people's stories?

Joseph: I want you to. I do not want anyone else manipulated as I was. Can I add something else to what you write? I would like to say I am sorry to my family and the other kids' families for causing this horrible thing to happen. I am not a bad person. I really love everybody, and I wish I could make what happened all go away. It hurts me to have caused such violence, and now I feel stupid for being duped by those horrible dead people who got me to do what I would never have done if they had only left me alone.

Joseph's ordeal holds lessons for all of us. We must watch what goes on in our minds to ensure that we act out of goodness and rationality. The stronger we become in our watchfulness and commitment to maintaining a positive state of mind, the more we will reap the many benefits, including harmlessness to ourselves and other people. Our actions reflect what is in our minds. Right actions come from right thinking, and we can train ourselves to employ only right thinking.

We have allowed the progression of violence and supported it by not opposing the entertainment industry's glamorization and commercialization of violence. Sensationalizing violence distorts our thinking and potentially some of our attitudes. If we collectively stop supporting the commercialization of violence, we will be taking an important step. Our younger generations and those who have difficulty separating fantasy from reality need us to stand up for them and protect them as they maneuver in a world that seems thirsty for violence.

Saad

In 2016, another mass murder took place in the United States. This time it occurred on the east coast. A young man of Middle Eastern descent used assault weapons to attack people in a nightclub. The people who died that night were enjoying a night of festivities when this young man ended their lives.

Saad planned the attack with the intent to kill as many people as he could. He killed or wounded about one hundred people that night before police killed him in a shootout. Saad was a U.S. citizen of Middle Eastern descent. While the attack was in progress, he called 911 to pledge allegiance to the Islamic State, implying that he was an Islamic militant.

Two days later, The Great Prophet Muhammad spoke to me and told me that he wanted to have a conversation with the young man. Muhammad instructed angels to bring Saad to me so I could act as an intermediary and connect Saad with Muhammad. A few minutes after receiving Muhammad's request for my assistance, angels brought Saad to me.

Angels: We have Saad. We are bringing him to you.

Kay: Angels, does he see you? Does he know you are with him?

Angels: As far as Saad is concerned, he is alone.

(Immediately, I sensed that Saad was close by.)

Kay: I am trying to reach Saad. Saad, come and talk to me.

Saad: Who are you? What do you want from me? Are you going to kill me for what I have done?

Kay: I will not hurt you in any way, Saad.

Saad: Then what do you want from me?

Kay: A friend of yours came to me and asked me to tell you that he wants to speak with you.

Saad: You are not serious, are you? Who would want to talk to me anyway? I am a cruel and hurtful person. I have evilness inside of me.

Kay: Are you willing to talk to someone who can help you understand yourself?

Saad: Who would that be?

Kay: Muhammad wants to give you some vital information about yourself.

Saad: I wonder if he is going to praise me.

Muhammad: Saad, what you produced through your violent actions causes me pain and sorrow. Your actions scratched the itch that you felt. You wanted to destroy people. You empowered yourself to judge other people and then to levy the justice of your judgment. Now let me ask you a question, Saad. What did you expect to gain when you set out to kill as many people as you could?

Saad: God's favor. I was defending God's values.

Muhammad: Which of God's values are you referring to?

Saad: Why are you asking me these questions? You should know what God wants.

Muhammad: Spell it out for me, Saad. What are God's values that you think you were upholding?

Saad: I targeted that place at that time because those people were not clean.

Muhammad: What does that mean?

Saad: They were not following sanctioned sexual expression, and they were not Muslim.

Muhammad: Saad, you are disturbed in your thinking, and you are covering up for yourself. I will tell you why you massacred those people. You are a fake, a phony. You do not strive to defend God's standards. You took it upon yourself to massacre innocent people to flex your power muscles under the guise of religious righteousness.

You pledged your allegiance to ISIS to become a big shot, frighten people and fulfill the urge you had within you to act violently. Face it, Saad, you felt weak and insecure inside, so you killed and maimed innocent people to prove to yourself that you were a powerful person. It had nothing to do with ISIS, did it?

Saad: Muhammad, forgive me. I was not truthful with myself. Now I regret the action I took. I beg your forgiveness.

Muhammad: Saad, you will have a hard time forgiving yourself. I am now taking you to a place where you will receive an education in basic principles you need to establish within yourself. You will not leave the educational center until you learn to love and respect all other people regardless of their sexual orientation or any other attribute they may have.

Saad: Muhammad, you have already taught me to be upfront with myself and not attribute my despicable actions to any other cause than my poor estimation of other people and my urge to be violent.

There is nothing like having the mirror of reality held up to our eyes so we can see the truth. It can be tempting to concoct excuses for our behaviors that mask our inner urge to misbehave. In Saad's case, Muhammad called him on his inner deceitfulness. Saad's violent urge took over and marred the lives of hundreds of people; not only those who died, were injured, or lost loved ones, but also those whose hearts felt broken by the terrible disregard for the value of every person's life.

After passing from physicality, Saad and other murderers are prohibited from mingling with the rest of the populations within the higher dimensions. First, they must learn to embody civil, respectful behavior while being detained in Reeducation Centers. These centers are enormously restrictive and exist to teach the basics of being a dependably honorable person. The residents of the Reeducation Centers only rejoin the afterlife's general population after they have reformed themselves and passed certain tests.

Since I began this work, I have made it a point to check on people executed for committing murder. Mercifully, there are fewer executions now than there used to be. I also routinely ask angels to investigate the whereabouts of murdered victims and to assist them if necessary.

The angels taught me that even for convicted murderers, their destination is the higher dimensions. I checked on many executed convicts, and a surprising number of them went right up after their executions. However, over the years, my angelic support consistently reported that an astonishing number of murder victims remained earthbound and did not transition into the higher realms.

This information puzzled me, so I asked the angels to explain why it is easier for those who committed murder to transfer into the higher dimensions than it is for those who were murdered. The angels explained that when people are murdered, it often comes from left field and throws them into a state of disorientation, which is a significant disadvantage for them. Many of them assume that their current disassociation from life, as they knew it, is all that is possible for them, and they do not realize that there is a better option available. When they do not have an automatic reaction of rising up and going into the higher dimensions, they are likely to wander around between dimensions for many years without knowing what steps to take to find their way into the elevated spheres.

On the other hand, the person convicted of committing murder often goes through an involved court process and long imprisonment before the execution date. This person has the opportunity to come to terms with his or her culpability. They know ahead of time when they will die and have plenty of opportunities to prepare themselves and atone for what they did. People who have repented for their crimes and sought forgiveness are very likely to go straight into the elevated realms after passing from their bodies. When convicted murderers make amends for their past misdeeds, they remove their obstacles to transferring directly into the desirable afterlife following their execution.

Tragedy in San Bernardino

We cringed in horror in early December of 2015 when a husband and wife team of terrorists made a deadly strike at a Christmas party for developmentally disabled people in San Bernardino, California. The husband and wife left their infant daughter with her grandmother and set off to perform a cruel and heartless act of terror. Sixteen people died that day, including the husband and wife terrorists, and numerous people were severely injured. The husband had a well-paying job and was a devout Muslim who did not display outward signs of terroristic tendencies.

Both husband and wife were undercover militants determined to follow the way of the Islamic terrorists, who had been creating havoc in many areas of the globe. Killing in the name of Islam to gain Muhammad's favor is a huge mistake that militants make. There is no favor gained by massacring people for any reason, especially from a world teacher such as Muhammad.

I waited several days before asking my guidance to check on all the people who died during the tragedy. From experience, I found that it often takes some days before suddenly deceased people are willing to part from staying close to their families, who are mourning their loss. After unsuccessfully attempting to make their presence known to their loved ones, the deceased finally resign themselves to the reality that their loved ones will never be able to detect their presence. Then the deceased become more interested in receiving angelic assistance.

I made a list of the people who died, including the two terrorists, and then I asked my angels to check on each one of them. Interestingly, of the sixteen people that died, half of them needed assistance, and the other half had already made their way into the higher dimensions. Except for one, those that needed help stayed together and were easy for the angels to locate. When I detected that the victims were present with me, I began a conversation.

Kay: Are you from San Bernardino?

A person: Yes, we are. We were instructed to wait while you were eating. Did you enjoy your food?

Kay: Yes. Thank you. It is snowing here, and a hearty breakfast is invigorating.

Another person: We noticed we do not have any need or desire for food.

Kay: That is how it is for everyone after losing his or her physicality. Did any of you happen to see angels nearby?

Person: No.

Another person: I do! Look there, another! They are all over the place!

Kay: They have come to take you on the best adventure you have ever had.

A person: We sure could use something good happening to us now.

Kay: (as I detect them leaving) Good-bye, everybody. Do not leave anyone in your group behind.

People: Oh, we are all here together.

At that point, we had accounted for everyone except the male shooter.

Kay to the angels: What do we do about the male shooter? Did he connect with any other people?

Angels: No, he is alone. We have not been able to get through to him. Will you try?

Kay to the shooter: I apologize for not pronouncing your name right. Can you hear me?

The male shooter: Of course, I can hear you. What do you want?

Kay: I would like to help you. You do not want to stay where you are now, do you?

The male shooter: I do not know where I am. There is nothingness here.

Kay: What did you expect? You must have known you were going to end up dead.

The male shooter: I expected Muhammad to congratulate me on my effectiveness.

Kay: Sounds like you killed and wounded innocent people to please Muhammad. Was that your motivation?

The male shooter: They were infidels.

Kay: I do not know what infidels are. Are they horrible, mean, and cruel?

The male shooter: They do not believe as we do.

Kay: What do you believe?

The shooter: I believe that infidels should be killed. That it is service to Muhammad to kill infidels

Kay: Is that why you expected Muhammad to come to you after you died?

The shooter: I really thought he would be pleased with what I did for him. I expected him to praise me. I did it for him. Wait! There he is! He did come, after all. I was right!

Muhammad: No. You made a grave error. How could it ever please me that you brought harm to people that I love as much as I love you? I am never pleased when people bring harm to other people. I am especially sickened when people inflict suffering upon others because they think I do not value them.

If my followers want to get my attention and please me, they will not come under the influence of anyone who espouses any kind of violence. Especially appalling is to use evil inside of oneself to poison the minds of my followers who do not understand my true teachings. Distortions of my teachings create divisions between people who do not know the truth.

116

I forbid my followers to come under the influence of those who twist and turn my true teachings. Desert those who kill in my name. Desert those that discount the value of any person's life and well-being. Extend the hand of friendship. Invite those you had looked upon as infidels into your homes. Extend them hospitality in my name. If you love me, you will put down weapons, look those who you may have thought were infidels in the eye and ask them for their forgiveness.

Shooter: Muhammad, forgive me. I was one of those influenced to kill infidels to please you. Now I feel horrible and stupid. How can I atone for my wrongdoing?

Muhammad: You will return to live on Earth again, but next time you will be a teacher who educates teenagers and young adults in my true teachings. Next time you will be a stickler for teaching acceptance and compassion for all people. You will represent me well.

Then Muhammed extended his hand. The shooter took it, kissed it, and smiled through the tears that were streaming down his cheeks. Undoubtedly, he was relieved that he would receive an opportunity in his next lifetime to compensate for the destruction he caused while he was here this time.

We who live on Earth know pitifully little about the original teachings of the great beings who were our world teachers. Those who came to teach us loving compassion and acceptance of all people are in the higher dimensions watching distortions of their teachings being used to incite people to turn against one another. I would love to have them come to us in person and teach us in their own words.

Each of them was kind and loving, and none extolled violence. We can determine to be the same way ourselves. If we all followed one religion that taught us to love one another and nothing else, we probably would be better off than we are today.

Douglas Oster

Executed for committing murder, Douglas Oster did not go right up into the heavens. When I inquired about him, the angels confirmed that he needed our assistance. They prepared me, so I knew in advance that they were bringing him when they maneuvered Douglas to me. As soon as I called out to him, he responded.

Douglas: Hey, lady, I heard you say my name. I am Douglas Oster.

Kay: Hi, Douglas. You probably do not know that angels have brought you to me so I can help you.

Douglas: How are you going to help me? I do not deserve much help anyway.

Kay: I read in the paper about your execution this week; you were executed for committing two murders. I thought you might need some help getting to heaven, so I asked the angels to look for you. Since they brought you to me, I know that you were not up in heaven yet. Am I right?

Douglas: I do not think I would be welcome there. I committed more than one gruesome act.

Kay: Would you like to go to heaven?

Douglas: Sure would if they would take me.

Kay: The angels are eager to help you. All you need to do is to go with them. They will take you into the light.

Douglas: I do not think they will come near me.

Kay: Look around you, Douglas, and tell me what you see.

Douglas: (In a stunned voice) An angel just winked at me. Maybe I am not so bad after all.

Kay: All you need to do, Douglas, is go with the angel. The angel will take you to heaven, where you will be welcomed.

Douglas: Are you sure? You know what I did.

Kay: I am sure because everyone is welcome. The angels have an interest in helping you. That is why they brought you to me.

Douglas: Thanks, lady. You are nice. You understand that I feel bad about what I did. I am truly sorry.

Kay: Have fun in heaven, Douglas.

Douglas: Bye, lady.

Douglas is another person that I did not expect to hear from again. However, after some time went by, he returned to chat with me. I was happy to have this opportunity. Before that time, I had not heard back from any of the other executed convicts that I had become acquainted with when we assisted them.

Douglas: Kay, remember me? I am Douglas Oster. You sure helped me out, and I stopped by to thank you.

Kay: Hello, Douglas. How are you?

Douglas: I am a lot better than I was when you first talked with me. I lived like an animal before I was executed.

Kay: What do you mean, Douglas?

Douglas: I only thought about myself and getting what I wanted. I did not care about anything else. I did not have the concept of love. As a child, no one loved me, and I grew up being dishonest and hurting people. I did not care what I did to anyone else. I was out to get what I wanted, and I was mean and cruel. I never did regret it when I killed other people. There were three. Not all at once. Different times.

Anyway, I came back to say that I am a new person now. Up here, there is nothing but love, really. Everyone loves everyone else, and no one takes advantage of or is mean to anyone else. I feel like a saint, and it sure feels good to me. I never felt like this, even for one minute the whole time I was alive. I felt crummy when I was alive. Now I can see what it would have taken to turn myself around when I was being my awful self on Earth.

Kay: What would it have taken, Douglas?

Douglas: Good role models, that is what I needed. My father abused my mother and me. She was alcoholic and very mean, especially when she was drinking. They both beat up on each other, and each beat up on me. I did not have much of a chance, really.

I did not do well in school. I was not bright and could not catch on like the other kids. Maybe because of my mother's drinking binges, even when she was pregnant with me. Maybe that affected my I.Q. I was a failure in school and resented the kids that had it all. Only a few of us had it tough. Most of the rest did okay.

I did not have any way to support myself, so I stole what I needed. I was not trustworthy. I did not have a trustworthy bone in my body. I disliked myself and everyone else.

I felt powerful when I stole that gun. I was going to be somebody and feel good about myself. I am glad that I was caught and sentenced to die. If I had stayed alive and not in jail, I would have continued to kill people.

It was my vengeance against my parents. That is what I think, and I will tell you why. As soon as I met you, everything turned around for me. I saw the beautiful angels and instantly felt love for the first time in my life. I would have gone with them anywhere. They could have taken me to hell. I deserved it. However, they didn't. They took me to heaven, and it sure feels good up here.

Do you know what I found out?

Kay: Tell me, Douglas.

Douglas: I found out that I really am intelligent, but I was right about my mother's drinking making it hard for me to catch onto things down there. I cannot tell you how good it feels to know that I am just as smart as anyone else is. I always had that hanging over me. I think my anger and my disregard for other people stemmed from feeling so worthless inside. I had a tough situation, no breaks, no breaks at all.

I do not want to go back ever again, but I have to. I have to overcome my foul temperament, which there is no sign of up here. They promised me that the next time I will have loving, respectful parents. There will be no excuses for me next time, and

I am going to show myself how well I can do. I am going to study hard and be an A+ student. Then I am going to be successful and helpful to young kids that are having difficulty in school. I may even be a schoolteacher. Now wouldn't that be something?

Kay: Sounds like a meaningful life you are planning for yourself, Douglas. I wish you great success with your personal development.

Douglas' story verifies that even people who have taken the life of another are not barred from heaven. The heavenly gates do not swing shut for those who commit crimes. However, this does not mean that people who commit crimes are not held accountable for the harm they inflict. They have the assignment of understanding their character deficiencies and working towards correcting them. Past regrettable behaviors do not ruin us. Everyone has the opportunity to amend their impulses and actions and then prove that they have reformed during their next life experience.

Rachael and Henry

A random act of violence brought together two people in death that never would have known each other during their lives. Rachael was a very successful woman who had a good reputation for making smart business decisions. Henry could not make life work for him. He was involved in petty crimes and was an outsider to society. One day their paths crossed, violence ensued. She lost her life that day. Days later, he lost his. Then they became good friends.

I had been following news stories about the shooting death of Rachael Carter. She was driving home one night after attending a movie, and a gunman shot her in what appeared to be a random robbery attempt. Police zeroed in on Henry Jones as a suspect. When police arrived at Henry's apartment to question him, Henry pulled out a gun and shot himself with the same gun he used in Rachael's slaying.

I asked my guidance to check on both of them, but I did not receive a response until two weeks later. Then, I began feeling the presence of unidentified people being with me. Along with feeling their presence, I kept hearing a man's voice repeatedly saying, "Rachael Carter, Rachael Carter, Rachael Carter." Then I heard his voice say, "I'll speak for us both."

Kay: Henry?

Henry: Yes. This kind lady should not be speaking to me because of what I did to her. I do not know what possessed me, why I shot her. I panicked. I was scared. It was a stupid thing to do. I could not think of how to get some money quickly. I was too eager to grab some easy money and did not realize that I would kill her. I did not have any way to buy food.

She was just a nice lady who happened to stop her car next to me. It happened so fast, and now here we both are. I am no better off. She has no life now. Can you help us?

Kay: Yes, I believe I can. May I ask you a question? Why isn't Rachael speaking?

Rachael: Oh, I can talk. Henry said he would protect me. We were not sure what would happen when you started talking to us, if you were going to do something hurtful or if you were safe.

Kay: I understand. I think it is great that you stayed together. Please wait just a minute. I need to get up and lower the temperature on the vegetables. I will be right back.

Rachael: Oh, I wish I could eat again.

Henry: Me too. They smell good.

Kay: I wish I could have you both over for dinner before you go to the higher dimensions. I would love to know what all happened to you after you died.

Henry: Rachael was easy for me to find. As soon as I shot myself and was dead, I saw her standing there. She came up to me. Then we talked.

Rachael: I was stunned to be staring at the man who shot me. He was as bewildered as I was when I first died. We started mending fences. It did not take long for us to like each other.

Kay: That is wonderful. Can you hear my timer? The dinner needs my attention. Before I leave, I am asking some wonderful angels to come and be with you.

Rachael: We can see them. They are delightful, carrying harps, singing. They want us to follow them. Henry and I feel safe and loved. We are going with them. Right, Henry?

Henry: Yes, Rachael. Hold my hand.

Afterward, I wished that I had thought to set aside cooking the dinner, so I could have asked Henry and Rachael more questions while they were still with me. Who would have guessed that two people who led such significantly different lives would have this natural compatibility and genuine caring for each other, even after one took the life of the other? They are an excellent example of working with the current reality instead of remaining stuck in the past's happenings. Fortunately, I received another chance to interact with them when they dropped by to pay me an unexpected visit.

Henry: Hey, we are back. Remember us?

Kay: I will never forget you two. Thanks for coming back. I missed you after you left. I was happy that you got the help you needed, but I wished we could have become better acquainted.

Rachael: Kay, we felt the same way. You were the only one that we felt close to, that understood our circumstances.

Kay: I am amazed by how different your backgrounds were, and even after all that transpired, your hearts opened to each other.

Rachael: Our hearts are still open to each other. We are sharing wonderful experiences now, and if we had not been brought together as we were, we would still be alive and strangers if we passed each other on the street.

Henry: Isn't that romantic?

(We laughed.)

Kay: Is there something you have in mind to discuss?

Rachael: We were thinking about our circumstances and how life was on Earth. People pass other people on the street and have no idea of what the other people are like or what they are going through in their lives. There is such a separation between people. Up here where we are now, everyone loves everyone else. You can feel it.

Back on Earth, you could not feel it unless you were with someone you knew that was special to you. On Earth, love generally stays narrowly focused. Up here, love is broad and all-encompassing. We like it here better. Even if we did not have each other, we would both prefer to be here. We are wondering why it cannot be more like this on Earth.

Henry says that it is partly due to class differences. Rich people do not usually spend time in poor neighborhoods; that kind of stuff. I think it is because, on Earth, people tend to keep to themselves more. There is a sense of unity up here that is not restrictive or limiting in any way. Everyone naturally cares about other people. If you need help with something, everyone who knows about it wants to be the one to help you. It is more like family – a healthy family atmosphere for all of us.

Earth is not like this. People do help each other, but it is not a generalized pattern, which everyone shares. On Earth, people mind their own business, keep to themselves for the most part, and do not want to intrude or interfere with other people's business.

Up here, it is the opposite. Everyone looks out for each other. We do not impose on each other, but every person here knows that they can count on every other person to come through for them. Interactions are loving but not pushy or overwhelming. No one dominates or competes with each other. Moreover, there is no withholding.

Kay: What do you mean by no withholding?

Henry: May I get a few words in, ladies? Back on Earth, people withhold assistance they could be giving to each other. They turn off the concern for all other people that we naturally have up here. On Earth, they choose those they will extend themselves to help and ignore the rest.

Now I realize that on Earth, there are many demands that we do not have here. We do not need to ration money so that we will have enough. Here everything is provided, and we do not need or use money. However, people on Earth can give a lot of assistance with little or no money. Look around and think about this, and you will get my gist. It is more about caring about people and doing what you can. And, do not forget about noticing them.

On Earth, people seldom look at other people and smile or say hello. Do you realize how good that simple act can make people feel? Just acknowledging someone else's presence feels good, heartwarming to both individuals. Saying hello and smiling at the people who provide services like the mail carrier, UPS delivery person, and garbage collectors is incredibly uplifting.

Those that provide services enjoy being acknowledged. They are not less worthy of a cheerful greeting than our own family is. On Earth, there are separate families. Up here, we all consider ourselves one family, I might add, one loving family that feels close to everyone else.

Believe me; it is far more pleasant to be here, especially for me. I could not, or would not, support myself honestly when I was alive. I had several strikes against me. I was of a minority race, and I was not very well educated. I came from a poor background with low expectations for myself. In hindsight, I admit that I could have done better, but with things such as they were, I fell into the shady side of life and did not really know better. Nobody accepted me for myself, until I met Rachael after I killed her, of all things.

Rachael is the most loving person that I ever met until I got here. Up here, everyone has her same attitude of caring, which was unfamiliar to me. I cannot tell you how much I love her. She means the world to me.

I know we will have to part at some point because I have a lot of learning to do. I will be coming back to Earth, hopefully under more favorable circumstances than the last time. I would love it if Rachael would come back with me, but she is more advanced than I am and will have other options. For now, we are enjoying paradise with each other.

Rachael: Kay, between the two of us, Henry and I have talked your ear off.

Kay: I cannot tell you how much I have enjoyed our visit and your insights. I will be thinking about what you both said. Please come back to visit me again. I love you both.

When I think about Rachael and Henry's description of what people are like in heaven, I picture in my mind how nice it would be if we were the same way on here on Earth. It does not seem that it would be difficult for us to extend ourselves to other people with eye contact and a smile. We would be happier and feel good about the warm responses we would receive in return. Coolly turning away from others instead of giving them a flash of warmth and connection deprives us of expressing some of the goodness we have inside of ourselves.

Paying attention to and respecting other people's presence is one way to get in touch with the tenderness that we have within us. When we arrive within the heavens without our earthly workloads and responsibilities, our attention naturally turns to the preciousness of other people. But, by then, it is too late to go back to the people that we ignored and tell them that we did care about them, although we did not show it when we were alive on Earth.

CHAPTER EIGHT

DID NOT EXPECT TO EXIST AFTER DYING

This chapter sends a message to people who believe that we only have one life to live and that nothing follows this lifetime. If you cling to this disbelieving mindset, you will be at risk of creating a confusing afterlife scenario for yourself. Better options than what you anticipate will be available, but it will be less likely for you to be able to perceive them.

This chapter is particularly insightful. The conversations that follow involve people who were confident that they would cease to exist after dying. As you will see from these stories, they made up their minds and did not consider an alternative point of view. Their conviction led them straight into a state of confusion after they passed from their physical body, retaining full consciousness but no longer able to navigate within the physical world.

The Lady Who Was Not All the Way Dead

One day a friend of mine living in California called to pass on a request for assistance. That morning she received a phone call from a person at her church who remembered that I helped them a year earlier when they faced a problematic circumstance concerning someone who had died. My friend said the person who called from the church expressed hope that I would come up with a solution for this predicament as well.

That morning, two women, who were good friends, came to the church requesting help with a most unusual problem. The women were desperate to stop the brazen paranormal activity that had been interrupting their sleep at night and frightening them half to death. These two women lived in different residences, but both were having the same chilling experiences.

Every night, while they were sound asleep, they each saw an enraged woman who unleashed a torrent of fury upon them and seemed to be demanding that they do something. She yelled and screamed. The angry woman was not completely understandable, and neither of her two targets had any idea of who she could be or why she kept terrorizing them. It seemed uncanny that they were both experiencing the identical invasive experience.

The paranormal activity had gone on for over a week, and each of the women felt psychologically disheveled. Now they were afraid to go to sleep at night. Neither of them had any clue as to who the woman was, why she was angry, or how to stop her from interfering with them while they were trying to sleep. When these two frazzled friends showed up at the church, they were desperate to find a way to halt their common recurring night terror.

The only clue that I had to work with was that they were both friends with another woman, who had died about two weeks earlier. Given my work, it was natural for me to wonder if these nighttime intrusions had to do with their newly deceased friend. Their mutual friend's name was Erica Wilson.

Shortly after I hung up the phone, my guidance announced that I had a visitor.

Kay: Is her name Erica Wilson?

Guidance: See for yourself.

Kay: Erica Wilson, are you here with me?

Erica: That is my name, but who are you?

Kay: My name is Kay, and this morning I heard that you died a few weeks ago and that you might need some help.

Erica: How can you help me?

Kay: I can better answer your question if you tell me about your situation. Two friends of yours are having dreams about you sounding angry and trying to tell them something they cannot understand.

Erica: You are darn right about that! You would think they would do something to help me out.

Kay: Like what?

Erica: I do not think I died all the way, and I do not know what to do about it.

Kay: Why do you think that?

Erica: Because you can hear me, can't you? If I were all the way dead, I would not be talking to you now!

Kay: You are not right about that, Erica. Even when you are all the way dead, you can still communicate with other deceased people, but the people who are still alive usually cannot hear you. Before you died, did you think there was such a place as heaven where people go after they die?

Erica: Not really. I thought that was made-up nonsense.

Kay: Well then, Erica, you are in for a pleasant surprise. You have indeed separated from your physical body, so you are deceased, and you have ejected from the physical world. It is also true that you still exist and retain your thoughts and memories. Indeed, there is an afterlife, which you are experiencing. Your problem, Erica, is that instead of not being all the way dead, your situation is that you have not gone all the way up. I am talking about all the way up into the higher dimensions of existence commonly identified as heaven. You just need a little help going all the way up.

Erica: So, I do not have to die all the way?

Kay: Your body died, but the essence of yourself is continuing to enjoy another aspect of living. What you really need is a boost to go all the way up, and then you will start to enjoy yourself. I can help you with that. Are you interested?

Erica: I do not have to think twice about your offer. You bet I am interested. What do I do next?

Kay: This is going to be fun, Erica. Look around and tell me what you see.

Erica: I just see you typing on your computer. That is all. No, wait a minute. Something is happening. I can still see you, but I think there are other people here with me now. I am not alone anymore. They are not people. They look like angels. There are such things? Really?

Kay: Yes, Erica, angels are real beings, and these angels are here to take you all the way up to heaven.

Erica: I can go?

Kay: Yes, of course. Everyone is welcome in heaven. Actually, you will be returning to where you were before you were born. You are going home.

Erica: I can feel myself gravitating toward the angels. I think you are right and I am supposed to go with them. What a surprise! I thought I needed help to die all the way, and instead, I get a trip to heaven, which does exist after all, with two angels. Lucky me! I am starting to float with the angels. They are cute. They have mischievous looks on their faces as if they know something that I do not know. They are right, aren't they? I would not have found out if it were not for your help. Thank you, kind lady, Kay.

Kay: You are most welcome, Erica. It is my great pleasure to help you to get all the way up!

Erica sounded like a feisty person whose beliefs boxed her into a corner with no apparent way out. The one advantage that she did have was that she was quick to change course when given the opportunity. Wonderfully for me, Erica returned to pay me a delightful visit that left me with a smile on my face.

Erica: Do you know who I am?

Kay: Erica Wilson?

Erica: You passed the test. Yes, it is me. I am back to say thank you for helping me out. When I died, I let go of everything and expected nothing further. I was petrified when the unthinkable happened. I still knew who I was and where I had been. I still felt like me. I thought a terrible mistake occurred, and I did not die all the way. Someone did not snip the last thread of life in me.

That is why I was screaming at both of my friends to finish the job. I thought I would be hanging there forever, almost dead, but still conscious. That is why I panicked.

Kay: Is it better for you now, Erica?

Erica: I am having the time of my life, and I still feel 100% alive. Isn't that a kick? I do not mind being here at all. It is very pleasing. I have new friends who also just left their bodies. We have *now-I-am-dead* celebrations. We are playful and like to throw parties for other people who are new up here, especially those who are lonely and may not have friends or relatives with whom they can connect. No one is forgotten about up here. We all belong, and we know it. It is the most wonderful feeling I have ever experienced.

Look for me when you get up here. If you do not have family or friends to welcome you, we will throw you a Now-I Am-Dead Party. They are great fun. You will love it!

Susie Leatherman

After Susie Leatherman died, she had a difficult time. She was not prepared for the challenge she faced of not knowing what to do, where to go, or how to attract assistance. It is challenging to get your bearings when you are in a confusing situation, which Susie was. She wandered around aimlessly until some angels shepherded her to me.

When asked to assist Susie, I received only a little background information. I learned that Susie was a friendly person who liked to entertain her many friends. She loved life and made life fun for herself and other people. Susie's life seemed ideal until she became ill in her later years. As her health declined and the illness became terminal, Susie fiercely clung to her life for as long as she possibly could.

After Susie passed, a mutual friend asked me to send some angels to check on her. When I contacted the angels, they said they would bring her to me, but they did not say when. About two weeks later, on the day before Thanksgiving, my angels said that Susie had been in the kitchen with me all morning. They explained that she was ready to go into the light, but she did not know how to get there.

Kay: Susie Leatherman, are you looking at me while I type on my computer?

Susie: (No answer)

Kay: Susie, I have some friends that are pretty close to where you are, and they told me that you are here with me now.

Susie: I did not hear anyone say anything, and I do not see anyone either. So how did you know I could see you? I see other people who are alive and do not know that I am there looking at them. What is your secret? Do you have ESP or something?

Kay: I really do have friends that are close to you. That is how I know. My friends want to be friends with you also. Do you mind if I introduce them to you?

Susie: I would love to meet some other people. I have been very lonely and depressed. I do not know what to do now. I go here and there, but there is not anything to do. I just watch the people I knew and the places that I am familiar with from when I was still living. I cannot do anything else. I just look at what I used to have as if I am watching a movie—nothing else.

Kay: My timer is going off. Excuse me a moment, Susie, while I check something I have in the oven. I will be right back.

Susie: What are you cooking? I think I can smell it.

Kay: Does it smell like cornbread?

Susie: That is it!

Kay: I am sorry for the delay. Susie, this is a wonderful opportunity for you to meet my friends. I am pleased to give you something to be excited about during the Thanksgiving holiday time. Now you might be surprised by what you are going to see, or maybe not. Are you an open-minded individual?

Susie: I do not really know the answer to that. I guess I am as open-minded as anyone else is. Do I have to be open-minded to meet your friends?

Kay: It is only because you have not been open-minded that you did not meet my friends by yourself. Susie, try to do as I say even if you do not believe that what I am saying is possible. They will not hurt you in any way. On the contrary, what you see will delight you.

Susie: You have a way of enticing me to go along with you on this. Okay, I will do what you say as long as it seems reasonable.

Kay: Susie, my friends are angels, and they have been watching over you even though you have not been able to see them. Since you are talking to me and can see me, if you want to, you will see and hear them, as well. They are in charge of helping you go on your way.

Susie: Where am I going?

Kay: I suggest that you ask them that question.

Susie: Do I pretend that they are here and talk to them?

Kay: Go ahead and talk to them.

Susie: Hello. Are there angels here that know where I am going to go? (Long pause) I do not know what to say! I have never been so surprised in all my life! I see your friends all around me, and they are angels, just like in the pictures I used to think were made up. They are real, after all, aren't they? They are smiling and looking so pretty. I cannot believe that I could not see them before. How long have they been here? Did they come when I started to see you?

Kay: No, Susie. They have been with you since you died. They have something to offer you. Do you see them outstretching their arms to you? They want you to go with them.

Susie: I feel safe and very happy all of a sudden. I want to go with them. Do you know where they are going? Is it somewhere that I would like to be?

Kay: Yes, Susie. They will take you to the higher dimensions, where you will see your friends and family members that passed before you.

Susie: Are they still around somewhere? Can I really see them?

Kay: Yes. They have been expecting you. Everyone who dies returns to the higher dimensions. As soon as your friends and family members joined the angels that came to fetch them, off they went to the elevated realms. Now you have the opportunity to go there with the angels. Are you going to go with them, Susie? Susie? Susie?

Guidance: She left with the angels that came for her.

In an instant, Susie saw what she had been unable to see before. All it took was the suggestion that she talk to the angels. Once she saw the angels, everything changed for her. Even if you convince yourself that there is no place to go after you die, you now know what to do if you find yourself in a situation similar to Susie's. Accept the actuality that there will be angels nearby and deliberately look for them. Even if you do not immediately see them, talk to them until your vision lights up and you see them smiling at you.

Mrs. Klein

Mrs. Klein was the elderly mother of a family friend. I did not know anything about her personally, but after she died, I sent angels a request to be sure she made it up all right. I was not aware of her beliefs until I had this conversation with her.

Kay to the angels: Is Mrs. Klein in the higher dimensions?

Angels: She is not in heaven. Mrs. Klein is here with us now. She refused to go. She is angry over the whole thing. Here, we will let her tell you.

Kay: Mrs. Klein, can you hear me?

Mrs. Klein: I do not know if I will talk to you.

Kay: Why not?

Mrs. Klein: You are going to interfere.

Kay: With what?

Mrs. Klein: I just do not have a good feeling about you.

Kay: Mrs. Klein, do you realize you are dead?

Mrs. Klein: That is what I was told, and I do not like it.

Kay: Do you miss your family?

Mrs. Klein: I like knowing what they are doing.

Kay: Mrs. Klein, are you interested in going to heaven with the angels?

Mrs. Klein: I do not believe in that stuff. I am on my own.

Kay: What if you are making a mistake and you are not on your own? What if there are angels who love you and will help you get to heaven.

Mrs. Klein: I do not believe it.

Kay: Would you like to see some angels who love and care about you?

Mrs. Klein: Show me.

Kay: Dear angels, please come to Mrs. Klein and let her feel your love for her.

After a brief pause:

Mrs. Klein: Oh, there are so many! They are lovely.

Kay: Do you believe now?

Mrs. Klein: Oh, I like this.

Kay: Are you willing to go with them to heaven where you will meet more beings that love you?

Mrs. Klein: I will think about it. (Long, long pause) No, I will go.

Kay: Mrs. Klein, have a nice trip to heaven.

Mrs. Klein: Ohhhhh.

Angels: She is gone.

This woman sounded like a character to me. Stubborn and strong-willed, she almost did not accept the assistance she needed. She dug in her heels and refused to budge. I wondered what it would have been like to live with her. Her family must have been very accommodating and flexible as they did their best to put up with her irrationality. Mrs. Klein is an excellent example of someone who probably would not have made it up to where she needed to be without special assistance that was as persuasive as seeing angels with her own eyes.

Darren Miller

I came to know Darren and his wife, Catherine, when we had dinner together a few times when they were in Houston. They were friends with my brother, Steve. Steve and Darren were both petroleum engineers, and they taught courses together in the U.K., the U.S., Asia, and other places around the world. Those dinners in Houston were delightful as we celebrated being together by dining at some of Houston's finest Middle Eastern restaurants. Each of us had an affinity for Middle Eastern food, and since Darren and Catherine had lived in the Middle East for many years, they enjoyed introducing us to their favorite dishes. Those were pleasurable experiences, and I enjoyed getting to know both of them.

Shortly before Steve and my sister-in-law Janis were due to leave on a trip to Europe, Steve called to say that Darren had died unexpectedly. Catherine phoned them that morning with this news. Steve and Janis had been looking forward to seeing them both toward the end of their trip, and now it looked like they would be attending Darren's funeral instead of laughing and celebrating being together again.

As soon as Steve asked me to check on Darren, the angels got busy and located him right away.

Angels: We have Darren Miller.

Darren: Kay, where am I?

Kay: What does it look like where you are? Tell me what happened, Darren.

Darren: Well, I was in the hospital, and then I left.

Kay: What do you mean that you left?

Darren: I do not know. I feel great, though. However, I do not know where I am. I am not home with Catherine. I am somewhere else.

Kay: Darren, do you realize that you died today?

Darren: That is what happened? (Long pause) No, I did not even think that I might have died. How did that happen?

Kay: Steve called to relay what Catherine told him, that you felt awful last night, so they took you to the hospital. I think Steve said that your kidneys and liver had been failing. Finally, this morning the doctors got you stabilized, but then you died.

Darren: I cannot believe how easy that was. I did not know that dying was not painful. It was so easy. What happens now? I assume I cannot go back.

Kay: Darren, would you want to go back? Wasn't your body failing and probably had been failing for some time?

Darren: Well, then, where else can I go?

Kay: Have you thought about where people go after they die? I mean, before this happened to you?

Darren: I did not think anything happened. Just nothingness.

Kay: Did you ever wonder if life might continue after death?

Darren: I was sure that nothing else happens. I never saw any proof, and I do not believe in that religious stuff. I thought that was how they controlled people. They told people to give money to the churches so they could go to heaven when heaven is just a fabrication intended to enrich the clergy's pockets. You know what they do.

Kay: You do not think there is anything to do after you die, but you are still alive, aren't you? And you are talking to me. Don't you feel as alive now as you did before you died?

Darren: You are right. I do, and I feel much better. Dying is good, but what happens next? I did not count on this, so I do not know what I should be doing.

Kay: May I give you a few suggestions? First, start thinking that you might be mistaken about there not being a place you could call heaven. Can you do that?

Darren: Now I am confused. Maybe I was wrong, but perhaps I am right. How can I know?

Kay: Darren, you may have to pretend for a minute. First, relax and clear your mind. Do not be worried about anything. Now, you do know how to pretend, don't you?

Darren: I am a logical, rational person. I do not fantasize. I work with facts and not fantasy.

Kay: I see. Well, humor me awhile if you would. Pretend three angels are standing near you. Look for them but stay relaxed and calm, and do not tell yourself that doing this is ridiculous. Are you doing it, Darren?

Darren: Well, I'll be darned. You were almost right. There are not three. There are about, let me count... seventeen! How did you know?

Kay: Angels attempt to help everyone who dies without knowing where to go or what to do. You are lucky, Darren, that you trusted me enough to follow the directions I gave you. Does it not follow, Darren, since there are angels, that there might also be a place called heaven?

Darren: I do not have to answer that. These angels have offered to take me there so that I can know for sure. I am going with them, Kay. I hope you do not mind.

Kay: I am delighted for you, Darren. Have a wonderful time with those angels.

When I called Steve and read him the report of my conversation with his longtime friend, Steve gave me a humorous tidbit. Darren used to teach a course on how to analyze uncertainly. Apparently, he forgot to apply the same principles to his analysis of what was possible for him after he died.

Douglas

Douglas was an exceptionally successful young entrepreneur who died at a young age from a fatal illness. When I asked about Douglas, the angels who were watching over him gave this report.

Douglas Austin is mystified that he is still conscious; this is one development he was not counting on. He had a hard time letting go of his diseased body because he was convinced that he would no longer exist as an individual and that he would be extinguished by dying. Douglas made it more difficult for himself and his family by extending his time in his physical body.

Now he enjoys feeling as if he were still in his physical body but without the illness, and he is trying to figure out what to do next. He is confused, irritated, delighted, and determined to reappear physically. He thinks he can pick up where he left off with his old life but in this new body that came from nowhere.

He ignores the angels. He is completely focused on getting someone who is still alive to see and hear him. His wife is his main target, and he is trying to get her attention. It is going to take him until after his funeral to accept that no one alive on Earth is ever going to see him.

What is amusing is watching his antics as he jumps up and down and tries to push his wife over. He thinks that if he causes her disruption, she will know that it is him. He is like a prizefighter trying to knock out his opponent, who is immune from his blows. He is entertaining the angels who are watching over him. He does not know he is drawing more and more angels to his sideshow.

After Douglas's funeral, my angels returned to give me their final report about Douglas. They said he loved all the tributes he received at his funeral and was delighted that so many friends and business associates came to say goodbye. By then, Douglas had given up hope of ever going back to his previous life.

As the funeral ended, he noticed that several angels were walking towards him, motioning him to come with them. Douglas thought that this was the first time anyone noticed him since he died. He was flooded with relief, and without an instant's hesitation, he embraced the angels.

About six months after my angels told me what happened to Douglas after he died, Douglas came to say hello to me.

Douglas: Hey, lady, remember me? I was the guy trying to push over my wife.

Kay: I sure do remember you, Douglas. You had several angelic bystanders laughing at your antics.

Douglas: It sure is different than I thought it would be.

Kay: What are you referring to, Douglas?

Douglas: The whole kit and caboodle. The entire dying thing. I did not know what would happen. I did not have a clue. I thought it was the end of everything, which is why I was so determined not to let go. I did not let go when I was so sick without any hope of getting better.

Then after I died, I still did not let go. I did not look ahead because I assumed there was nothing there. I hung on as long as I absolutely could. Then after dying, I tried to turn around and jump back to where I was before. Who would want to be terminally ill again? I am happy that I did not hurt my wife by trying to push her over. After all she went through with me sick for so long, she did not need me pounding on her.

Kay: So you feel a little guilty about that?

Douglas: Guilty and stupid. The angels I saw walking over to me after my funeral had been hanging around since I died. I did not pay attention to them because they seemed to be coming from my imagination, not really real. I guess you could say that they were in my peripheral vision – kind of on the side – not in my main focus. I was not looking for angels.

I was completely dead set (Do you like my pun?) on one thing and one thing only – getting back into my physical body. Not my diseased body. No, I did not want that. I wanted to keep feeling great as I did when I left my physical body. I did not think that through, did I? I wanted a conundrum. I wanted to be back where I was before I died, but I wanted to feel the relief I felt being out of my body. I wanted it both ways.

OK, back to the angels. Those rascals let me carry on until I gave up all hope of ever being noticed by someone alive. My funeral did it for me. There I was trying to shake hands with and thank everyone who came, especially the people who said such nice things about me, and they all walked right by me. No one noticed that I was there. On the one hand, I was exuberant because so many people were there. On the other hand, I was crushed because no one noticed that I was standing right there next to them. I was definitely invisible.

I felt alone, truly alone. Then I saw those angels smiling broadly and motioning for me to go with them. They looked familiar, like I had seen them before. My mind flashed back to the figures in my peripheral vision. I started paying attention and realized that those almost invisible angels had been hanging around me ever since I floated free from my body. They were waiting for me to notice them while I was focusing on other things. I had to change my focus to be able to see them clearly.

Kay: What an interesting story, Douglas.

Douglas: I thought you might want to know. That is why I came back to talk to you. If you die ... wait a minute. Let us begin again. When you die, do not look back. Look forward. Give up on the life you left behind and see what is right in front of you.

I would look for rascal angels if I were you. Seeing them is the ticket to your rescue from being lonely. They might be hard to notice, as they were for me, but maybe not. You seem to know what you are doing better than I did.

Kay: Douglas, thanks for the advice. I will remember what you said.

Most of us are like Douglas. We focus on what we desire, even when that which we long for is unobtainable. Sometimes we can develop such an intense fixation on what we desire that we do not pay enough attention to what else is going on around us. The cost to our well-being may be negligible or significant, as in Douglas' situation.

Douglas did not want to accept his current reality, so he looked the wrong way, backward instead of forward. Keep in mind that when we fly free of our physical embodiment, no matter what condition our physical body was in at the time of our passing, our spirit body feels like a wonderfully restored version of the same body we had while we were alive on Earth. Instead of tightening up and becoming frightened as we pass from physicality, our best reaction is to optimistically look forward to all the wonderful experiences we are about to encounter. And, do not forget to look for angels!

CHAPTER NINE

HOLDING ON
TO LOVED ONES

———

A significant and common obstacle, which keeps some of us from automatically transferring into the higher dimensions immediately after exiting from our physical form, is remaining single-mindedly focused on our relatives or friends, who we dearly love and feel responsible for supporting. Although our physical separation from them is permanent and irreversible, and we cannot do anything to change that, we still may feel compelled to remain close to them. Usually, we stay committed to being with them because we love them dearly and are trying to help them somehow, but occasionally, as in this next story, there can be other motives.

Judy

Judy and David were happily married for several years, but after Judy contracted breast cancer, she became angry and vindictive toward David. The malignancy seemed to bring out a sense of emotional devastation in Judy, which she took out on her husband. Her psychological state reversed from what it had been during the early years of their marriage. Finally, dealing with problems resulting from the malignancy soured their relationship and led to divorce. A few years later, she died. They had not spoken since their unpleasant divorce five years earlier.

Four days before Christmas, I received a phone call from my friend David. I had met David's former wife, Judy, and knew that she had been battling cancer for a long time, so I was not surprised to hear about her passing. David called me the very afternoon that he received the news that his ex-wife died. After receiving this information, he told me that he decided to phone a few people who knew Judy but most likely did not know of her passing. David said he felt great until then, but he suddenly became violently ill after making the last phone call.

He felt feverish, and his body was convulsing with other symptoms of illness setting in. He was especially upset about being sick this particular day because he planned to attend a Christmas party that evening. His disappointment at having to miss the party motivated him to call and tell me about his situation. As he was explaining what was wrong with his body, he had a creepy thought. What if Judy, in her spirit body, somehow overheard him talking about her while he was on the phone and was causing him to get sicker by the minute?

My mind was spinning. I had not run into this possibility before, nor have I since. Frankly, I thought it was impossible for Judy in her spirit form to have the power to do this to David. I promised him that I would ask my angels if Judy was somehow involved in creating his deteriorating physical condition. The last thing David said to me before our conversation ended was, "Thanks for doing whatever you can to help me. I sure want to go to that Christmas party".

Immediately, I sent for the angels, but Judy's spirit was in the kitchen with me before the angels arrived, and she was raging. As Judy's fury descended upon me, I became terrified. Reasoning with her did not work. It was futile. When the angels came, they had no better luck than I did in calming her. They tried several different approaches to talk her into going with them, and she rejected every one of them outright. She was like an angry hornet, hell-bent on stinging.

The angels regrouped and came up with another idea. This time a choir of angels singing Christmas carols surrounded Judy. As the angels came close to Judy, Mother Mary appeared carrying a baby in her arms. Suddenly, Judy was quiet and reverent. Mother Mary offered to place the baby in Judy's arms, which she accepted. Judy's heart flew wide open as she cuddled the baby in her arms. Judy could not take her eyes off the baby, and she did not object when the whole group began to gently ascend upward. The angels continued singing as they all left together, and Judy experienced the joy of holding a newborn baby as she floated into the heavens.

I was in awe of what I had witnessed. A short time later, I called David and reported what happened. He said that the information I gave him made sense because Judy had five children before they were married, and she always had a special love for children. I detected a background noise over the phone, so I asked David where he was. He answered that he was in his truck on his way to the Christmas party. He joyfully exclaimed, "I feel great now."

I was relieved for both David and Judy that she had given up her determination to hang around him to drum up as much trouble as she could. I had only been with Judy one time before she died. That day Judy was calm and cordial. However, when David phoned and was telling me how Judy was raging at him, she suddenly began to attack me. I was scared. I cannot tell you how relieved I was when she became distracted by the infant in her arms and then left with Mother Mary and the choir of angels. I thought that was the end of that; however, sometime later, Judy returned to talk to me and explain what motivated her behavior toward David.

Judy: Hi, Kay. I am civil now. I sure treated David terribly. I blamed all my health problems on him, and he always did his best to help me. I used him as my scapegoat. I butchered him.

Kay: That is a strong statement, Judy. What do you mean butchered?

Judy: You know our backgrounds. I had all the money. My family was wealthy, and I inherited all kinds of assets. David was virtually penniless but oh, what a brilliant and creative person he is. I loved him dearly until the cancer showed up. I blamed him for my coming down with cancer. That was horrible of me. I did not do this at first, but as time went by and I actually got better, I decided that it was because of him that I got cancer in the first place.

I became enraged at him. Nothing he did could make me happy. He was searching for cancer cures and taking me to various practitioners to find help for me. That is when I started improving. It is because of him. He loved me, and I began to hate him.

Kay: Judy, why do you think you started to hate him?

Judy: I do not know. There is not any rational reason. I kept thinking that this sickness could not be happening to me. It just could not be. I had been a very controlling person. Believe me, I controlled more than the purse strings. I called almost all of the shots just because I had money, and he did not.

I can see that he is a much better person than I was, and I treated him miserably, especially during the divorce. I did not want him to have anything. I wanted him to be penniless. I was mean, nasty, and filled with vengeance.

When I saw the movie of my life, it hurt. I wanted to say, "No, that person was not me!" However, there I was, seeing myself. Undeniably, it was me. I wish I could apologize to David. I wish there were a way to wipe the slate clean. There is no erasing what I did. Now he is left, the creative genius that he is, still struggling all these years later. I could have been fair with him, but I would not consider it then. I wanted to put a financial stranglehold on him, and I did.

Thank you for letting me get this off my chest. I wish I could make this up to David. Please tell him what I have said. I am truly sorry, and I wish it were not too late to make it up to him.

One other thing. I want to warn you. We have to rectify our mistakes. I am due to experience the other side of the coin next time. In my next lifetime, the only thing I will inherit will be a set of financial difficulties, one after another. I am going to have to swallow a piece of the bitter cake I shoved down his throat.

I was impressed with the way Judy came clean about her treatment of David. Here is an excellent example of 20/20 hindsight, which we all have when we enter the higher realms after we die. If we could set aside our need to blame others for what happens to us that was not actually their fault, we might preserve valuable relationships that we end up destroying. This example refers to a marriage relationship, but I cannot help but wonder how many other personal or business relationships dissolve when one party holds the other accountable for acting out of line when the accuser is unjustified in their thinking. Too often, as we live our lives, we hold other people responsible for the unpleasantness that we conjure up.

The Entertainer

Unexpected death leaves no time to say goodbye and creates a heartache that is difficult to endure. This entertainer's unforeseen death came suddenly one night. He had been rehearsing for a new concert that was to open in a few weeks. His death evoked a lot of sadness and a deep sense of loss for those who admired his creative genius and humanitarianism.

I did what I usually do when I hear about the passing of someone who might need assistance. After contacting my angels to request that they check on this person, I waited. After a short while, I felt the deceased person's presence with me. Then the contact began.

The entertainer: I do not feel safe talking to you.

Kay: Do you have something to say to me? Do you need my help?

Entertainer: I am a famous person, and I have three children that need me. Now, what is going to happen to them?

Kay: I am sure your family will be certain that your children receive excellent care. You have such a big family. I expect that they will do whatever they can to ease the children's pain from losing their father. However, there is one thing I can do for you.

You probably came to me for this reason, although you may not have been aware that it was important for you to speak with me.

Entertainer: Can you get a message to my children and tell them that I love them with all my heart?

Kay: I would gladly deliver your message if that were possible. You know yourself that I would not be able to get through to them or your family members. Moreover, if I could, none of them would believe that I was telling the truth.

Entertainer: I wish there were a way. I did not even say goodbye.

Kay: I am very sorry this happened to you.

Entertainer: Thank you. I must say I am relieved.

Kay: About what?

Entertainer: I had so much pressure on me. I could tell that my body was not strong, but I thought I could get back on top. I was not looking forward to my next performance. I was afraid I could not put on as great a show as I used to, that people would be disappointed because I could not do all the things I used to do so easily. None of that matters now, does it?

Kay: No, it does not. What does matter is what you do next.

Entertainer: I have not thought about that. Are you going to tell me what I should do?

Kay: I can explain a wonderful option you have. May I …

Entertainer: Does it have to do with where you are supposed to go after you die? I do not see any pearly white gates. What am I supposed to do?

Kay: Had you not been so focused on your children, you would have seen the angels who came to escort you. They are with you now, and if you look around, I will bet they are easy for you to notice. Tell me what you see.

(Silence)

Angels: He is with us now.

This famous entertainer immediately gravitated to the angels as soon as he saw them, showing what a simple matter it is to recover from being displaced after dying. The entertainer is another person who surprised me by coming back to visit. One day, with little notice, my guidance informed me that this entertainer would like to speak with me again, and they promptly connected us so we could have a conversation.

Entertainer: Hello, again. Remember me? I have been doing some great things since I have been up here.

Kay: I would love to hear about them.

Entertainer: It is easier to...

Kay: I cannot hear you very well. Will you speak louder?

Entertainer: OK, I will speak up. When I got here, I was all excited. I felt that there were no limitations. I could create music that sounds different from anything on Earth. I dance effortlessly and have been teaching people how to do the steps I made famous. You know, before I died.

Everything is easy. I think about what I want to create, and right away, I have it ready to try out on my pals up here. I have people dancing the steps I do, and they feel great about it. It is fun for me, too. I do not have to deal with the headache part of being in show business. I have the fun of it without the rest. I love it.

At first, I felt bad about what happened to me. No one else was responsible. I did not manage my emotions or my will, so I ended up causing problems for myself. I felt so bad and miss my family but especially my super children. I had a hard time not being able to apologize to my children for leaving them.

I have made peace with myself. (Long pause) I want to tell you something. There were lessons I just did not get. I could not let go of the things that happened to me when I was a child. I felt abused and resentful, and I let that color my life. I became overprotective and afraid of people. I did not want to get too close. I did not want to be defenseless like when I was a child. I exaggerated my fears and felt like I needed protection all the time. I do not think I would have brought so much misery down on myself if I had not been abusively treated when I was a child.

I heard you were writing a book. Some angels stopped by and told me. They said that if I wanted to help other people by giving them advice, this would be a good opportunity. I thought about what they said and decided to speak up. I have three suggestions. The first one is to parents. Treat your children with respect and do not take out your vindictiveness on them. You know your kids are defenseless so lay off them! You have so much to give your children that will help them to have high self-esteem. Build them up. Do not cut them down.

My next suggestion is for the rest of the people. I should have said all the people. Movie stars and entertainers are as real as anybody else is. Let us have normal existences and leave us alone when we are not performing. Do not make us have to protect ourselves from intrusive fans that have no boundaries. It is tiresome and frustrating not to have the freedom to live without harassment from photographers, reporters, and screaming fans. You are always a target, and it is disruptive to people who make their living as a public figure.

We are no different from anyone else. We need to enjoy a nice day with our families, alone, without fans and photographers hounding us. I am speaking up for all the people in the public eye: actors, musicians, and politicians. We all need to be treated respectfully and not intrusively. I guess you can tell that I feel adamant about this.

Kay: Yes, clearly. Please continue.

Entertainer: My third suggestion is for all people everywhere. Love each other. Put your arms around each other and take care of one another, even people you do not know. It is not hard to love everybody. It is easy. It is easier to love everyone than to stir up trouble.

As I see it, the problem is that we learn our behavior from watching what other people do, and then we duplicate it. Children do this. Well, so do adults. People need to start doing the right thing themselves and maybe start a new trend. If enough people start to love and demonstrate this love through kindness, courtesy, and eye contact, others might catch on and start doing the same thing. This is just a suggestion, but I think it could work.

Kay: Thank you. I will be sure to include your suggestions in my book. Anything else you would like to say?

Entertainer: One last thing. I would like my children to know that I am with them. I am keeping track of them growing up, and I love them. They cannot tell when I am there checking on them. I wish they could see and hear me. I have tried. It has not worked so far, but I will keep trying. I love them with all the strength and power of my mind and my heart. Thank you for letting me say these things. Now I have finished.

Some time went by, and then one December morning, this entertainer paid me a return visit. He had something specific on his mind when he began this conversation.

Entertainer: I left something unsaid during our earlier conversation.

Kay: What would you like to say?

Entertainer: I want my children and everyone else to know that there is a glorious place where we go to recover from the stresses and trials of our time on Earth. Where I am now, everything is pleasant. No one picks on anyone else. Everyone is civil and considerate. There is no need to be frightened of dying. People are better off here where I am than in the schoolhouse of earthly experience.

At this point, I have no compulsion to return to the testing ground of life on Earth. Earth is a schoolhouse that does not look like one. Everyone on Earth has the assignment of becoming a better person, which in itself is not dangerous. I am reluctant to return for my next lifetime on Earth for fear that I will pick up where I left off, withdrawn and frightened because of hurtful family dynamics. I am not going back until I am ready. I am comfortable right where I am.

Kay: Thank you for this lovely return visit. May I have your permission to include our interactions in this book of instruction that I am currently assembling?

Entertainer: I do not want to miss the opportunity to help protect children from becoming marred for life due to oppression from any other person, and especially from a member of their immediate family. Protect your children. Honor the preciousness of all people but most especially the children. My burdens from childhood stuck with me throughout my entire lifetime. I am grateful to you for allowing me to participate in your efforts to inform people to place loving arms around other people, especially all the world's children.

Whether we are rich or poor, famous or ordinary people, our most important goal in life is to honor and respect all other people. When we make no effort to achieve this lofty goal, we create karmic consequences for ourselves. Our lives teach us lessons, which help us to evolve. When we are cordial and supportive of others without picking and choosing who deserves our respect, we are making real progress.

Anton and Marnie

Anton and Marnie had a deep abiding love for each other during their marriage. Before Anton reached old age, he contracted a terminal illness and prepared to leave the love of his life. People with terminal illnesses are not just at the mercy of the illness's progression, as most people may think. How people feel about dying and their willingness to release from their bodies, and how willing their loved ones are to set them free also determine how long they take to complete the dying process.

In my eyes, Anton and Marnie are heroes. Their love was selfless, and their support for each other was unconditional. I did not have the pleasure of meeting them, but after Anton passed, Marnie sent word to me through a mutual friend that she would treasure a communication from Anton if that were possible. A few days after Marnie's request was relayed to me, Anton came into my field of perception and began to speak.

Anton: Kay, I would like to introduce myself. I am Marnie's husband, Anton. Two angels, who stopped by to say hello and tell me that Marnie would like to hear from me, directed me to you. I have always felt sorry for people who lose their spouses, but I am telling you that I am feeling great from up here where I am now. I would much rather be the spouse who dies than the spouse who has to live without their lifelong partner.

When I died, I was surprised that I felt so good. I went from being wasted away to being robust and active again. My first impulse was to turn around and go back to Marnie. I wanted to tell her the good news that I was back to my young self again. Then I stopped myself. Actually, there were angels there that stopped me and told me that it was impossible and that she would not be able to see or hear me. That crushed me. I wanted to share my good news with her and show her how healthy I became when I died.

As much as I enjoyed my life with Marnie, I would not go back to it. I will tell you what I would do if I could. I would go back there, grab her by the hand and pull her up to where I am now. She would love to be here with me. No headaches. No backaches. You feel like a kid again, robust and energized. It can be playtime or worktime, whatever you chose. I am playing now, but I am planning to make myself useful in time. Time is kind of a joke up here because there is not any. Time does not exist. There is no need to sleep or eat. It is almost like living in a dream where you do what you want and go on one adventure after another.

Having the best dream possible is the way I would describe how it is where I am now. No one calls it heaven, but everyone is happy and completely contented being here. Some people say they are going to be reborn on Earth again soon and are not looking forward to being there. They would rather remain here.

Kay, do you mind if I dictate a note to Marnie?

Kay: Anton, I am happy to give you the opportunity to communicate with Marnie directly.

To my dear Marnie

Thank you for letting go of me. I would have stayed longer if you had clung to me. I was impatient and wanted to get on with the inevitable. I knew I was dying, and I did not want to fight it. I am a realist and an adventurer. I was very interested in finding out what was going to happen after I died. I had a good feeling about it being an adventure, and I was not disappointed in any way. If you had clung to me, I would have held on longer. You did not put me through the tug of war that many people go through with their terminally ill loved ones, determined to hang onto them as long as possible.

I knew I was free to leave, and I could not wait to escape living as a terminally ill person. To me, hanging on until the very last second that I could stay alive was abhorrent. I knew I was not skin and bones. I knew there was more to me than my physical body because I am the same person that I was when I was a child, then an adult and then as a sick person.

My body changed, but the self that is me was the same all along. I reasoned that the *me-ness*, my personal identity, was still going to be OK even without my body. I figured it was like dreaming when your consciousness separates from your physical self and goes on an adventure. That is exactly what it was like. After I took my last breath, I floated out of my body. It turns out I did not need it after all. So here I am, still me but liberated from being attached to a diseased body.

Marnie, without your support, I could not have done it. I would have stayed if you really needed me to, but you wanted what was best for me. That is the highest standard of caring that there is. I love you with all my heart and want you to know that your selflessness allowed me to bypass pain and suffering that would have been even more devastating. You gave me the freedom to leave my terminally ill body, which is a wonderful act of loving-kindness.

You know we will be together again. We have another lifetime to share, another gift for us both. We are intertwined. Two as one in good times, and there will be many more of them because our love is deep and pure.

The point of including this message from Anton to Marnie in this section about holding on to loved ones is to demonstrate what selfless love can do for a dying person. Unconditional, selfless love encourages a terminally ill person to follow their inclinations, acting as comfort but not as a deterrent when they are ready to fly free from their physical body. On the other hand, if the terminally ill person is not prepared to release from their body, comfort them, soothe them and accompany them along their path until they become ready to give up their bodily attachment.

Keith Langdon

I received a request from a friend of mine who was a massage therapist. She had clients whose family had suffered a loss of significant consequence. Unexpectedly the beloved patriarch of their large family died of a heart attack while vacationing. He had headed up a large corporation, which was undergoing some difficulty during this time, which may have contributed to his heart's weakened condition.

When I inquired about him, my guidance responded, "Angels came for him two days after his funeral. Again, he refused to go with them. We are bringing Keith Langdon to you."

Off in the distance, I heard a man's voice complaining and saying, "You are taking me from my family. I am not going to leave them, but I will meet with this person named Kay. I do not know why I am going to her. I have never met her, do not know her, and would rather not leave my family to make her acquaintance."

Guidance: He is here, but he is hesitant to speak to you.

Kay: Mr. Langdon, may I call you Keith? My name is Kay.

Keith: Why are you writing things on that blue paper?

Kay: Ah, so you can see me. I am recording our conversation in case it is appropriate to give this to your family to read.

Keith: What are you up to, Kay?

Kay: For many years, I have helped deceased people who take a detour instead of going directly into the heavens after they die. Typically, when people do not automatically transfer into the heavens, it is because they do not see the angels or other loved ones who come to escort them. I work with angels devoted to helping people such as you make that divine connection when it did not happen automatically at the time of death. Did you see the angels that came to take you to heaven?

Keith: There were two who were smiling at me and motioning me to go with them. I did not consider going with them at that time.

Kay: And why is that?

Keith: I vowed to remain as close as possible to Laura to help her keep her strength up. It is not right that she has to deal with this on top of everything else. She is a remarkable woman, the love of my life, and I could not bear to leave her. Therefore, I waved the angels off and told them to come back later.

Kay: I am sad that you had to leave your wife. (I feel his pain. His immense feeling of grief and loss has come over me, as well.) Keith, I think I am feeling your pain. You have endured so much. It feels to me like you have a broken heart.

Keith: My heart is aching, and I am crying. The tears just will not stop. No one understands how helpless I feel. Our good life dissolved. Now I find myself talking to you, and you can hear me, but my wife cannot hear me. I put my arms around her and tell her how much I love her, but she does not notice. She is so brave and trusting. I admire her very much. I have tried to show our family that I am still around. I wish that they could tell that I am still with them. I would like you to give your notes of this conversation to my wife.

Kay: I promise that I will. Keith, my guidance told me that the angels came to fetch you two times, and both times, you refused to accompany them. The angels brought you to me today, so I could help you change your mind. The sad fact is that you can no longer support your family. You are keeping a great many angels and divine beings waiting. They have a warm welcome planned for you, but twice, the guest of honor has stood them up.

If you go with the angels, you will not regret it for an instant. They are a lively group, and you will have a lot of fun. Once you enter the higher dimensions, you will feel more at home than at any time when you were on Earth. You will be able to go back and forth once you become acclimated, so you will be able to return to check on your family.

Keith: How do you know this?

Kay: From personal experience. Both my mother and my sister Louise have gone into the heavenly realm. After each of them died, they came back frequently to check on their husbands and other family members. They also gave me messages for their family members. When they first passed, they came back often, but after several years, I only heard from them occasionally.

Keith: Hmmm. Do you think you could get a hold of those angels again?

Kay: I am sure that I can. Look around you, Keith, and tell me what you see.

Keith: I see a brightly lighted golden path. What do I do next?

Kay: Keep looking for the angels. You might want to call out to them.

Keith: Someone told me to step on the golden path. I am going to do it because I believe you.

Kay: (I can hear Keith laughing as a great number of angels on both sides of the path are cheering and clapping.)

Keith: Now I feel foolish but also very happy. I know that I should go with them. The same two angels that came for me the first time are walking towards me. I have made my decision. If you talk to my wife, tell her I love her and will always carry her and all of our children and grandchildren with me in my heart. I am going with the angels, but I will be back to check on my family.

Before I leave, I want to tell you that I deeply appreciate the help you have given me. I guess I made a couple of wrong choices when I ignored those angels before. If you had not talked to me today, I would have remained in my miserable state. I can tell that where I am going will be much better than where I have been. Tell my wife and our family that I will always love them, but now I am going to have some fun.

Kay: I will.

Keith: Do you do this for other people?

Kay: Whenever I can help, I do. I ask my partnering angels to check on deceased people I knew personally or people who died under challenging circumstances. These wonderful angels locate the person I inquired about and report their status. Then when those that missed their divine connection are ready to progress into the heavens, the angels bring them to me as they did with you today.

Keith: That is how I got here?

Kay: Even though you were not seeing angels, they maneuvered to bring you to me so we could talk.

Keith: Well, it is good work you do, Kay. I am very happy to have met with you today. Thank you very much.

Kay: It has been my pleasure, Keith.

Then Keith turned away from me and reached for the arms of two angels. As he did this, a cheer arose from many other angels that had gathered alongside the golden path. As Keith and his two angels started walking on the path, the path expanded and became a golden platform under all the angels and Keith. A comforting beam of light engulfed all of them, and they all floated up into the light.

Continuing to feel responsible for our precious loved ones can be a significant handicap after one passes out of their body and can no longer maneuver within the physical dimension. Even if our loved one was totally dependent upon us when we were alive, we cannot continue our commitment to them. Unfortunately, they will have to accept the challenge of living without our physical presence supporting them. Our best option is to transfer directly into the higher dimensions and then, from that elevated state of existence, return to visit our beloveds and observe how they are getting along with their lives.

We must transfer into the higher dimensions to gain the ability to navigate back and forth between the earthly realm and the higher realms. Many people who greatly care about their loved ones still alive on Earth make it a point to visit them regularly, in the beginning. Then after becoming more nestled into the higher realms, they tend to visit less frequently. Newcomers to the higher realms adapt quickly and immensely enjoy their new circumstances, which hold unlimited appeal.

CHAPTER TEN

CRITICAL SELF-JUDGMENT AND SELF-LOATHING

Some of us are our own worst enemies. As if our lives are not challenging enough, some of us introduce more difficulty by being hypercritical of ourselves and unwilling to soften our constant self-harassment. Those of us that have this problem behave like an old vinyl record, which becomes stuck, and then keeps going over and over the problem area. Becoming anchored in one's overly strict self-assessment creates a painful existence that is no one's fault but our own.

Almost none of us earns an A-plus in life. Life does not work that way because we are confronting our weaknesses as well as enjoying our strengths. Our report cards reflect how well we are doing. Some of us earn higher marks than others do, but what matters most is our level of improvement. Each of us is on a specifically designed study program. We are the ones who, before we were born, designed our challenges to advance our level of development. To compare ourselves with anyone else makes no sense because their strengths may be our weaknesses, and vice-versa. However, our strengths may elude us if we focus too severely on our shortcomings.

The deceased people in this section encountered difficulty because they under-rated themselves and undermined their well-being. They are not unlike those of us who come down too hard on ourselves, creating feelings of worthlessness. Instead of continuing in this manner, we can give ourselves a break by focusing more on our beneficial qualities that we may have pushed into the background of our awareness.

Willis Armstrong

One morning, angels brought a deceased man to me. I had heard about his passing, so I asked my angelic partners to check on him. I did not know him personally and had no background information. When the angels brought him to me, they told me that they had appeared to him as regular people. He did not realize that his visitors were angelic beings.

Kay: Willis, I have been expecting you. Can you hear me all right?

Willis: Who are you anyway? Why should I talk to you?

Kay: I have been checking on you since you died to see if you were ready to go on to heaven.

Willis: And? So, am I ready yet?

Kay: That is up to you. You can remain where you are if you prefer, or you can leave that place and go to a higher level of existence, which will be much more enjoyable.

Willis: I do not have to go?

Kay: No. You decide what you want to do.

Willis: If you are talking about heaven, I do not think they will let me in.

Kay: Why not?

Willis: I screwed up a lot. Hurt people. I did not act nicely; I let many people down, especially my family. I would not fit in there anyway. I have always had trouble fitting in. I do not know what to say. I do not know what to do. I have trouble getting along with people.

Kay: Willis, that is not enough to keep you out of heaven.

Willis: I thought you had to have a good record to get in.

Kay: That seems to be a common misconception. From my experience, everyone has a place in heaven waiting for him or her after their physical form dies. When we finish living on Earth, we go back to where we were before we were born. It is like going home after taking a trip. After a person has been gone on vacation or a business trip, it is time to go home.

Willis: If that is how it really is, I have been gone from home long enough. If they will take me, I want to go. What happens to me if I cannot get past the front gate?

Kay: As I said, I have not known of anyone who did not get in. I have known people who lived disappointing lives because of their character flaws, but they still received a warm welcome. I am sure you will sail right in and be very happy to be there. Your disinclination is holding you back. Your deceased friends and family are waiting for you to overcome your stubbornness. There is a party planned for your arrival.

Willis: A party for me?

Kay: Yes. That is only a part of the welcome you will receive.

Willis: How am I going to get there?

Kay: Some angels are going to take you when you are ready. It has to be your choice.

Willis: I think I would be a fool not to at least try getting in.

Kay: You are right. There is no reason not to try. Are you ready?

Willis: Where are the angels?

Kay: Look around you. Do you see anything different than before?

Willis: (smiling) Yes. I see the people that have been staying near me. They are angels, aren't they? Are they the ones that are going to take me?

Kay: Yes they are. Go with them. They are lovely, and you will enjoy being with them.

Willis: Okay, lady. You sure are nice. I will be knocking on heaven's door and telling them that you sent me.

Kay: Have a wonderful new life in heaven, Willis. Goodbye.

Guidance: He has gone with the angels.

Sometimes being our own judge and jury can result in overly harsh sentences. Throw in low self-esteem, and we may slip into self-loathing. Although it may be a challenge, the best antidote to feelings of inadequacy is to pay attention to the positive aspects within ourselves, shining the light of awareness upon them. When we engage in lopsided self-evaluations, we are asking for trouble. Let us remember to pat ourselves on the back for our positive traits and actions, even though we may wish our list were longer than it is.

Tobias Soto

A relative requested that I ask angels to check on her friend's father. He had been sick, but not with a terminal illness when he died unexpectedly.

Angels: He needs help. He does not know where he is. We will get him. (Pause) He does not want to come with us. He is irritated, angry, filled with self-loathing. We are going to send a child, actually a young angel who works with us. She is with him now. At this moment, he is crying. He said he loves children. He said he feels like a child, a lost child.

The young angel is holding his hand, and he can feel her love flowing into him. He is relaxing. He stopped crying. She whispered something into his ear, and now he is smiling and nodding his head. The young angel told us that he agreed to go with her when she said she wanted to give him a tour of heaven.

He is not afraid anymore. He is laughing and telling the young angel how sweet she is. Now he is asking her questions like, "Where am I? How did I get here? Am I dead now?"

She said she would answer all his questions and that she would stay with him as long as he wanted her to. He trusts her, and he has agreed to see what it is like in heaven. They are leaving together.

Tobias was a tenderhearted person who could not straighten out his self-concepts. He dwelled on his negative aspects and withdrew support for himself. Tobias turned off the spigot of self-esteem because he would not let himself off the hook of strict accountability. Rather than striving to improve those behaviors that made him ashamed of himself, he sunk into despair. Although we all must strive to improve ourselves and not give up on becoming a better person than we have been, let us give ourselves a break and be kind and forgiving toward ourselves.

Samuel Parker

When Samuel Parker came to my attention, I did not have much confidence that the angels would find him. Although Samuel had been deceased for many years, his niece kept him in her thoughts and prayers. She loved him dearly, and when she learned that it might be possible to discover if he made it up to the heavens all right, she asked if my angels would check on him.

When I inquired about Samuel, the angels were pleased to give his niece this report. "After Samuel's death, he wandered around between dimensions for several years. Finally, after allowing himself to relax his critical self-judgment, he had what was a new thought for him. He wondered if he might be acceptable to God, so he asked God if he was. The answer came instantly, as he was surrounded with white light and whisked into the heavens by angels."

Sometimes we are like a dog chewing on what we see as our deficiencies as if they were a delicious bone, which we cannot stop chewing. If we relax our self-harassment and, instead, become understanding and sympathetic, we give ourselves the gift of ending our self-imposed punishment. This is one gift, which only we can give ourselves.

Dominic Carson

A family member brought Dominic Carson to my attention after attending Dominic's funeral. Some of my relatives and friends, who know about my efforts to aid deceased people, inform me about their acquaintances who might need assistance. Over the years, this has provided many people with special delivery service into the heavens. It has been my pleasure to play a part with my angels in the elevation of deceased people who needed assistance.

It is a big stretch for some people to believe that it is possible to communicate with deceased people and seek help for them from someone who does not walk around with a halo around her head. While we are alive, we tend to limit what we think is possible, especially if we have not experienced it ourselves. Thankfully, I have had relatives and friends who are open-minded to seeking angelic support for people they knew who died and might need assistance.

When I asked my guidance about Dominic Carson, they responded immediately.

Angels: He has been with you the whole time you were having dinner.

Kay: I could feel the stronger than usual energy but did not know what it was signaling.

Dominic: Are you talking about me?

Kay: Yes. I felt your presence while I was eating dinner. Dominic, I met your son Davis one evening in Houston. He is a friend and business associate of my brother, Steve. One night, Davis, Steve, and a woman who worked with them flew into Houston. I gave Davis and the other person a ride to their hotel. That is how I met Davis. Years later, after Steve attended your funeral in Estes Park, he asked me to check on you to be sure you made it up into the light. Did you get up all right?

Dominic: That is why I wanted to talk to you. I did not have any trouble going through the tunnel. I released from my body, and I seemed to float into the tunnel. Then I ended up in another dimension where everything is light and airy and kind of shiny. Where am I?

Kay: That is the question you wanted to ask me?

Dominic: Someone told me that you would be able to tell me where I am.

Kay: Are you still in the new place now, or did you leave it to visit me?

Dominic: As soon as I heard that you could tell me where I am, I ended up in your kitchen watching you eat dinner. So, I am here with you, but how did I get here, and where is there?

Kay: I am surprised that you did not see some angels who could answer your questions. Evidently, you did not have any trouble leaving your body.

Dominic: I was ready. I could not wait to leave it and get on with what comes next.

Kay: Did you see your friends and relatives who had died before you?

Dominic: No, nobody that I knew.

Kay: That is unusual from what I have heard from others that died. No one greeted you and showed you around?

Dominic: Only a few ladies, but I could not understand what they were saying. I have been discouraged because I do not know what to do next. What am I supposed to do next?

Kay: Dominic, I really do not know what you are supposed to do next. Let us see if we can locate some angels that can help you. (I am calling angels to assist Dominic.) Dominic, I think some angels have come to be with you. Do you see them?

Dominic: No. I do not see anybody except you.

Kay: (I mentally ask the angels what to do next. They tell me that they are right next to Dominic, and they instruct me to tell him they are there.) Dominic, there are angels right next to you. Try to see them.

Dominic: I still do not see them.

Kay: Try touching them.

Dominic: I just bumped into something or maybe someone. Let me feel around. I feel two someones, but I still cannot see anything.

Kay: Are you sure you cannot see anyone?

Dominic: Not yet.

Kay: Are you afraid of anything?

Dominic: Well, a little afraid that they will tell me that I am not good enough to go to heaven.

Kay: That could be your problem, Dominic. Maybe fear is keeping you from seeing the angels and others who came to greet you. You have already prepared to go to heaven because you went through the tunnel into the light. You arrived in heaven, but it seems like you prevented yourself from seeing the wonderful people there.

Dominic: Are you sure I am qualified?

Kay: Yes, I am sure that you are qualified. Now look again to see if you can perceive any angels.

Dominic: Oh, you must mean those two over there that are smiling at me.

Kay: I am happy that you are letting yourself see them. Can you hear them also?

Dominic: Yes, they are offering to answer my questions and take me to see my already deceased friends and relatives. Maybe I did qualify after all.

Kay: Sure seems like it to me, Dominic. Are you satisfied that they are going to give you all the help you need?

Dominic: They are telling me not to worry about anything anymore because they will stay with me until I am well settled.

Kay: I think you are in very caring hands, Dominic. You are going to have fun discovering your new situation and being with your dear ones.

Dominic: We are all leaving now. I can feel the pull to go with them. I am going to be okay. I am glad you met Davis so you would know of me and give me this help. I am on my way.

Kay: Goodbye, Dominic. Have a wonderful time in heaven.

I believe that it is an important objective to advance our awareness of our deficient behaviors. Yet, it has to be of equal importance to think of ourselves as fit human beings that may have made mistakes, but nonetheless, are precious and capable of becoming better than we were before. Loving ourselves despite our shortcomings is a challenge that we can meet.

Some of us have a sound, mostly accurate self-assessment, but many of us do not bother to evaluate ourselves at all. Those of us who are strict in our self-evaluations may be the most willing to look at ourselves critically, but there are potential potholes along this path. A single-minded focus on our faults does not necessarily lead to correction, but it definitely may lead to self-loathing. When we finally decide to treat our weaknesses with compassion and congratulate ourselves for our strengths, we will feel more satisfied being who we are.

A Challenging Uncle

One of my relatives asked me to check on their spouse's uncle, who had passed away a few days earlier. This man had many redeeming traits that made him a joy to be around. He was fun, kind, and helpful to people in need, good for a joke at any time, and always the life of the party. On the other hand, he was often tough on his wife, children, and some of his siblings. Unfortunately, as he got older, he became less pleasant and more challenging for those closest to him. After he died, I asked my angels to see if he had gone up to the heavens and their reply was one of the most enjoyable responses I can remember.

Angels: He was dragged up kicking and screaming, but he calmed down quite well when he realized where he was going. Initially, he thought we were taking him the other way.

CHAPTER ELEVEN

DID NOT KNOW THEY WERE DEAD

—

It may be hard to believe, but some deceased people do not realize that they died. To them, their lives are continuing as if no interruption had taken place. It used to be inconceivable that a person could pass out of their body and not realize that a tremendous change has occurred. Now I wonder just how often this happens. This first story is a charming example of neighborly compatibility and the network of friendships that sometimes exist when deceased people band together to form a community.

The Hilltop Hotel

On the way home from our family reunion in Kentucky, my husband and I stopped at a hotel well-known for its natural hot springs and gangster history. Before we left Houston, Mike checked on the internet to make a hotel reservation for that evening. After viewing several possibilities, he decided on the Hilltop Hotel, built early in the twentieth century and recently renovated. When I asked Mike why he chose the Hilltop Hotel, Mike answered that he liked its architecture and location near the historical district. However, later he acknowledged that he mainly chose it because he felt drawn to it.

We arrived late in the afternoon and, after driving around to see some sights and get our bearings, we checked in at the Hilltop Hotel. We immediately fell in love with its charm and particularly the old-style design. The tile work, the high ceilings, and the layout of our room reminded me of the few times I stayed in Chicago hotels in the 1950s when I was a child. Mike and I both felt like we had zipped back in time.

After settling in, we went for a short walk and talked about where we would like to eat dinner. We both agreed that we wanted to return to the Hilltop Hotel and have dinner there. When we entered the dining room, it was about 5:30, and we were the only patrons except for another couple that was just leaving. After we ordered our meals and with the rest of the dining room empty, the waitress came over, sat down with us, and we started chatting. It did not take long for us to realize that she had something on her mind to tell us. She drew close to us, and in a hushed voice, she confided to us that the hotel was haunted.

Immediately our eyes lighted up, and of course, we encouraged her to keep talking. We were curious to hear the details. She continued by saying that their manager called the staff together that morning to report evidence that the hotel was haunted. He explained to the staff what happened the night before, and the only determination that he could come to was that the hotel was haunted. The old service elevator, which had been out of commission for decades, was running up and down all night long. He could hear it from the room where he was staying.

That was all the waitress said before another couple entered the dining room and required her attention. After that, the dining room filled, and she was busy the rest of the time. We were both disappointed that we did not get to hear the rest of her story.

When dinner was over, we paid the bill and were leaving the restaurant when we noticed the manager standing at the front desk. Since we were eager to learn more, we stopped and asked the manager what happened the night before. To our delight, he was eager to tell us. "Last night, I was on duty until 10:30, and when my shift was over, I went home to spend the night. When I got home, I could not get in. I had locked myself out of the house, and after trying unsuccessfully to find a way in, I decided to go back to the hotel to sleep.

"I took one of the vacant rooms on the fourth floor and laid down on the bed. As I was dozing off, I heard the old service elevator going up and down. The elevator stopped at different floors; the doors were opening and closing as they do when people are getting on and getting off. But that elevator was disconnected many years ago. It is not connected to any electrical power source."

The manager explained that they had shut off the electrical power and locked the elevator about twenty years ago. He had the only key that would have opened the elevator in his pants pocket the whole time. He reached into his pocket and showed us the key. It was on a large key ring with numerous other hotel keys that the manager kept in his possession. No one could have used that elevator, yet, it went up and down all night long. The manager concluded his story by saying, "I laid in bed wide awake for the rest of the night paralyzed and afraid to move. This hotel must be haunted."

Mike and I were gleeful. After we said goodnight to the manager and headed to our room, Mike looked at me and said, "It looks like you have some work to do." I was excited. I had not run into this type of group discarnate entity activity before. When I asked my angels if deceased people lived in the hotel, they immediately confirmed that they did.

Angels: There are 23 of them: ten men, ten women, and three children, which they share. We will bring them all to you. (Lengthy pause) They are all gathered here.

Kay: Hello, everyone. Can you hear me?

One of the invisible residents: Yes, we can, but who are you anyway?

Someone: Don't be rude, Henry.

Kay: I am spending the night here and heard about the service elevator running up and down all night long. That elevator cannot operate without electrical power and the key to unlock it. So, I thought I would check to see if there were what some people, like the manager, would call ghosts living here.

Henry's voice: We are not ghosts, or are we?

Edna: Of course we are, Henry. Nobody can see us, and we live in this old hotel, coming and going like everybody else, but we do not pay a penny. We just help ourselves to whatever we want and make a little mischief.

Kay: Well, it is time for the mischief-makers to go into the light.

One of them: I am afraid.

Another: Me, too.

Someone: I do not want to go anywhere.

Someone else: Well, I do. I am tired of living here. Count me in.

Kay: It is time for all of you to experience a wonderful event. Now look around and tell me what you see.

One of them: Angels are blowing golden trumpets. The sound makes me want to go with them.

Someone: I am leaving. I am tired of living at the hotel. I am going with these angels. They had better not leave without me.

Someone: Do not go, Charlie.

Charlie: Sam, you are going too! Come on now.

Angels: All 23 went into the light.

I chuckled inwardly and felt satisfied that the Hilltop Hotel's invisible residents had gone with the angels. I went to bed, fully anticipating that this was the end of that episode. However, well before six in the morning, I awoke to the feeling of many sets of eyes peering at me. I knew I was not alone. The moment I opened my eyes, many voices started talking to me. It was as if someone had informed a network of deceased people that there was something potentially good for them, going on at the Hilltop Hotel, and they all came over to check it out.

As I communicated with my angels, they told me that forty-five people were there with me while I was waking up. The angels explained that many more people gathered during the night because word travels quickly in the astral plane. The astral plane is a level of experience just beyond the physical plane of experience. Deceased people pass through the astral plane on their way to the more elevated levels of existence.

At that point, I asked the angels, "How should I handle this?"

Angels: They saw what happened last night and know you can help them. Go ahead and talk to them.

Kay: Hello, everyone. I have a feeling you know that I can help you move to a glorious place to live, and you want to take advantage of this opportunity.

People speaking in a chorus: Yes, we do.

Kay: Do you know of other people who might want to go? I can wait a few minutes while you go to get them.

Someone: I have friends in Chicago.

Kay: Then go and get them and anyone else you find.

Someone else: My cousin is in Phoenix.

Kay: You go too. We are not going to leave anyone behind.

Someone: We all know of several other people, but we did not want to leave. We were afraid to leave. We thought we might miss our opportunity if we did. We just waited until you woke up. We are delighted that you could tell that we were here.

Kay: Do you want to go and fetch the others?

Someone: Yes, if you will wait for us to return. But, please do not go away without giving us the chance to get out of here for good.

Kay: OK, it takes me about 15 minutes to do my hair. Come back by 7:15 to 7:30. Then I will call the angels to come for all of you and your friends.

As I dry my hair, I hear voices saying, "Yoo-hoo, we're back," and "We're ready." I ask, "Has everyone returned?"

Someone: No, people are still coming.

(I waited a while longer.)

Kay: Has everyone assembled?

Someone: We are only missing 3 or 4. Look, more are coming.

Kay: Let us begin. Others may see what is happening and come along. Is everyone ready to meet some lovely angels?

Someone: I am.

Someone else: Me, too.

Someone else: So am I.

Kay: OK. Let us invite some heavenly angels to come and show you the way to heaven.

Someone: Will they have trumpets like the angels last night?

Kay: I do not know. Look around and tell me what you see.

Someone: Oh, look. This is too wonderful. They are playing jazz this time. It is an angelic jazz band!

I sense all the people rush over to see the music-playing angels. The jazz band acts as a magnet drawing deceased people from all around. People are laughing with delight. More deceased people are coming, attracted by the music and the commotion. I cannot hear the music, but I see the angels and the people gathering around them.

Slowly the jazz band starts to elevate, and the people stay with the band. The whole group is floating into the higher dimensions together. A few people turn back, and with big smiles on their faces, they wave to me. More people are racing to catch up with them.

Now the band and the people are nearly out of sight, but other angels are posted nearby to help those who come late. A few deceased people are still showing up. When they arrive, angels immediately take them. The angels pledged to remain there to escort people into the heavens as long as they continue to come.

By then, it was about 8:30, and people were still coming, but my services were no longer needed, so Mike and I went to breakfast. This was one of the most joyful experiences that I have ever had working with angels to uplift those caught between worlds. The Hilltop Hotel and its residents will always have a special place in my heart.

As time went by, I often wondered how they acclimated to being in the higher dimensions and if any of the hotel mates stayed together. Henry and Edna answered this question for me when they returned for a visit.

Edna: Remember us? We used to be ghosts at the Hilltop Hotel.

Kay: I will never forget the two of you and your friends there.

Henry: We made a nice little life for us at the Hilltop Hotel. I did not mind it one bit, but after being here, I would not want to go back.

Edna: Me, neither. I did not know how great life could be until we got up here.

Kay: What have you two been up to in your new location?

Edna: Henry and I still enjoy being together. We could have gone our separate ways, but we were used to each other. We like to dance and go to parties. We tried playing cards, but it is no fun. Everyone knows what cards everyone else has.

Henry: We tried taking some classes but got tired of that. We would rather play than learn about stuff.

Edna: We sound boring, Henry. We travel a lot. We did not mention that. In addition, we visit with friends, Henry and me. We never met a person who did not become our friend. We have friends all over the place.

Kay: So, do you live in a hotel?

Henry: We know you are teasing. There are no hotels here. We do not need to sleep or eat, for that matter. We are always on the go. There are so many people here to get to know. That is what is most important to us.

Kay: You two are sweet. Anything else you would care to mention about your life now?

Edna: People are good. Everywhere we go, we meet more people that are wonderful. I wish Earth were more like it is up here. On Earth, we knew wonderful people, but you had to be a little choosy. Some folks seemed nice at first, but then watch out! Some of them sure got angry sometimes, and others were fussy or peculiar.

At the Hilltop Hotel, we were all compatible, but some people that we liked a lot moved on, and we missed them after they left. Some of them we never saw again. Up here, all we do is meet more people who become our friends, and we can find them any time we want. We send them a thought message like, "Shirley, where are you now?" and then we will be standing right in front of her laughing. Just thinking about someone you would like to see zips you right over to where they are. Lickety-split. We zip over to people we have met all the time to see what they are up to.

Henry: We are like little kids playing and being happy.

Kay: It has been great hearing from you both. Say hello from me to the other folks from the Hilltop Hotel whenever you bump into them. I certainly enjoyed getting to know all of you, and I am happy that you are still living where you can come and go as you please and do not have to pay a cent.

Henry: You can't beat it!

Pauline

I had a lovely network of spiritually-minded friends when I lived in Texas. One of the most memorable is Pauline, who had a loving heart of gold. She radiated a gentle, loving presence whenever I was with her. We were in mediation groups together, which allowed us to spend time visiting about what was going on in our lives. Pauline's life changed direction when she met and fell in love with her sweetheart. They both preferred to live in the country. Therefore, Pauline left Houston, and they moved to a home with space for their many animals.

Abruptly, Pauline's life ended one morning at 6 a.m. while she was outside feeding their animals. I was surprised to hear that she had died since she was still in her fifties and appeared healthy. When I heard about her passing, I asked my angels to give her my love. I knew with absolute certainty that Pauline would have immediately transitioned into the heavenly realms. Much to my delight, my angels brought her to me so we could speak with each other.

Pauline: Do not feel bad about what happened to me. It was my choice to leave. I longed for my real home, and my husband needed the challenge of being without me. He will grow through this experience. I cannot tell you how wondrous it is on my side of life. Earth was a wonderful experience, but life is difficult, and the lessons are many. Now I can relax and investigate whatever my heart desires. Over here it is wonderful, calm, peaceful but very exciting too.

It is preferable to remain here, but I know I will be back for another go-round on Earth because I did not learn how to value myself. I thought I did when I was there, but now it is obvious to me that I did not give myself as much opportunity to advance myself based on my abilities and work ethic. I settled for less because I did not think I could do better. I was not happy working so hard to support myself, but I did not see another way. Now I realize that if I had valued myself more, I would have put myself in more supportive situations. So, I will be back to learn to take better care of myself.

Kay: Pauline, what happened when you died?

Pauline: In an instant, angels, who were giggling because I was so surprised to see them, surrounded me. I did not realize what happened to me, that I died. I just thought, "Oh, now I can see angels." It was a happy time. No regrets. No hesitancy to leave my physical body. I flashed instantly through a light beam surrounded by sparkling effervescence that was familiar.

The angels stayed with me and took great delight in introducing me to beings of light who were familiar. These were my friends from before I came to Earth last time. It was a happy time for me. Such a surprise! In one instant, I am in a sparkling place surrounded by giggling angels and old friends.

During this conversation with Pauline, I realized what a wondrous gift she received. She did not have to go through the aging process or experience anything traumatic during her death. Her passing was so smooth that she did not realize that she was deceased. Because she was so close to being an angel herself, it did not surprise her to see them surrounding her. Many of us have this angelic connection but are not conscious of it. We may not have any awareness that angels are with us until the instant we pass from our bodies, and there they are sparkling with delight at the shocked looks on our faces when we first notice them.

One day from out of the blue, Pauline stopped by to visit with me after years had gone by.

Pauline: Hi, Kay. I have decided not to wait any longer. I am coming back.

Kay: Pauline, it is great to hear from you again. It sounds like you are ready for another earthly experience.

Pauline: I decided to make this next lifetime my last, so I will give myself as many experiences as I can. I want to sample a luxurious lifetime. I do not want to be lazy. It is just that every time I come back, I seem to struggle to support myself. I have never stood up for myself to ensure that I receive fair compensation. This next lifetime I am not going to settle for less. I am going to become an expert in a field that pays exceptionally well, and I am going to invent proprietary products that will pay me royalties. I will work hard, be paid exceptionally well, retire early and live the good life.

Kay: Pauline, that sounds great! I am very happy for you.

Pauline: I knew you would be. Do you remember when I got all those fleabites on my legs when I did temporary work for that oil company in Houston?

Kay: I sure do. You had fleabites up to your knees.

Pauline: Even further up sometimes. Wearing pants and long socks did not help much. Those fleas were vicious, and this was up on the seventh floor. We all had them. Fleas bit everyone who worked on that floor. We complained, but our complaints were ignored. We were only temporary workers, and the company did not care what was happening to us. I bet that if their executive offices had flea-infested carpeting, they would replace it immediately.

Well, no more of that for me. For my next and final lifetime on Earth, I am going to be treated well. I will not tolerate anything other than respectful treatment, and I will have the talents and resources to reposition myself if I am not in a good situation. The same goes for my personal life, too. You know that I am a kind and exceptionally loving person.

Kay: That is very true, Pauline.

Pauline: Well, I used to think that being sensitive and loving meant that I had to give myself away and take a back seat to other people. That is why I settled for less during my last lifetime. I was off-balance and did not realize that I had myself to love and care for too. This time I will still be my gentle, loving self, but I will love and take care of myself as well. I am going to restore proper balance, and this will be a big achievement for me.

Then, I am going to top it all off by retiring early and living a luxurious lifestyle. Not opulent, really, but for me, what I have in mind will seem luxurious compared to my other lifetimes. I will own my own home free of debt, and I plan to travel and enjoy myself.

Kay: Pauline, will you be an American again?

Pauline: No, I do not think so. I want to live in another part of the world. I am actually considering the Middle East for several reasons.

I know you like Middle Eastern food.

Kay: My favorite ethnic food is Middle Eastern. I have an authentic Persian cookbook, which I cherish. I love their use of sour fruit like Persian limes and sour cherries in their dishes. Their food has an intriguing flavor, and it can be challenging to identify the mystery ingredients.

Pauline: Well, it is not only for the food. My reasons are cultural. I would like to live in a part of the world that has different traditions. I do not think there would be so much animosity on Earth if we all knew each other. I respect almost every person I have gotten to know and understand. Right now, I am leaning toward finding a suitable place in the Middle East in which to be born.

I know what you are thinking, that it might be tough living there. I do not plan to be a female next time. We can choose if we prefer to be male or female. I had lifetimes when I was a male. Most of the time, I have been female. I want to be a strong, successful male for my last lifetime, and I want to help women gain the rights and freedoms they deserve. I think I could do this more effectively if I were an open-minded and accepting man with enough personal power to make a difference for women.

Kay: Paula, you have put a lot on your plate. This sounds like a very ambitious and powerful lifetime you are planning for yourself.

Pauline: I do not know if it is realistic to do all of this. I may have to scale back my ambitions.

Kay: If you can accomplish all this, you will be leading a life that is totally opposite of your last one.

Pauline: That is exactly what I am trying to achieve, and I think I may be able to do it. I am still considering and planning. I do not feel in a hurry to return, but I would like to challenge myself and make my last shot a peak achievement.

Kay: Pauline, this has been a treat for me to be with you again. Thank you for coming to visit with me. I wish you success in planning a most ambitious final lifetime for yourself. May I ask you a question? After you have lived your last lifetime, what will you do?

Pauline: When we become qualified after many, many lifetimes of improving ourselves, exciting options open up. I do not know all of them. I have not had a complete explanation, but one that I do know sounds interesting. I want to join the angelic core that defends and protects disabled people, especially disabled children on Earth. After proving to myself that I can do more and be stronger than I knew myself to be, I want to do the same for disabled children.

You know I am not happy unless I can express my loving nature. I would like my love to flow to disabled children who need to gain confidence in themselves. I am going to be their angelic cheerleader who whispers in their ear, "You are stronger than you think you are. There is a lot you can accomplish that you do not think you can. Try harder and tell yourself how great you are. Most of all, feel good about yourself. Always feel good about yourself."

Kay: Pauline, this will be a great assignment for you. The same pep talk that you plan to give to the children is one that all of us should give ourselves and all children placed in our care.

I would love to hear from you again if you are so inclined. I love you dearly, Pauline. Thank you for coming to visit me.

Pauline's saying that she was interested in joining an Angelic group gives us a tip that perhaps some of the angels are graduates of the school we are attending here on Earth. People who have died often mention what they are going to do when they return to Earth for their next lifetime. Pauline is the only one that I have communicated with who said that this next lifetime would be her last.

She also is the only one that said she might become part of the Angelic teams. I have wondered where all the wonderful helper angels originate. Now I know that some of them are Earth graduates with a clear understanding of the support we need while we are here and are qualified and willing to help us.

Mrs. Morrow

Mrs. Morrow was the mother-in-law of a friend of mine. She was a matriarch who controlled her large family after the death of her wealthy husband. I had heard that Mrs. Morrow was in the hospital for a lengthy time, and when I had lunch with my friend, Carrie, I asked how her mother-in-law was doing. Carrie responded that her mother-in-law died a few weeks earlier, and the family was sorting out her possessions and distributing them to different family members.

I confided in Carrie about my involvement with angels and offered to check on her mother-in-law if she would like me to. I mentioned this casually, not expecting that her mother-in-law would necessarily have had any difficulties. However, as Carrie continued talking about her mother-in-law, I changed my mind. Carrie was describing warning signs that Mrs. Morrow might still be hanging around.

The most shocking clue occurred when their housekeeper, who had also been the housekeeper for her mother-in-law, walked into Carrie and her husband's house the previous day. As she entered through the front door, the housekeeper became white as a ghost and kept shouting, "Mrs. Morrow is here! Mrs. Morrow is here!" The frightened housekeeper almost passed out and needed assistance to the sofa so she could lay down.

Carrie and her husband did not know what to think about the housekeeper's outburst. At first, they tried to overlook the housekeeper's turmoil, dismissing it as over-emotionalism, but as they thought about what she said, they could not help wondering if it could be true. So, when I offered to have angels find out if her mother-in-law was still hovering around, Carrie did not hesitate for an instant. Yes, she wanted me to check on her mother-in-law.

When I called upon my angels to check on Carrie's mother-in-law, they immediately complied. They did not have any trouble finding her. The angels showed me Carrie's mother-in-law sitting in a hospital bed as if she had not died. She was propped up on some pillows barking orders to nonexistent nurses.

When I spoke to her, she noticed me and declared with scorn in her voice, "I've been abandoned. Nobody pays any attention to me anymore. You are the first one in a long time that has come to see me. Just look at me. Look at what I have to wear. This ugly hospital gown because my family will not bring me my good lingerie. I look so shabby. They do not pay me any mind at all. I apologize to you for being dressed like this."

After a short pause, she continued to complain. "No one comes to visit me anymore. They leave me here and go about their lives as if I did not exist. Do not think that I do not know what they are doing. I know exactly what they are doing. They already took the family portraits out of my house. Now my portraits are hanging in their houses. That is not all. They are emptying my house of all my things. Those are my things they are taking. They are going to sell my house. I do not know what has come over all of them."

I tried talking to her and explaining that she was dead now and that her family did not mean to hurt her feelings. She did not want to accept that she was no longer living and kept insisting that I was wrong and should not be saying that to her. She was hardheaded and difficult to persuade. Although she admitted that no doctor or any hospital staff member had come to see her for a very long time, she still would not concede that perhaps she was dead. I had just about given up any hope of being able to set her on the right track when angels suddenly appeared at the sides of her bed. Mrs. Morrow broke out in a broad smile, and her eyes began to shine brightly.

One of the angels handed her a beautifully wrapped package decorated with a rainbow of ribbons. With her eyes sparkling, Mrs. Morrow carefully opened the box, and then, with a grin and a nod of approval, she held up the elegant dressing gown given to her by the angels. This gown was precisely what she needed. Next, one of the angels spoke and suggested that they could take her shopping, which would be a whole lot more fun than staying in the hospital. She eagerly agreed, and off she went with the angels.

The next day I gave Carrie my notes from the conversation I had with her mother-in-law so Carrie could give them to her husband. Later I asked how her husband reacted when he read what his mother had said. Carrie responded that when her husband read his mother's words, he became very pale, his knees went weak, and his hands were shaking. I asked Carrie, "Did that sound like his mother?" She said, "Exactly like her."

This was not the end of my involvement with Mrs. Morrow. One day she returned demanding to speak with me.

Mrs. Morrow: Young lady, come here. I want to talk to you. I want you to know what those angels did for me.

Kay: Tell me, Mrs. Morrow, what did those angels do for you?

Mrs. Morrow: They took me shopping all right, but when we got there, the store disappeared, and there I was looking straight at my granddaddy. I felt like I was six years old, and I knew he loved me more than anybody else. I could feel it in my heart. I had the same feeling when he put his arms around me and gave me a kiss on the cheek.

Then he started calling me "young lady" and chuckling. His eyes were dancing and mischievous. I then realized that he did not look any older than he did when I was six years old. So, I asked him how that could be, and he laughed again and said, "How old do you think you are? Do you still feel like an old lady sitting in your hospital bed after you died?"

Well, that is when it hit me. I did not know that I was dead. I thought those angels took me shopping. I did not put things together. That is why I asked to come back and have a few words with you. I want you to know what I found out in case you do not already know. I have tried to tell my family, but they cannot hear me. You are the only one I know back there that hears me talking to you.

Kay: Mrs. Morrow, you are easy for me to hear. Please continue.

Mrs. Morrow: What I found out is that I was wrong. I was so sure of myself that I did not listen to what other people had to say. If someone said something that I did not believe, I would think to myself, "That's baloney," and dismiss whatever it was that they said. My point is that I was unteachable and hardheaded because I would automatically reject whatever I did not believe, and I always thought I was right.

I guess I was born that way, just thinking that I had enough answers to suit myself and did not need anymore. I never did like to hear what other people had to say. I was always right in my own mind and did not need any other information.

Now I see that I put up a wall around me for security. I was a queen in my domain. I determined how things were in my domain, and that was enough for me. I was my own expert and rule maker. I had no reason to budge. I had the answers and what I thought had to be the way things were. I was my own expert until I got here.

Kay: What do you mean, Mrs. Morrow, until you got there?

Mrs. Morrow: Well, it is funny here. Without trying, you really do know how things are, but it is also unsettling because now it turns out that how things really are is so different from what I had decided. I took information from my long-held thoughts and opinions and called them facts. I did not care to investigate other people's perspectives. Theirs were automatically faulty just because they were not mine. Do you get my drift?

Kay: Yes, I believe I do. It sounds like you did not necessarily have an open mind to investigating other people's perceptions.

Mrs. Morrow: I did not think there was any point to it. I kept myself insulated from truths and facts because of my own hard-headedness. You know, I did not want to learn from other sources. I had to be my own expert, so I kept myself locked in my own little realm of security. I kept myself comfortable with my mistaken thinking and locked out what I could have learned from other people.

Now, I am telling you this, dear, so you will not do the same thing. If I were still alive, I would be saying, "Here, I have this right." However, from where I am now, I am saying, "There were many things I did not have close to right, even though I thought I did."

Kay: Thank you, Mrs. Morrow, for your advice. You are saying that where you are now, you perceive with clarity and that you did not perceive with clarity when you were still alive, although you thought you did.

Mrs. Morrow: I actually prevented myself from understanding with more clarity because I would not let myself learn from others who thought differently or had a different opinion. I put my blinders up and stayed snuggled in my own beliefs. Do not do this. It is not a good thing to be narrow-minded and rigid.

Kay: I will heed your warning, Mrs. Morrow. Thank you for returning to caution me.

A Private Man

A young genius unexpectedly passed away in middle age. He was a very private person, so I will not go into his background information other than to say that many people mourned his passing. As I usually do when it comes to my attention that someone has died, I summon the angels who specialize in investigating whether or not the person who passed needs assistance. I sent out the call to my angels the day after this person died, and about three hours later, I had my answer.

Angels: We have brought him to you.

Kay: Can you hear me?

The man: Who are you?

Kay: My name is Kay. Now I live in Littleton, Colorado, and help people make the right connections after dying, supporting their transfer into the heavens.

The man: How did I get here to where you are?

Kay: Angels maneuvered to bring you to me. You cannot see them, can you?

The man: I do not see anyone but you, writing on some paper.

Kay: Where do you think people go after they die?

The man: So I am dead. I was not sure. At first, I thought I was asleep and dreaming, but now I am not sure. You are the first person I have spoken with ever since ...

Kay: Since when?

The man: Well, I do not know. Since I fell asleep is how I think I should respond, but now I am not so sure. How can I tell if I am dead? How can I tell if I am alive? I pass all the tests for being alive. I am my own self, but it is lonely here. I am by myself; there are no other people here.

Kay: May I give you a tip?

The man: Sure, go ahead.

Kay: I can understand why you may be feeling some anxiety right now.

The man: Some anxiety???? You would be too if you were where I am, wherever this is!

Kay: Do your best to relax your mind.

The man: Now what?

Kay: Think about the most wonderful thing that has ever happened to you.

(Short pause.)

The man: Wow! Did you know they were there? Let me count them. Thirteen, and one is holding an infant. I have never felt this elated in my whole life!

Kay: You did not tell me who *they* are.

The man: Now they are laughing. You knew all along, didn't you? Angels are surrounding me.

Kay: Now, do you think that you may have died?

The man: From the look of things, I must have, but I do not mind one bit. The angel carrying an infant is approaching me. She wants to say something. She is saying that this infant is symbolic of all the infants born without the ability to survive. When they pass from their bodies, they flow directly into the waiting arms of an angel who takes them straight to a nursery within the heavens.

She says that the maternal angels who care for them are a most wonderful substitute for their physical parents. She is telling me to tell you and other people that children, who passed from their body, receive very special attention from the sweetest angels who specifically request to minister to children.

This angel also says that parents whose children are dying can help their children by showing them pictures of angels and explaining that angels like these will take care of them, love them and play with them when they are in the wonderful place called heaven. In addition, for children, who are old enough to understand, tell them that there is no sickness or disability in heaven. Everyone in heaven has a healthy, perfectly functioning spirit body that feels like their regular human body but without any problems.

Kay: Oh, this is wonderful to hear.

The man: Thank you for being concerned about me and asking angels to check on me.

Kay: You are most welcome. I am happy for you. I know that you will be very much at home within the heavens.

The angels know whom they are dealing with when they come to the aid of a deceased person. They relate in ways that are especially meaningful to the person who needs their assistance. When the angels appeared to this man, one of them held an infant in her arms. She was demonstrating the angelic attention and kindness extended to all children who pass from their bodies.

Only those who have experienced it themselves can understand the heartache endured by parents who lose their children. That pain may cut more deeply than in most other tragedies. The angels who came to assist this man give us joy, knowing that special divine care flows to children whose bodies cannot sustain physical life. Beloved angels envelop the children in their arms and care for them within the heavens.

An excellent way to introduce children to the concept of angelic protection is to teach them about guardian angels. Guardian angels are a particular class of angels who are primarily devoted to the protection and care of children. We all had a guardian angel assigned to us when we were born.

When children are young, they are especially receptive to learning about guardian angels and accepting their presence as a reality. Some of us learned to say a prayer to our guardian angel before going to sleep at night, which made us more likely to feel a closeness with them. Saying these prayers also induced feelings of being peaceful and protected as we fell asleep.

As children grow older and their lives become more complex, devotion to one's guardian angel may seem to be childish. Often children's belief in guardian angels falls by the wayside when they enter their teenage years. When we think about all the decisions that teenagers make and the repercussions of some of those decisions, it is evident that every teenager could use the gentle influence of a radiant angelic being. The best friend a teenager could have is their special angel to help them navigate the challenges of the teen and even preteen years.

If you would like to initiate a relationship with an angel, send out a prayer request to the angelic realm for a volunteer to come and stay with you and protect you. Every night before falling asleep, mentally talk to the angel that will have responded to your invitation and express your gratitude for their presence in your daily life. Making that nightly connection will strengthen the ties between you. Believe me; this is not a fantasy. Who among us would turn down the constant companionship of a blessed angel who is devoted to our well-being?

CHAPTER TWELVE
YUGOSLAVIA AND AFRICA

There were two extraordinary occasions involving collaborative efforts with my angelic partners when we uplifted exceptionally large groups of deceased people into the higher dimensions. During the summer of 1999, my attention turned to more ambitious undertakings than my usual involvement. My friend David Sleeper knew about my working partnership with the rescue angels and stopped by to visit. David lived in the Big Bend area of Texas and came to Houston from time to time. When he came to our area, he would usually stop by to say hello. David was one of the few people who knew about my work with the angels, and he enjoyed participating with me.

During this particular visit, David suggested that it might be possible for us to help large groups of deceased people all at once. This thought had never occurred to me. Honestly, I was lukewarm to the idea, but he persuasively insisted that it was worth a try. He wanted to pitch in to be of assistance. His theory was that the two of us working together might generate a stronger energetic connection, leading to aiding a more significant number of people. Our plan was for David to meditate with me before connecting with my angelic collaborators and then remain energetically connected as the angels and I worked together.

David happened to have his tape recorder with him that day, and because he did, we have a transcript of what occurred. Before we began, we discussed what our immediate objective would be. We were both distressed by the happenings in Yugoslavia. The Bosnian war brought about inhumane savagery, which displaced thousands upon thousands of people. The combatants targeted a large number of people for eradication. As the world watched in horror, families were broken apart and rendered homeless. Populations were starving. No one had an exact count of the number of people who died. I am not sure there was an official number because many people disappeared and were never seen again.

We both agreed that we would focus our attention on aiding the deceased people of Yugoslavia. We had no idea if what David proposed was doable, but we thought we would do our best to assist them. Since we had not before combined to do this work as a team, we did not know if our proposal to help Yugoslavia's deceased people would be effective. I began by asking my guidance what procedure we should use. The angels that guide me, although silent up until this point, had an immediate response.

Guidance: There are hundreds of angels ready to assist your efforts. This is a glorious undertaking. Many Archangels are going to be helping with this process, including Archangel Michael and his angels. Angels will be involved in various capacities.

Kay: Thank you. Then we will get started.

(David turned on his tape recorder.)

Kay: A great mobilization is taking place. Angels are in place and ready to go. With my inner vision, I am beginning to witness many deceased people being uplifted into the heavens. They are being taken up one by one, not as a group but as individuals. Each angel is assisting one person. Every individual is receiving personal assistance.

Moreover, there is wailing and crying, and it seems to be growing louder and more widespread, a lot of crying. More and more people are starting to see the angels. These people felt displaced forever, not only without a home and just existing in a no man's land, but without ever being with their loved ones again. They had accepted this as their misfortune, which they could do nothing to alleviate.

Now that angels are appearing, there is great excitement, joy, and gratitude but still a lot of crying and wailing. There is an emotional mix. I see people with outstretched arms and angels coming to uplift them, a very exciting happening.

Guidance: Divine hands are here to help. Angels are ready to go, but the human connection is necessary. There must be concern from the human heart for the well-being of others. This upliftment is a lovely expression of the highest form of this type of assistance. No ego or personal agenda is involved, just a desire to provide help for another that the other desperately needs and cannot obtain on their own.

Kay: Great numbers of people are going up to the heavens, and I can see them being welcomed. When they get into the light, more extended hands are there to take them. These desperate deceased people are being delivered into welcoming arms. Many of them are crying. Some are very joyful, but for the most part, this is a heavy emotional experience, and many tears are being shed. There are a lot of hugs and joyful tears, as well as very emotional tears.

Perhaps all the tears are joyful, but some seem heavy. Maybe they are crying out of them all of the distress that has ... That is what it is. They are crying out the despair built up within them because of their horrific experiences and the personal losses they encountered. Their crying is a release, a way to wash away the fear and heaviness. This event is joyful, although there is heavy crying of release.

Angels are taking these displaced people into the heavens, one by one, gently wrapping their arms around each one individually and soothing them. Many people swoon at the sight of the angels and instinctively reach for them. Others who do not consider themselves worthy of going with the angels hold back and refuse to accompany them.

The rescue angels keep going back and forth. This activity is going on for as far as I can see with my inner vision. Hundreds and probably thousands have gone up already. Some people are lagging behind the group because they created misdeeds that they regret. They are fearful of being punished. Soon angels will assist them as well.

Thank you, dear angels, who love and care for these people. Thank you, archangels, and thank you, David, for thinking of this. That is your job. You are skilled at identifying ways we can combine our efforts to help people.

A sizeable number of people are turning the angels down. Angels are offering to help them, and these people are saying no. The angels are taking the ones who are willing and eager. There are plenty of those, and I am observing that there are children too. Now I asked guidance when those who are turning the angels down will receive assistance, and the answer is "not for a while yet."

David: Think about what must be going on.

(A long time goes by.)

Kay: The angels have almost completed taking those who are willing to go with them, and they are searching to be sure that they have not missed anyone who is ready. As I watch them, it seems that those they are approaching now are rooted. They seem to be stuck, not willing to release. Now it is time to deal with them.

David: Go get'em, angels!

Kay: Wait, this is interesting. I have not run into this before. I hear angels speaking to them in their own language.

Angels: We can communicate with these people because our directed thought transcends language. They receive the communication that we send them using mental telepathy, and they respond. We are trying to make all these people as comfortable as possible. We communicate with them directly, giving them the message they need to hear in their own language.

We will hold them in our arms and tell them how important they are, how their lives were not meaningless, and that those hurtful experiences do not reflect on who they are in the eyes of God. Even though some have caused happenings that they now regret, they are acceptable in God's heaven. Not only are they acceptable, but they are also important, and we angels are here to help them. They have to accept that God is more forgiving of them than they are of themselves.

Kay: This is a most beautiful, loving approach. Now I see angels holding individual people in their arms and looking lovingly into their eyes while speaking to them in what sounds to me like a Slovakian language. I cannot understand what these tenderhearted angels are saying, but I can see that people's faces are transfixed with awe and wonder. This approach is working. Almost all of the people are raising their arms to signal to the angels that they are ready to go with them. There are only a few stubborn ones, kind of grumpy and mumbling.

David: Wounded humans.

(More time goes by.)

Kay: Now angels are going back to those who are still having difficulty. They are going to raise them up. The angels, with their arms around individual people, are stroking them tenderly. Two or three angels are caring for each person, consoling them. The angels are pouring love upon them, which melts the people's resistance. Many of these people begin to cry.

They do not feel worthy to receive such divine treatment, and they are letting go, like when you fall into a heap after being highly emotional and feel completely drained. These people are releasing their tension, blame, and regrets. They are letting go and clinging to the angels who are taking them very gently with tender concern for their well-being. I do not notice anyone declining angelic assistance now.

After some time goes by, I try to see if there is anyone left. Angels are looking, too, to see if they missed anyone.

Guidance: This completes the uplifting of the disembodied people who suffered not only the conflict that took their lives but also the horror of continuing disruption after they died. The people have gone on to the higher dimensions with great relief and release from continual distress over being stranded between worlds.

They were in the bleak situation of seeing their loved ones in the physical world as their loved ones continued to take the brunt of the conflict. They shared a common desire to protect those they left behind, and it was disheartening not to be able to jump in and help them in any way. They were ineffective in shielding those they still felt responsible for defending.

Much benefit has happened today, and we thank you for participating and initiating this transference of people from the In-between into the higher dimensions.

Kay: A question David has is how many have gone into the heavenly realms today.

Angels: There were thousands of people. An exact number will not be given. The main thing is to understand is the great benefit they each received. Even if it were only one person, it would be significant, and of course, the significance multiplies because of the tragic circumstances and the vast number of people involved. Many people have arrived in the higher dimensions today because of your efforts, your willingness to extend yourselves to help them.

Kay: We thank the angels who helped the people of Yugoslavia today. David would like to ask if Africa would be a good place to turn our attention next.

Guidance: Many places have a need, but Africa is definitely one of the areas where it would bring the most benefit. It is not only because of what happened in Rwanda but also because of the continent's history, how much abuse there has been, and the AIDS epidemic. There are many people there dying of AIDS. There has also been much starvation on that continent.

Many people have had desperate situations at the end of their lives, keeping them from exiting their physical bodies in a peaceful frame of mind. These circumstances often cause the hang-up where one cannot transfer from the physical realm into the higher dimensions. As to your question, the answer, of course, is yes that Africa would be an excellent next step, the next place to perform this service.

David: So let us make that our plan, perhaps when we get back together in August.

Kay: Okay, sure.

David: Everybody?

Angels: We will be here to support your efforts. We work together. We cannot do it without you, and you cannot do it without us.

One month later, David was back in Houston and paid me a visit. We both had the clearing of Africa on our minds. After angels collaborated with us to help the people who died in Yugoslavia, we were eager to collaborate with them again. We did not record this event; however, my memories are distinct because of the strong impact it made upon me.

As in our last combined effort, we began by sitting and meditating together. Our intent was firm. We requested angelic assistance to uplift all the displaced people in Africa who had failed to transfer into the higher dimensions. We did not know how many there would be or that they would be such a complex group to assist.

The session began with my internal overview of the deceased people in Africa. Within my inner vision, I saw massive numbers of disembodied people almost elbow to elbow. They were not looking at each other or communicating with each other. They ignored other people as they shuffled around in a dull, dazed state, looking lost and bewildered.

As I watched them, my guidance clarified that these disheartened people did not communicate with each other because they spoke so many different languages. They could not understand what the others were saying. There did not appear to be any organization or effort to accomplish any goal. The people appeared to be completely listless.

My guidance explained that the deceased in Africa mixed with people of other tribes, which number in the thousands, and they all speak different languages. Because there were more than a thousand African dialects, it was difficult for them to find people they could communicate with. The vast numbers made it unlikely for them to bump into deceased family members or acquaintances.

The people looked drab and gloomy as if they had been in this state for eons of time. Nothing constructive was going on. No interactions. There were no smiling faces, just dreariness in untold numbers of people shuffling around, going nowhere.

Somehow, these angels could communicate with the masses of people and effectively arrange this major orchestration. Angels got right to work, and they knew precisely what to do. They circulated among the deceased people making announcements. They defined certain organizational areas and issued instructions for the people to assemble into their tribal groups. I knew that people understood the angelic communications because right after the angels gave their instructions, people started moving around.

Their prior slow shuffling gave way to deliberate action. People became enlivened. As I continued to watch, I began to see flashes of recognition between some people. These sparks of recognition preceded warm embraces and joyous laughter. People were reconnecting with others of their tribes, including deceased friends and relatives, and began to feel revitalized.

This organizational phase seemed to take a very long time, and I was delighted to be watching what was going on. After the angels were satisfied that people had understood the instructions and had moved into their tribal groups, those angels in charge of each particular group issued each person brand new clothes native to their tribe. I watched as angels distributed neatly folded, brightly colored clothes to each person. Joyfully the people donned their greatly appreciated new clothing. Happiness and cheer spread among everyone. There was nothing other than smiling faces and sparkling eyes dancing with delight. It was enthralling to see these beautiful people become revitalized.

Within my inner vision, I saw certain areas, which the angels said were indicative of what was going on throughout the continent of Africa. I cannot imagine how many angels were involved in organizing this vast number of people. The African people looked bewildered but in a good way. They were experiencing leaving the pit of despair that they expected to go on endlessly, and now they were feeling confident because they were receiving the exact help they needed. Everything was going great.

The angels' next step was to deliver rows and rows of an enormous number of colorfully decorated busses floating down from the sky, enough to accommodate every tribal group. I cannot imagine how many of these heavenly busses were arriving to transport all those the angels had come to rescue throughout Africa. I watched spellbound as these multicolored whimsical-looking busses unexpectedly appeared. These were not ordinary busses. Each bus was decorated with splashes of red, blue, yellow, green, and other bright colors in bold designs. The busses resembled giant-sized cartoon creations, which made everyone's eyes sparkle with delight. This scene, which I watched with my inner vision, swelled my heart with complete joy and happiness for these dear people who had suffered such misery.

I wondered what the angels were up to when the busses began to appear, but soon it became apparent. These fanciful busses played an essential part in reassuring people that they would be in a better place than where they had been, thus relieving any lingering anxiety among the precious people. This most creatively designed transport system produced the immediate impact of delighting and entertaining everyone.

The angels in charge organized each ethnic group and directed them to board their designated busses, which the people were eager to do. Once they were seated, music erupted from all directions as each busload of people began to sing their ancestral songs. At the top of their lungs, they sang with all their might. Through their songs, they poured out feelings of pure joy and enormous relief, as well as the delight of being reunited with others in their tribe. In every direction, people in busses were singing different songs in a variety of African languages.

An enormous number of archangels directed the organization of all these groups. It was apparent that the people felt relaxed, cared for, and safe. Then as I continued to watch, ever so gently, one by one, each bus began to lift and slowly float upward toward the heavens. Multitudes of angels flew around each bus while the singing continued uninterrupted as all the busloads of people took off for the heavenly realms. From my perspective, I was standing on the ground, watching the progression of events and dearly wishing that I could be there when they arrived in the heavens to welcome them. I estimate that all of these events took about two hours for me to view.

Afterward, David and I were gleeful with the outcome of our determination to uplift the deceased people of Africa, helping them to ascend into the heavens. I would never have thought of such an ambitious undertaking myself. However, because of David's desire to aid as many people as possible, vast numbers of Africans received the help they needed. Before David left that afternoon, we started to chat about what our next project could be. Soon we realized that both of us were exhausted after our endeavor to aid the deceased people of Africa and did not feel up to choosing our next project.

After this session, my body began to signal that something was going wrong. It did not start until shortly after David left, and I started cooking dinner. I began to feel shaky and light-headed, and eating some food did not settle me down as I hoped that it would. My body started to feel like it was going haywire. My energetic system seemed to be all scrambled, and I became very weak. As the hours went by, I started to convulse with dry heaves. My reaction continued all evening long, and it was very frightening to be unable to stabilize my body. I had not been feeling ill until after our session to clear the African continent, so I figured that the way I was feeling was related to what we accomplished that afternoon.

When I questioned my guidance about why this was happening to me, they replied that the vast number of people involved with the African clearing put too great a strain on my energy field. They cautioned me against putting myself into the same position again by explaining the following. They said that although it seems like I am only watching what is going on, the energetic connection that makes it possible for deceased people to see and interact with angels flows out through my body's energy field to every person.

This connection puts an overwhelming demand on my energetic resources. It can destabilize my body, even if I have the energetic support of other people who contribute, such as David did. My guidance instructed me to safeguard myself by not working on such large numbers of people all at once, as in the African situation. I was sad to abandon this most helpful way to assist a vast number of people, but my physical deterioration afterward was deeply unsettling. Hence, I followed this instruction from my guidance.

There is a fervent desire within the angelic realm for partnership with people who are willing to work for the good of humanity, as these two instances imply. It is comforting to have angelic beings who care about our welfare and are more ready than we might imagine to collaborate with us when we extend ourselves to help other people. I suggest that we take the point-of-view that my friend David Sleeper frequently expressed. He often said, "Put the angels to work. There are a lot of unemployed angels who are just waiting to be put to work." It might be a good idea to invite some angels to come along and participate with us when we extend ourselves to help another. I suspect that there are unemployed angels who would be willing to collaborate with each of us.

CHAPTER THIRTEEN

THE IN-BETWEEN

———

In retrospect, it is hard to believe that my angels cautioned me not to attempt to aid such large numbers of people after the Africa endeavor because they requested my assistance with a much vaster undertaking ten years later. I will tell you about this after I give you some background information. The material that I am presenting now is of paramount importance for every person to understand.

Previously, I referred to the In-between as the default area where deceased people continue their existence when they cannot perceive their better alternative. There are different levels of the afterlife, and people in the lower levels cannot perceive activity in the more advanced levels of creation. We accept as being real, that which we can hear, see and feel. While we live in the physical world, we know what it is like to be living here. Because we do not have consciousness within the ascending levels of existence beyond the third dimension of solid matter, we may think other dimensions do not exist. Going only by that which we can confirm with our senses does not give us the entire picture of creation.

Creation is vaster than our human minds can conceive. We live our physical lives within one level of creation. After we pass from experiencing our current level of creation, we lose our dense physicality. As we slip out of our physical body, we find ourselves wholly conscious but without the hindrance of having to navigate within a physical form. Our navigation system lies within our minds. We think about where we want to be, and instantly we find ourselves transported there solely by our will. After we pass from our physical body, our mind takes over as our navigation system. Without a physical form, we are free to maneuver our spirit body anywhere our mind directs.

After we exit from our physical body, there are options open to us. Those who remain attached to the family they left behind are at risk of missing their divine escort. Every person who passes from their physical body receives an escort into the elevated dimensions of existence; however, many deceased people cannot detect their escorts. When a deceased person does not perceive their escort, they wander around in a vast section of creation that the angels call the In-between. The In-between is a swath of the afterlife, which closely adjoins Earth, and this is where deceased people congregate when their convictions do not include transporting to a most desirable place after dying.

People who die distaining the concept of a gratifying afterlife are not likely to find their way to their best destination. People who pass from their bodies fearing retribution for past misconduct lock themselves out of experiencing a swift ascension into a more desirable place to exist. We create our own obstacles when we embrace mistaken perceptions about what happens after we die. Some of these misperceptions come from earthly religious authorities, who repeatedly teach erroneous information previously taught to them.

What we believe and anticipate sets the stage for what happens to us after we pass from our body. I caution everyone to keep your mind open to other possibilities than what you may expect to occur. Be open to finding your best option and always carry a very high vibration. Remain peaceful and calm. Think positively and expect the best to happen. Look for the presence of elevated beings, relatives, or dear friends who predeceased you.

When people pass from their bodies unaware that a most appealing alternative is available, they do what comes naturally. Initially, they remain attached to the physical world as a voyeur watching the activity and sometimes attempting to affect some kind of influence upon it. Residing in the In-between is extraordinarily confusing because no other options seem to be available. Instead of being a place, the In-between is a range of availability open to those who pass from their physical form without perceiving the divine beings who are present and attempting to help them. At death, angels offer every person assistance, but the low vibrational level induced by fear often prohibits newly deceased people from perceiving the angels' presence.

When they pass from physicality, deceased persons will not run into difficulties if they focus their attention on going home to the heavens with joy in their hearts. Having this focus creates high vibrational frequencies. These frequencies enable them to perceive the presence of those who have come to retrieve them. A vibrational threshold exists between the three-dimensional world and the higher levels of existence. When deceased people do not have a high enough vibration to pass through this threshold, they remain below the threshold, lost and confused. In this state, they do not know where they are, how they got there, or what else they can do.

The elevated levels of existence require newcomers to release from all earthly involvements. When it is our time to pass from our bodies, we need to be looking forward to the grand adventure that lies ahead for our best outcome to materialize. If we dwell on our fears, judgments, regrets, anger, or vindictive feelings, we close a door of opportunity as we approach our death. We prevent ourselves from easily perceiving our best path forward.

When newly deceased people rise above the low vibrational threshold, they are on their way to creating wondrous after-death experiences. They will readily perceive the presence of their angelic assistance and others who are special to them who now reside in the elevated realms, such as their already deceased friends and relatives who come to greet the newcomer. When people pass from their bodies, all will go smoothly if their energetic vibrations are higher than the low vibrational barrier.

Deceased people, who cannot perceive their higher dimensional support, remain in a lost and confused state of existence. They are not mistreated. They receive the same attention as those who easily traverse the low vibrational barrier. Their problem is that since they cannot perceive the higher vibrational support that is being extended to them, they remain in a confused state, not knowing what to do.

We all have the potential to execute a perfect landing straight into the heavens after we pass from our bodies, giving ourselves the trip of a lifetime if we do not get in our own way. High vibratory levels give us wings to fly high into the heavens after we die. They act as our protection. Depressed vibratory levels act as an anchor that keeps us rooted in the In-between.

Within the In-between are people who vary in personal development. Most of the people who are in the In-between are much like the people whose stories appear in the previous chapters. They were in a low vibrational state as they passed from their bodies for reasons such as committing suicide, suddenly dying in a fatal accident, or being murdered. Unless they turn their fortunes around by raising their vibratory rate, they are likely to remain stuck in the In-between. I have included instances where people in this In-between state freed themselves and instantly gained access to the higher dimensions. Both Samuel Parker in Chapter Ten and Sara at the end of Chapter Four explained how easily they accomplished this.

The In-between may be difficult to comprehend because our typical perceptions have not included an energetic boundary between our physical Earth and the elevated dimensions, which we commonly refer to as heaven. We are used to thinking in terms of physical boundaries, set and defined in terms that we who live on Earth can understand. The actual separation between the Earth and the heavens is energetic. If you happen to be a deeply spiritual person who practices withdrawal into deep meditation you will have experienced ascending vibrational frequencies.

I like to refer to this state of ascending vibrational frequencies as being halfway to heaven. Within this state of effervescent purity, you feel like you are indeed halfway to heaven. When abruptly disrupted from this state, it is particularly unpleasant. Swiftly going from very refined energetic vibrations down to the lower vibrations of Earth consciousness is unsettling.

After dying, there is a sort of crossroads that the deceased must navigate. People with clear consciences, who have led beneficial lives and are confident that the elevated dimensions exist, will find themselves pulled in that direction. Other people who are frightened and do not have a clear picture of what is available to them, or those who have led lives of treachery or dishonesty, often run into difficulty. They slip into existing in the dream-like state of the In-between.

The extreme differences between the elevated vibrations of the heavens and the depressed vibrations of the In-between, cause people within the In-between to be unaware of the existence of the higher dimensions. Within the In-between, people remain adrift, going from place to place, having no idea that they could extract themselves and transfer to a more satisfying existence. It is almost impossible to change one's perceptions when the circumstances you are experiencing are all you have to go on. There is no one in the In-between to educate the other residents there. Those who are enlightened have already advanced themselves into the elevated realms.

Especially in the beginning, deceased people stranded in the In-between create existences that fit their personalities. Many deceased people wander around in groups of various sizes. Some even form communities, as you read about in the Hilltop Hotel story. Most people are as pleasant after death as they were when they were alive; intrinsically, they are no different. A certain number of them are quite sociable and are attracted to being with people like themselves. Some wander around alone or with one or two others whose company they enjoy.

There is no exact procedure followed when people cannot detect their angelic assistance and end up wandering in the In-between. The people within the In-between experience their reality lacking direction and purpose. They know that they still exist, but no one can explain where they are, how they got there, or how to get out. None of the other people there can help them. None of them knows how to access a better alternative.

When they first arrive in the In-between, most people curiously investigate their new parameters. Usually, after completing the initial testing of their new environment, many people nestle into the upper levels of the In-between, with most of them engaging in repetitive activities. There is no personal development. Their behavior is the same as it was when they were physically alive. People who were hurtful or dishonest do not rise above that level of self-expression. Within the areas of the In-between, people carry on activities that do not advance their self-expression.

The In-between is as real to them as our lives on Earth are to us, but being in the In-between delays inner growth and development, whereas our lives on Earth seem designed to foster our evolutionary progress. At least we have the opportunity to set our sights on this objective while we are here, whereas the people within the In-between do not have this opportunity. One could exist in that state forever and end up no more evolved than they were when they initially entered it. Even if we set up an agreeable situation for ourselves initially, such as those who maintain an interactive social life, after a while, we tend to tire of the tedious repetition and sink to lower levels of confusion. Then hopelessness takes hold.

In some cases, deceased people, who are aggressive and harbor evil intent, use their wills strongly enough to interfere with a living person's mind and decision-making, as the Las Vegas shooter and Joseph encountered in Chapter Seven. These are extreme examples of what can happen when evilness flexes its directed power. Just as we have people of terrible character, who harness their activity to destroy the well-being of others on Earth, the In-between also has them.

Failing to transfer into the higher dimensions after dying casts one's consciousness into an alternative level of experience. People are not aware that they are engaging in a dream-like reality because that is all they can perceive. Those who die without carrying the elevated vibrational frequencies required to relocate into the higher spheres of existence remain in a disturbed dream-like state. In this state, they wander around interacting with other people who are in the same predicament. Being with others such as themselves who also cannot perceive any alternatives leads them to believe that this situation is all that exists.

When we die in a low vibrational state, we immediately become confused and disoriented and do not know what to do next. Our low vibrations keep us unaware of those who now reside in the higher vibrational reality. Low vibrations keep us from perceiving our previously deceased friends, relatives, or angelic beings who have rushed to our side to assist us. Adding to this hindrance is not having the impulse to seek divine assistance as we sidetrack into the default place called the In-between. We entrap ourselves between worlds. The In-between is not purgatory, nor is it hell. No judgement is rendered upon anyone.

After dying, the next step is to join our escort that has come to lead us forward into the heavens. Our deceased relatives or friends who now reside in the heavens may arrive to accompany us into the elevated dimensions. Angels are also available to accommodate our transfer from Earth to the heavens, but usually, they remain in the background. They are quick to step in to assist when the deceased person does not have a personal escort. All bases are covered to help us navigate where we are supposed to go next, and note that where we are supposed to go next is the same for all of us.

I cannot overemphasize that we are all welcome within the higher dimensions. No one is prohibited from entering as a form of punishment. All people go back to where we were before we were born, and we are the only ones who judge ourselves. When we reenter the higher dimensions, we review our performance from the lifetime we just completed. We watch the movie of our life, and we render our own honest assessment of how we performed. By that point, we have lost our distortions regarding our intentions and actions while we were alive, and we openly accept the many plusses and minuses of the record we created for ourselves.

The In-between is massive and contains inestimable numbers of people. If the person I ask the angels to locate is residing in the deepest parts of the In-between, that person must have been there a long time, and the angels face a daunting task. Finding a particular longtime resident of the In-between is almost impossible for the angels. Angels have a hard time identifying one lost person from another in those areas where the vibrational rates are the most depressed. Even angels who have been trying their best to infuse some higher vibrations into the deepest parts of the In-between are rarely able to affect any improvement. The people's despair is too strong to allow the angels' efforts to have much impact.

When Archangel Michael asked me to collaborate with him and multitudes of angels to elevate the residents of the In-between into the higher spheres, I did not think twice. I immediately said yes. I was more than willing to accept Archangel Michael's invitation to participate in the angelic plan to evacuate the people stuck in the In-between, including those in the deepest, most dreadful parts of the In-between.

I was incredulous that there was such a plan afloat and that I was requested to participate. It was natural for me to say yes. I was very willing to pitch in to do whatever I could to assist. I did not know what this would entail, and, in retrospect, I do not think Archangel Michael or his angelic forces did either.

There was enormous preplanning that went into this operation. I initially received bits and pieces of information, and over time, as more information came forth, the full plan emerged. The angelic plan was to evacuate all the people stranded in the In-between. Under this plan, the angels needed to search each of the many levels of the In-between, looking for forsaken people to assist.

To comprehend this more clearly, think in terms of a sky scrapper that goes down instead of up and covers the length and breadth of a whole continent. Then think about it occupied with millions of people scattered on different levels. Now you have some idea of the complexity involved. Then throw in that these people do not know where they are or how they got there. There does not seem to be a way out of this building. Then notice that there are no exit signs, no elevators, and no one to give directions to the rest of them.

The people within the In-between live in confusion and despair, especially those who have been there a long time. It is not that angels have avoided trying to transfer them out of there. People in the low vibrational frequencies of the In-between do not detect the presence of angelic beings. The energetic vibrations, particularly in the lower areas, are far too dense for people to notice that angelic beings are present and doing their best to communicate with them. It is as if the angels are not there, even when they have their arms around people within the In-between.

It is similar for us living on Earth. There is such a huge difference between our energetic vibrations and the high vibrations of angelic beings that even if angels are standing next to us, we cannot detect their presence. Now you have an idea of what the angels were facing.

The angels asked me to assist their efforts by establishing linkage, which would help them overcome an overwhelming obstacle. Archangel Michael explained that they were facing several roadblocks. One of them was the inability of people within the In-between to perceive and communicate with the angelic forces coming to recover them. Archangel Michael asked if I would join their effort by setting up the initial announcements and instructions for the people in the In-between. He expressed that my involvement would probably last about two weeks, and by then, the intervention would be well underway.

My job evolved into far more than the initial plan presented by Archangel Michael. My first assignment was to issue early broadcasts to the people within the In-between, telling them that a wonderful event was about to occur. These preliminary contacts served the purpose of giving them time to prepare for a big change ahead and create excitement that this change would bring them vastly improved living conditions. Archangel Michael's plan was for me to communicate to the residents of the In-between that beautiful new residential areas were opening, and all of them were invited to relocate to these most appealing places.

There was quite a stir when I projected my spirit body into the In-between and made these preliminary announcements. It seemed that everyone was thrilled at the opportunity to go to the new residences, and many sought reassurance that they would be included. As I met with individual groups, I automatically instilled within them the higher vibrations, which they required to be able to perceive the angelic communications.

Archangel Michael had prepared me in advance by implanting potent energetic frequencies within me that I could pass along to those in the In-between. These frequencies were flowing from me into them and from them to everyone else with whom they interacted. In this manner, we created our initial hooking-up of the people in the In-between with the ability to discern the angels' presence. I was in nearly constant contact with individuals and groups of people drumming up readiness to cooperate with Archangel Michael's plan to elevate them out of the In-between.

Sometimes I am conscious that I am in my spirit body as I travel to the people I assist. I maintain my consciousness in both my physical body and in my spirit body, which I sometimes project into the area where I am assisting people. I cannot explain how this occurs, just that it does. I think it could be a natural consequence of spending so much time between dimensions instead of remaining grounded only in the physical dimension.

Archangel Michael confided in me that he decided to limit the information in our announcements to the fact that people would be relocated to a most desirable place to live. He did not want me to mention anything about relocating into the higher dimensions.

He did not want to discourage anyone from relocating because they objected to where they would be taken.

He was specifically referring to people who would object to relocating to any place referred to as heaven. He said that this could create a big obstacle to relocating quite a large number of people. Archangel Michael conveyed that many people in the deepest parts of the In-between are terrified of going to a place called heaven because they fear that they will be harshly treated and punished for their actions when they were physically alive. He did not want anyone to refuse to go out of fear of suffering retribution for past behavior.

Archangel Michael was in charge of logistics. He drew volunteer angels together from all over the heavens to participate with him and his legions of angels. Angels prepared the new residential areas in the higher dimensions to receive as many people as anticipated, extending the space if needed. The angels who staffed these areas were familiar with the difficulties of moving from the In-between's lower frequencies to the higher frequencies of the heavens.

The master plan was to initiate this orchestration in one area of the globe and then advance to the adjoining areas with the angels working their way all around the world. Archangel Michael hoped that all we would need would be one sweep around our planet. He planned to begin the relocation in Tokyo, relocating the residents of In-between from that area. Then, from that starting point, he would direct his angelic forces throughout Asia, continuously transferring residents of the In-between into the higher dimensions. He and his angelic forces planned to move from one continent to the next, liberating and uplifting the people in the In-between from around the world.

Periodically Archangel Michael gave me an update on how the people of the In-between were reacting to our announcements about them moving to the new residential areas. He also informed me about the angelic forces' progress as they organized and got into their positions to start the mobilization. I did not receive the planned starting date until a few days before the mobilization was to begin.

On a Tuesday morning in February of 2010, Archangel Michael visited me and announced that all the angels would be in place and the mobilization would commence in two days. He instructed me to wait until Thursday and then start making announcements to the people within the In-between, informing them that the relocation to the new residences had begun. Neither Archangel Michael nor I were aware that eavesdroppers were listening to our conversation.

These people had to be from the upper levels of the In-between, where the vibrational frequencies are high enough to grasp what people in the physical world are saying. They heard me asking questions of Archangel Michael. Although they could not have heard what he said because his communication was beyond their ability to detect, they could hear what I was saying. Based on the questions that I was asking and the rest of my part of the conversation, they pieced together the organizational plan.

Shortly after my conversation with Archangel Michael concluded, I began to hear from our eavesdroppers. There were only two or three of them. They were highly excited and offered to help spread the word. Well, you can imagine what happened. Our planned Thursday commencement was out the window. The angels were scrambling to try to stay ahead of the rush of excitement that was sweeping the In-between.

As Archangel Michael's angelic teams worked their way through the In-between area by area, he kept me informed of their progress. What they universally found was that there were many more people within the In-between than they expected. They had no way to know precisely how many were stuck there, no way to count them. People had been accumulating in the In-between for eons of time. Many of them had sunk to the lowest levels with millions upon millions of other people.

My contribution did not end with my first assignment. As soon as the mobilization began, streams of deceased people found their way to me as if I were a lighthouse in a storm. They all needed help, so I called whichever angels I could connect with to take them to the new residential areas. All available angels were put into service. I wish I could fully convey to you how the heavens were organizing during this time. It was as if all the heavens were acting in concert to pull up every dislocated person throughout the In-between, and it seemed that everyone in the angelic realm had signed on to help.

None of the people who transitioned out of the In-between into the heavenly realm received any form of retribution. All were accepted, embraced, and helped to adjust. Their vibrations were monitored and gently elevated, guaranteeing that the extreme rise in energetic frequencies would not disorient them. The teams of angels were sensitive and caring and made everyone feel welcome at the place where they truly belonged. The transferred people expressed overwhelming joy and happiness, as well as tremendous relief.

Most of the people within the In-between were eager to move to a better place to live, although at first, some had reservations, and more than a few dug in their heels, refusing to budge from where they were. After the first rush of people relocated, it became apparent that many others were reluctant to leave. They did not believe the promises that seemed too good to be true, and a significant number of them refused to leave even the deepest and most horrible parts of the In-between. No amount of persuasion was adequate, and the harder we tried to persuade them, the more adamant they were that they were not going anywhere. Some even withdrew and went into hiding places to keep themselves safe from the angels, which was a discouraging problem.

Then something wonderful happened. One man, who had been elevated from the In-between to the new residential areas, came and paid me a visit within my energy field. He had a plan to convince the holdouts to move to a much better place to live. He volunteered to return to the In-between and attest to how lovely the new residences were, to convince the holdouts to drop their stubborn refusal to take advantage of the divine assistance flowing to them.

This selfless man had integrity and the power of persuasion. He worked tirelessly and singlehandedly created momentum to relocate in many of those who had stubbornly refused. Angels worked beside him, transporting all who reconsidered and got up their courage to relocate.

People who had already relocated observed what was going on in the place they were fortunate to have left. They especially watched with special interest this particular man, who was singlehandedly saving stubborn, frightened people from remaining stuck in the same situation that he had been in. This outreach encouraged many newly relocated people to follow the example of the first man who returned to help the rest.

These remarkable volunteers went back to the dreadful place from which they just liberated themselves to tell the people still there how beneficial it was to be in the new residential areas. Their presence had an immediate positive effect, and they were able to move up vast numbers of reluctant people who accepted their glowing reports. These volunteers had credibility with the people who did not believe the angels' descriptions; however, many people within the In-between were still very tough to convince.

The volunteer movement grew, expanded rapidly, and created a remarkable turnaround in the stalemate that had arisen. These remarkable volunteers could barely tolerate the environment of the In-between after adapting to the heavenly vibrations. To return there for even an instant took enormous compassion and dedication to the others who were still in that regrettable situation.

Groups of volunteers worked as long as they could tolerate and then went back to the relocation area and rounded up other returnees to take their place. One particular woman, who returned to help the fearful ones, worked tirelessly for an extraordinarily long time with tremendous vigor and determination. I will never forget all these compassionate volunteers, especially the man who started the volunteer movement and this particular woman.

As the mobilization went on, a close partnership evolved between the rescue angels and me out of our joint determination to do whatever we possibly could to relocate every person. Not everyone in the In-between had been alerted that angels were coming to relocate them to better residential areas. Some people were so far down in the lowest parts of the In-between that they did not receive the communications most of the others had. Since they had not been alerted, they did not know that the angels were coming and that they should be looking for them. Although the angels were not visible to these people, the angels managed to maneuver many of them into my presence so I could communicate with them.

Sometimes my angel partners would inform me that they were bringing people to me, and other times, they would send them to me unannounced while they immediately returned to the In-between to fetch as many more people as possible. It was as if the angels put a marker within my energy field and told the people they were assisting to go straight to the marker to receive the help they needed. Suddenly, day and night, people needing help would show up within my energy field. Sometimes I easily saw them, and other times, although I could not see them distinctly, I strongly felt their presence right there with me. When I detected them, I telepathically communicated with them.

I was shocked by the massive number of people being sent to me to prepare them to connect with teams of angels that would take them the rest of the way. Many people streamed to me in groups of various sizes. It was common to have groups with thirty to one hundred people, and many times one thousand or more people would come together. Because I usually could not detect how many people there were, I started asking how many were in their group for no other reason than my own curiosity. With one request for assistance, I asked, "How many of you are there?" The mellow response came from a gentle male voice, "Table for one?" He deeply touched my heart.

Another memorable exchange came as I was preparing a large group for their lift-up. One particular woman became quite excited and starting making a commotion. In a nervous, exhilarated voice, she kept repeating that she could not leave yet because she needed more time to plan for her entrance. She was certainly drawing a lot of attention to herself. This behavior was puzzling until angels answered my question and told me who she was. They said that she was a glamorous movie star in the late 1950s and early 1960s who committed suicide at the peak of her career. Even as I chuckled about her desire to prepare for her grand entrance, I felt shocked and saddened that she had been stuck in the In-between for so long.

One afternoon I went grocery shopping. I just started putting a few food items into the grocery cart when my angels warned me that I should go home immediately. Right after they gave me this instruction, I began to feel very weak and light-headed. That was enough for me, so I did as they instructed. I quickly left the store and drove the short distance home.

As I entered the house, my body went limp and started trembling and shaking. I felt an overwhelmingly powerful energetic connection between my energy field and that of a very large group of deceased people who were being sent to me. As I wondered what was going on, within my inner vision, there started to appear, disheveled people – men, women, and some children, looking severely beaten-down, plodding along, all in a line. They were streaming forward out of utter bleakness. I watched this scene as my body became weaker and weaker. I felt their emotional desolation, their hopelessness.

My vision settled on the man walking in front, leading the long line of people who were barely able to walk. When I asked how many people there were in their group and what happened to them, he was the one who answered. He said he did not have an exact count, but there were over two thousand people. A few ruthless men had held them in captivity as slaves, and they had not had an opportunity to escape. I asked him how they could get away now, and he responded that the men who enslaved them got up and left when they heard about the beautiful new residences to which they could relocate.

For the first time, these slaves were left unattended by their captors and were finally free to walk out of the deepest bowels of the In-between. Uncontrollable tears poured from my eyes, and I started shaking and mentally screaming to Archangel Michael, "Archangel Michael, hurry, hurry, come quickly, come quickly! Bring legions of angels with you! Come now! These people need your help! Hurry, hurry!" Repeatedly, I shouted into the heavens to get assistance for these desperate people.

I cry even now when I remember what happened that day. I came face to face with a terrible evil that was not a god's judgment or damnation. This situation is the closest thing to hell that I have run into the whole time that I have done this work, and this hell was created by what some people did to other people.

Later, when I asked Archangel Michael what happened to the men that enforced slavery upon so many other people, he replied that they were confined in a Re-education Center within the higher dimensions. These men would not mingle with the general population until they took responsibility for their reprehensible actions and atoned for all their cruelty. Archangel Michael explained that these men would have to endure the pain and heartache they caused. Part of their instructive process was to experience all the harm they inflicted upon every individual enslaved in the In-between and those they harmed throughout their lifetime before they passed from the Earth.

This program to uplift the people of the In-between in mass, to where they should have been all along, lasted in full force for over three and a half months, and for me, it lasted a lot longer. For many months after the main upliftment, I had stragglers showing up in my inner awareness, asking for help. I wish I could say the entire In-between was cleared, but it would not have remained clear even if it had been then. People continue to pass out of their physical bodies and enter that low vibrational dream-like state of the In-between, not knowing that they have a much better option.

As I participated with these incredible angelic teams to uplift people caught in the In-between, I thought about the distressing situations the people there had endured. People trapped in the In-between feel hopeless and deserted. They are not aware that they do not need to be there. If they were aware that there is a much better place for them and knew how to elevate their vibrations to go straight up to the higher realms, there would be no In-between.

The In-between can ensnarl any one of us, especially if we run into extraordinarily difficult death circumstances. Becoming trapped in the In-between does not necessarily mean that one is not an inherently good person. Here is an example to clarify what I am saying.

One of the people I was instrumental in aiding, not during the clearing of the In-between but later, is Tina Barns. I got her name from one of my usual sources, the newspaper. When I inquired about Tina, angels brought her right to me.

Kay: Tina, I feel you here with me. Did the angels find you?

Tina: Yes, I have already been to heaven with them. It is a nice place, a miraculous place for me.

Kay: What do you mean, Tina?

Tina: I had given up hope of finding my way out of the In-between.

Kay: What happened to you?

Tina: I was in a group of people, and we were wandering around together. We did not know what else to do. It was uneventful – all that wandering. I do not know how long I was there. It must have been a long time. Then from out of nowhere, I heard someone playing a harp. I followed the sound and found a small group of musicians singing my name as they played their harps. They looked like regular people until I got close enough to look into their eyes. Once I looked into their eyes, I knew who they were — angels who came to help me.

Kay: How did you know?

Tina: Their dusty-looking clothes disappeared as soon as I looked into their eyes. They were radiantly glowing angels disguised as musicians!

Kay: Then what happened?

Tina: They said they were taking me with them and asked if I would like to bring along the rest of our group that traveled together. This offer made me very happy. You have no idea how dreary and sad we all felt. We felt pushed down so low because nothing good ever happened to us.

Kay: Then what occurred?

Tina: When I wanted to know why the angels were singing my name, they said you sent them to find me. Immediately, I wanted to thank you, but the angels said that before that could happen, all of us were going to take a newcomer's tour of heaven, which we did. Never had any of us been so excited and happy, very happy. Then we had a choice. We could have gone to a giant party for our whole group, or we could pay you this visit to thank you for helping us out. We did not want to put off coming to say thank you, so here we are. (All in a chorus) THANK YOU!

Kay: You are so welcome. I could not be happier that all of you returned to the higher dimensions. How wonderful. I wish everyone still caught where you were, could go up too.

Tina: Our whole group has decided to go back and find more people who are as we were, lost and sad. The angels said we would all go together, and they invited more angels to come along. We are going on a rescue mission!

Kay: Tina, this is wonderful news. I have not heard of this happening before. Find as many people as you possibly can. Maybe the angels would be willing to make several trips. Maybe your whole group could become rescue angels yourselves.

Tina: That is something to consider.

Kay: God bless all of you precious people.

Angels to me: We thought you would like to know.

Kay: Thank you, dear angels. I am so very pleased for them. How did Tina hear your voices? Where she was, the vibrations must have been very heavy and depressed.

Angels: Tina had been an angel herself, but after her savagely inflicted death, she could not remember that she had been an angel who incarnated on Earth as a regular person to help people. After being murdered, she remained traumatized and unable to detect the other angels that came for her. It looked like she was hopelessly bewildered, but Tina still carried within her the remembrance of angels singing and playing instruments. When Tina heard their voices calling her name, she was finally able to recognize their presence. Her memory awakened when she looked into their eyes. Then her mind lit up with a spontaneous desire to stay by their sides.

Tina had the best possible recovery from being disoriented and lost within the In-between. There is no way to know how many residents of the In-between are, in reality, evolved people who underwent severely challenging life circumstances. At the beginning of this story, I did not tell you that Tina was a prostitute murdered in a hotel room. Even wonderfully evolved people may encounter terribly difficult life circumstances. Let us not turn up our noses at people who are struggling to survive or judge them harshly. Have you heard the saying, "There but for the grace of God go I"?

I do not want anyone to take an unnecessary detour after their death because they are not aware of the dynamics of our afterlife transition. The In-between is not a place designed to punish people. The term In-between refers to a holding area for people who died without knowledge of or belief in the existence of a desirable afterlife, which is available to every person. When our energetic vibrations are at depressed levels, we jeopardize ourselves as we pass from our bodies. If there is one time in our lives when it is essential to sustain elevated energetic frequencies, it is when we fly free from our physical body at the time of our passing.

Within the higher dimensions, particular centers support people needing what we might define as restorative services. These restricted support areas exist to rehabilitate people. Many people advance to the higher dimensions' entry-level in an unsatisfactory state that does not qualify them to mingle with the general populations. These people remain under supervised care until they have overcome their impediments. Instead of sending people to jail, they remain confined in Re-education Centers until they reform themselves and prove that they are harmless to all others. Being harmless to all others is a strict requirement within the elevated realms.

People who have a history of abusing people, such as the men who enslaved thousands of people within the In-between, are respectfully treated. However, they enroll in an incredibly insightful educational program. Part of their education is to experience all the abuse they brought upon other people. They will personally feel the distress, terror, and pain they inflicted upon others. There is no better way to educate an offender than to have them swallow the bitter pill, which they forced down other people's throats.

The men who enslaved the group of people within the In-between are indicative of the type of person confined to a Re-education Center upon their arrival in the heavens. Those who are restricted for cruelty will not qualify to leave the Re-education Center until they have taken responsibility for their severe hurtfulness and disregard for the preciousness of all people. They must prove that they have overcome their former dishonorable tendencies and can embrace the pristine standards of the elevated realms to graduate from the Re-education Center.

People arriving within the heavens often need specific types of assistance. Commonly, people require special assistance because of the problematic or frightening conditions people endured before dying. In Chapter 6, Samuel Sutter describes the Restoration

Center, where he remained as he recovered from his harrowing death experience at the hands of an Islamic terrorist executioner. In Chapter 14, Jeff Kelley tells us about his and other Alzheimer patients' experiences in their Restoration Center. They took their time pleasantly enjoying each other's company as their mental faculties were being restored before they set out to mix with the general populations of the heavens. Other Centers address different issues, such as the Behavioral Adjustment Center, where Marie was detained because of her abusive behavior. Her story also appears in Chapter 14.

I hope this fuller picture of what happens when deceased people become lost after dying will not frighten as much as instruct. I would rather you found out about the In-between by reading about it than by experiencing it. There is no reason for any of us to end up there when forewarned and have what we need to know to avoid it altogether.

CHAPTER FOURTEEN

PERSONAL MESSAGES FROM PEOPLE WHO PASSED

———

As a young child, I had a clearly defined perception of what it was like in heaven. My vision of heaven was a big freezer filled with ice cream. I could see it in my mind's eye. It sat in a dark void space and gave me incredible comfort that I would be able to eat as much ice cream as I desired when I died and went to heaven. Since then, my perceptions of heaven have changed, and now I base them on more solid underpinnings.

Nothing delights me more than receiving direct information from people who describe their experience of transferring to the area of Creation that we refer to as heaven. Forthright honesty flows from residents within the higher dimensions; honesty and clear assessment. Their communications give a fuller picture of what motivated their choices and actions when they were experiencing life on Earth. In some cases, becoming aware of their joys, regrets, and whatever else they decided to convey gives us the inside track on how we might feel when we arrive where they are.

Meaningful insight into what it is like in the higher dimensions flows from these communications. Repeatedly we receive confirmation of the wonderful treatment and respect given to everyone. By familiarizing yourself with these conversations, any fears you may have will most likely fall away. Each of these messages has something of value to deliver. In them, we learn that dying and returning to the higher dimensions will instantly restore clarity and release any self-deception we may have engaged in while we were alive on Earth.

As we live our physical lives, we often entangle ourselves in the different angles and twists we use to justify our actions. Then after dying, when we arrive within the higher dimensions, our thinking instantly becomes rightly perceptive. There is no discoloration of our true intentions for taking the actions we did. Our enlightened self-assessment is completely honest. We face the good, the bad, and the ugly. We do not punish ourselves for our failures, but we do take full responsibility for every action we took while we were alive on Earth, and primarily those actions that produced a negative impact on someone else.

We also pay rapt attention to the progress we made while we lived our physical life. We come into these lifetimes with an agenda to accomplish, so afterward, it is fascinating for us to see how we did. Our most fulfilling moments occur when we assess our performance and know deep within our hearts that we measured up. We accomplished our goals giving us the satisfaction that we have led a successful lifetime.

The following conversations with deceased people are enlightening. In some of them, we see what people did when they were alive that they came to regret, but only later when they understood the negative result. Sometimes our choice of behavior brings about harmful repercussions for other people. It is easy to assume that what we do does not carry a detrimental effect, particularly when we did not directly intend to create difficulty for someone else. Very few of us focus on monitoring our impact on other people, and those of us that do are often tempted to discount what we did that was detrimental.

Aunt Patsy

My friend Kate and I were talking one day when she mentioned that her favorite aunt had passed away the week before. Her

Aunt Patsy and her father were sister and brother. I knew Kate's father, who had died a few years earlier, and other members of Kate's family, but I had not heard Kate mention her Aunt Patsy. It did not surprise me when Kate said that her aunt was a very accomplished woman because Kate herself had many talents and diversified skills. I became curious when Kate told me about her aunt's honors and accomplishments, so I decided to look for her obituary online.

At that time, I did not have a computer, so I asked Mike to look it up for me on his. He pulled up Patsy's obituary, and as we were reading it, my body got that light, tingly feeling that signals an angelic presence. Then my guidance chimed in and announced, "There is a message for you." I asked if the message was from Patsy, and they answered, "Yes." I grabbed paper and pencil and sat down to record what Patsy had to say.

Patsy's Message to Kate

Patsy: I have a message for Kate.

Kay: I will be happy to give Kate your message. May I call you Patsy?

Patsy: I am pleased for you to call me Patsy. I love that name. I want to tell Kate that her father and I are going to give her a wonderful party. She will have to wait until it is her turn to take the glorious trip I have just taken. I know just what I will do for her. I will have a choir of angels singing her favorite songs. Her father and I will greet her with all our love combined. We will honor her. We will celebrate her life.

Then her father and I will show her around. She will see the glory that my eyes behold. She will be as ecstatic as I am now. We will rejoice together.

Kay, thank you for allowing me to reach back to tell Kate what I would like to say to her directly.

Kay: You are most welcome, Patsy. It is an honor to perform this service for you and my lovely friend Kate.

Patsy's plan for Kate's welcoming party is an example of one of the grand welcoming celebrations spoken of by those who have experienced theirs. Each person who returns to the afterlife experiences whatever is most significant to him or her. Some people want to be quiet and by themselves to ponder the events that just occurred as they passed into spirit and arrived within the heavens. Some folks cannot wait to get the party rolling, and yet others immediately seek the quiet company of those they were closest to who predeceased them. There is not only one type of arrival for everyone. Each arrival is designed to give every individual that which means the most to them.

Even though Kate and I were good friends, I had not told her of my work with angels until her Aunt Patsy gave me this message. With some hesitance, I explained to Kate that I communicated with her aunt and that Patsy gave me a brief message for her. First, Kate looked surprised, and then she became excited that her Aunt Patsy had sent a message for her. Kate eagerly read Patsy's message. Then she broke out in a bright smile, put her arms around me, and gave me a big hug.

The delight that these messages bring is not limited to what the deceased person conveys. It is also in the personal touch of having someone you hold dear confirm that they are still in existence and that even though they are not physically present, they are still holding you close. You know you are important to them and that the love you had for each other still endures. Often, when our beloveds pass from this life, we experience a lost and empty feeling. Our connection to them seems severed. It is comforting to know that their love and commitment to us do not end when they relocate into the higher realms. We remain in their hearts forever as they remain in ours.

Shirley Kinney

When Shirley passed, my brother, Steve, wondered if she might send a message to her husband. Steve and my sister-in-law,

Janis, were friends with Shirley and her husband, and they were doing their best to support him after Shirley's death. Steve was not concerned about Shirley's ability to find her way to the higher dimensions. He said she was the kind of person who would make it up without any difficulty, but he wondered if she might have something to say to console her grieving husband. It did not take long for the angels to locate Shirley and offer her this opportunity, which she eagerly accepted.

Shirley: I am a little overwhelmed by the thought of reaching James. First, I have a question for you. Why do you talk to dead people?

Kay: I do it to help in some way or another. You are not offended, are you?

Shirley: I am curious.

Kay: Do you have something prepared to tell James?

Shirley: Yes, I want to start with darling. Okay, here goes.

Shirley's Message to James

Darling,

You would not believe what I have seen since I died. It has been wonderful. Jesus met me. He put his arms around me and said he has been keeping an eye on me. He watches over certain people, and I am one of them.

He introduced me to Mother Mary. She is just as I pictured her, very sweet and gentle. She took me to visit some people I know. We had a good time laughing about how afraid people are to die. I was not afraid, but most people are. They would not be afraid if they could see this place. It is prettier than any place on Earth. It is full of happiness, no sadness or fear. People stay busy. They enjoy themselves because they are so happy. We talk to each other and compare our expectations of what heaven would be like. Nobody I have met was even close to figuring it out. It is much nicer than we thought it would be.

We are just as alive as we were before we died, but now we enjoy good health. I have joined a group of people who like to dance. It feels good to be able to dance. I move about so easily here, no more aches or pains.

There is a lot I will be experiencing once I adjust to being here. I get to choose what I want to do. I do not know what all the choices are yet, but I will have the freedom to visit you. During this time, angels are taking me to be with you. It is wonderful to have them helping me. They said I would be able to visit you whenever you need me the most. We are still closely connected because the bond of love is strong between us, and it will remain.

I want to give you a signal, so you will know I am with you. Look for the fragrance of my perfume. When you smell it, I will be there with you.

You are going to like it here, James. You will be able to hear perfectly, and nothing will be difficult. You will be happy and excited just like I am. When you come here, I will be the one to help you. You will not even know you died. You will think you are somewhere else that is an exceptional place. You will not believe how much fun it is when you talk to angels, and they take you on little trips to see things that exist in heaven.

It feels like you are on Earth, except that everything is perfect. There is no suffering or pain. No one is disadvantaged or disregarded. Every person is treated honorably. Moreover, everyone feels good about himself or herself. There are no feelings of insecurity here. Everyone is happy and contended.

Be happy for me, James. Soon you will be with me, and we will be together again. I will visit you. We will remain connected with each other. Do not be sad or disappointed that I am no longer with you physically. I am holding a spot for you in heaven. You will not have to worry about finding a place. Your place will always be next to me.

As I looked over Shirley's message to her husband, I thought about how difficult it is to be the one left behind. The one who departs the earthly life to go on a grand adventure feels exhilarated, while the person left behind may be lonely and despondent. Especially when death is the separator, the one who remains physically alive may feel disoriented and lost without their partner. With a better understanding of what happens after transitioning to the afterlife, the partner left behind might be comforted that they have someone they dearly love watching over them and holding a spot for them in heaven.

Dad's Friend and Mine, Chet Harrigan

Dad had a special friend whose name was Chet Harrigan. They knew each other before they each moved to St. Elizabeth's Assisted Living. Chet moved there first and recommended this residence to Dad. Dad felt fortunate to have a pal already living there when he moved in. Both Dad and Chet were devoted Catholics, and they loved living at St. Elizabeth's for two important reasons; they could attend Mass every day and, the food was wonderful.

When Dad was at St. Elizabeth's, I made it a point to have lunch with him and Chet every week. These were memorable times as we talked about how the Broncos football team was doing and if the dining room would offer spumoni ice cream that day. St. Elizabeth's always offered several flavors of ice cream, but spumoni was our favorite, and they did not always have it on hand.

One day we decided that we did not care for ice cream unless they had spumoni. We asked the waiter, and when he said they did not have spumoni that day, I just said what popped into my mind. I spontaneously declared, "No spumoni, no business," which the people seated around us thought was funny. Smiles and laughter broke out. After that, every time the three of us took our seats in the dining room, the first thing we did was ask about the availability of spumoni ice cream and pass the answer on to the other diners. Those weekly lunches were fun.

After Dad passed, I visited Chet at St. Elizabeth's, and we had an interesting conversation. Chet told me how he was ready to die and could not understand why God had not taken him yet. Chet was probably in his late eighties by then, and he was living with a deteriorating physical condition. He was not comfortable in his daily life and was in a hurry to pass on. Other residents in the assisted living also wondered why God did not take them because they felt ready to go. Chet asked me my opinion, and I did not know how to respond.

When I heard that Chet passed, I knew that he would have made it to the higher dimensions without a hitch because he was a truly good person, and he was ready. I asked my guidance for a report on how he was doing. Shortly after making my inquiry, the angels brought Chet to me so we could speak with each other.

Chet: Kay, I figured out what took me so long to die.

Kay: What was it, Chet?

Chet: I did not want to entirely let go of everything.

Kay: I do not understand. What do you mean?

Chet: I kept planning. I still had things I wanted to do. I felt miserable, so handicapped, but I still held on tightly to life. I told myself I was ready to die and kept wondering why God did not take me. I thought it was all up to Him, that He was keeping me alive. Now I realize that I was not ready. He allowed me to stay until I gave up every plan and desire that I had. When I finally let go of everything, my time came.

Kay: This is interesting, Chet.

Chet: The rest of it was pretty much as I had expected. My deceased wife was by my side as I raised up out of my body. We looked at each other and laughed. I was not frightened. I was overjoyed, and so was she. It felt so good to be together again. She held my hand, and I could not stop looking at her.

You know the rest – about the tunnel of light and all that. It was wonderful. I am glad I finally made it up here.

Your dad says to say hello and to tell you that they even have spumoni ice cream here.

Kay: (I was shocked to hear him say this.) I thought you did not eat when you were in heaven.

Chet: (Laughing) We do not get hungry, but we can remember the taste of spumoni ice cream. We can recreate it to experience the flavor again, but we do not really eat ice cream.

Kay: Thank you, Chet, for coming to talk to me. I am very happy for you.

Chet: Me, too.

After my conversation with Chet, I wondered what Chet wanted to do before he died. This curiosity was playing on my mind when he came back and resumed our conversation.

Chet: I wanted to save enough money to give each of my grandchildren something when I died. I did not have much, but I would have a little left to save for them every month. I was determined to have something to give them.

Kay: Did you meet your goal?

Chet: I finally gave up. I told myself this was the best I could do. Giving up was what I needed to do for myself. I do not think it made any difference that I did not leave them a significant gift. They all loved me and knew that I loved them deeply. I wanted to return to clarify the reason I delayed my trip to heaven.

Kay: Thank you, Chet. Do you have anything else you would like to say?

Chet: No, I do not think so. Wait. I do. Do not be afraid to let go of everything, absolutely everything, when you are waiting to die. I delayed my death without realizing what I was doing. I could not wait to separate from my body and go up to heaven. I thought there was no reason for me to remain alive, and God was ignoring the prayers that I kept praying. I thought He was ignoring me.

I found out that He heard all my prayers and knew I wanted to come back to Him, but I had to wait until I stopped wanting the few things I wanted. When I decided not to want anything anymore, I came right up here. This is what worked for me. Keep it in mind when you are old and ready to go.

Kay: Thank you, Chet. I will keep it in mind.

Chet, Dad's friend, and mine answered one mystery of life, whether they have ice cream in heaven. Chet also gave us a valuable tip about letting go of absolutely everything when we feel ready to go on to the afterlife. When there is nothing left for us to accomplish or enjoy by being alive, we can start the ball rolling to return to the higher dimensions by letting go of all of our attachments.

We need to stop worrying about our loved ones, and we need to withdraw into a state of utter peace and calm. We cannot release our hold on life until we stop looking ahead to the future. Letting go is more involved than just saying that we are ready to move on. We have to put a stop to our wanting and our planning.

Marie

When I lived in Texas, I had an unusual neighbor, an elderly woman named Marie. Marie was in her mid-eighties and full of stories about her earlier years spent in Montana. Marie was self-absorbed and very talkative. She had lost her husband several years earlier and liked to talk about the past. I ran errands for her when Marie needed something at the store and helped her to have new dentures made. She was pretty self-sufficient until she could not drive her car anymore. She hated to give up those car keys. After that, it was not long before her family came to move her to an assisted living facility near their home in Dallas.

I did not expect to run into Marie again, but one evening about fourteen or fifteen years later, she popped into my mind, and I mused about her time living next door to me. In retrospect, I think she had been hanging around me, wanting to communicate with me from the world of spirit, but was hesitant to speak up. When I mentally asked who was with me, she came forth with a swift and direct reply.

Marie: Kay, you know who I am, don't you?

Kay: Is this Marie, my next-door neighbor from long ago?

Marie: Kay, I want to come clean to you now that I am not the same person that I used to be. You know what a stinker I was, my poor daughter-in-law. I was as mean and nasty as I could be to her. She was sweet and tolerant of me while I held my nose up in the air, convinced that my son was far superior to her. I was an evil woman. I tried to undermine their marriage so I could have my son to myself.

I know how unhappy I made her whenever I came to visit. I undermined her at every turn. She would cook a nice dinner for my husband and me, and I would turn up my nose and announce that we did not eat those foods. My husband was so disappointed in me when I did that. He loved her cooking, especially those foods I had complained about.

Kay: Marie, were you that way with other people, or did you just target your daughter-in-law?

Marie: If I had a chance to be uppity, I took it. I was a petty person. When we went to a restaurant, I would be arrogant toward the waiters and servers. Inside I felt inferior, and I blamed someone else for my feelings of inferiority.

Kay: Whom did you blame for your feelings of inferiority?

Marie: My husband, of course. I used to lord it over him that the other man who wanted me to marry him came from a well-to-do family, and if I had married him instead, I would have had a lot of money. I often said to my husband that I should have married John.

Kay: Did you mean it? Did you really think you would have been better off if you had married John?

Marie: Kay, you met my husband before he died. There was no sweeter man on Earth. I was looking for a scapegoat for my feelings of low self-esteem. I did not deserve to have the wonderful husband that I had. How he put up with me, I will never understand.

Kay: What else do you want to get off your chest, Marie?

Marie: My father sexually abused me when I was a child. He was a highly respected doctor in our small town. My mother never said a thing when dad said he wanted my sister and me to take turns sleeping with him. I do not know if she knew he was inappropriate with us. She may not have. No one ever said anything. It just happened.

Kay: I am sorry to hear that happened to you, Marie. May I ask how this affected you when you got older? And your sister, what happened to her?

Marie: We never spoke of what our father did to us. We each married very nice men. Her husband was as nice as mine was. Both were sweet, considerate, and very personable. Everything outwardly looked normal. My sister and I each gave birth to one son. I was almost forty when my son was born, and in those days, that was very old to be having a child.

The sad part of this story is that both my sister and I molested our own sons. I do not want to go into detail, but the effects on them were devastating. Memories of the abuse flooded my nephew's mind when he became middle-aged and made him severely depressed and unable to continue his work. He drifted around for several years until he could finally reestablish a good flow to his life. Then unexpectedly, he committed suicide in his early sixties.

As for my son, he has had gender identification problems his entire adult life. He is as athletic as his father was, but he likes to cross-dress and have homosexual dalliances even though he is married. I do not think that it is a coincidence that both of our sons have struggled with issues of sexuality. I feel directly responsible for creating my son's gender identity issues.

Kay, I was an intelligent person, but I did not lead a clean and decent life. I undermined my son's and my daughter-in-law's marriage in many ways and took advantage of any way I could think of, to press my uncivil behaviors upon them when I came for visits. They should have kicked me out and told me to come back when I learned to behave respectfully and courteously.

Kay: Marie, I feel sorry for you. It must be hard for you to understand your poor self-expression and the hardship you imposed upon other people.

Marie: When I first arrived in heaven, I was confined to a Behavioral Adjustment Center. It was there that I got myself turned around. I had to face what I did not allow myself to see when I was alive. I knew that I had been an ignorant, hurtful, and actually dangerous person. I did not like admitting this to myself. If I could have hidden this understanding, I would have. It was tough owning up to the reality of how I was when I was alive. I was shocked that I was admitted into the heavens. I did not deserve to be there.

I did not deserve recognition for my good traits because I had so many bad ones, but my positive qualities were also acknowledged. There was no question about my inability to mingle with the other residents until I had spent time in and graduated from my Behavioral Adjustment Center. As soon as I arrived within the heavens, I was whisked away to the Behavioral Adjustment Center, where I stayed for quite a while. Others there were graduating and moving on to the open areas of the heavens where you can move around freely. I was confined for an extended period because my ingrained traits were not letting loose. I was deeply disturbed in my perceptions about sexuality, and those did not mitigate easily.

Now I plan to reenter the physical world, and I am hoping to perform a lot better than last time. I should. I have had a lot of determined effort put into straightening me out, but you know how I was. I was one tough cookie disguised as an old lady.

Kay: Yes, Marie, I do know how you were. I was astonished by how your daughter-in-law could tolerate your disruptive visits and your cruelty towards her. I have a question to ask before you leave. If I remember right, you were approaching your late nineties when you died. Did you have longevity genes? Why do you think you lived so long?

Marie: I was afraid to die because I was convinced that there is only one life and you do not exist anymore after you die. No one could convince me otherwise. I thought that all the talk about going to heaven was made-up nonsense. I would not even consider that it might be true. I am glad that I was wrong so I could get myself straightened out and receive another chance to become a more dignified and accepting person. Does this answer all your questions?

Kay: Yes, Marie, it does. This has been a very interesting conversation. I hope that when you do come back to lead another lifetime you will be successful in making all the improvements that you have planned.

Marie was a person who only thought about herself. She was a self-centered and abusive person. She felt superior to other people and did not care who she hurt. She was the center of her universe and disregarded her impact on her husband, her son, and other family members. She and her sister brought the same evil upon their sons that had been pressed upon them. It is of utmost importance to refrain from sexually abusing a child. To do such imprints a horror upon them that will disrupt their life, and unfortunately, may lead them to continue the cycle of abuse. It is never all right to act out sexual or other forms of abuse upon any other person, and it is entirely abhorrent to mistreat a child.

I felt sorry for Marie's husband and her daughter-in-law, who she looked down on and antagonized. Marie did not have any sense of personal accountability, and she let her nastiness fly. Some people have little concern for what they do to other people. They continue dishing out their brand of disruption and hurtfulness because it is their natural way of being.

There is only one way to handle such a person. Stop them in their tracks. Do not tolerate their antics and, if need be, even when dealing with a close relative, keep them at a distance. Do not allow them the opportunity to bring their brand of evilness and disregard for other people into your presence or your children's presence. Let them know why you choose to keep your distance from them, so they clearly understand the cause.

No adult is too powerful to stand up against if he or she is being abusive. Even the meekest among us must learn to roar with objection and disgust when anyone, including authority figures or one's own relatives, act abusively toward children or adults. We must be perceptive and not overlook signs of abuse. We are here working to create a better world for our children and people everywhere. Let us not hide or tolerate any form of cruelty or exploitation.

Jeff Kelley

I met Jeff in college when he and my future husband were roommates. I was dating Mike, and Jeff was dating my sorority sister, Angela. The four of us shared many good times even before I married Mike and Jeff married Angela. A few months after Mike and I married, we moved to Texas. When we returned to Colorado to visit our families, we would often get together with Jeff and Angela. We loved being with them and catching up with all the news about our friends from college.

After living in other states for about forty years, Mike and I relocated back to the Denver area to be close to our son, daughter-in-law, grandchildren, and many other warmhearted family members who live there. We eagerly looked forward to reconnecting with some of our friends from high school and college. We were especially looking forward to seeing Jeff and Angela again since several years had elapsed since we were last with them.

Jeff was not the same as he used to be when we saw Jeff at Mike's fiftieth high school reunion. There were subtle differences, such as when Jeff looked at me, he smiled warmly, but I could tell that he did not know who I was. Later Angela confided in me that Jeff had Alzheimer's disease, but he was still functioning pretty well at that point. During the next few years, however,

Alzheimer's disease progressed rapidly, and then Jeff passed. After attending Jeff's funeral, I asked my angels to check on him.

Angels: Jeff is in a Recovery Center where he is cared for as he gains recognition of who he is. All his memories will return as he views the movie of his life. Right now, he is acclimating to his surroundings, which are not frightening in any way. It is too soon for him to do anything other than to regain his composure after releasing from the bondage of the body.

About a week and a half later, angels brought Jeff to me.

Jeff: I have been briefed that you can hear me speaking to you. Kay, can you really hear me?

Kay: Yes, Jeff. I hear you. I understand that you would like to talk to me. Are you ready to begin?

Jeff: There is a lot to say. I did not know what Alzheimer's would be like.

Kay: Was it horrible, Jeff?

Jeff: I would not call it horrible, exactly. It was more like fading into somewhere else.

Kay: I do not understand what you mean.

Jeff: I usually knew what was going on, but more and more, it became harder to respond. It was as if I was watching myself being myself, but sometimes I could not control the part of myself from which I was separated. I know that this is hard to understand because, for you, these two parts of you are together.

I could see myself being angry and aggressive. I could also see myself when I was sitting there, non-responsive. I could not control the part of myself that I was separated from, which was the hardest part. I could not tell people *thank you* for the care they gave me. I saw how kindly they treated me, and I could not respond to tell them how grateful I was.

My sons were compassionate and loving. There cannot be more kind, compassionate, and loving sons anywhere. They stood by me until the very end, as did both of my wives. I consider Lorrie as my second wife. She and Angela, but especially my closest friend Lorrie, kept me going. I wanted to see her and be with her. I wanted to stay for Lorrie.

I held on as long as I could. The end was more pleasant. I was sitting there unresponsive, but I actually felt better. The part of myself that I had separated from was not a problem anymore. That part no longer seemed to exist. Except for a dull connection that was barely discernible, I had separated from that action part of myself. I knew they thought I could die at any moment, and I was not afraid. Something inside of me wanted to stay, so I stayed as long as I possibly could.

While I was in the hospice, I started to catch glimpses of religious figures. There are a lot of them there. They talk to other people like me. All of us who were dying had visits from these religious figures. I did not know who some of them were, but it did not matter. They were all friendly. I could tell that the other hospice patients enjoyed their company as much as I did.

When I had no other choice, off I went. I was out of the hospice. In an instant, my life ended, and I felt much better. All of a sudden, I felt completely normal again. I still could not remember enough to connect all the dots, but I remembered enough to know that I was still me. What I mean is that I was completely comfortable and not disoriented anymore. I knew myself and again felt connected with the action part of me. Now I was whole again. The two parts of me were back together.

I do not know who was there with me, but other caretakers were there, but they were not from the hospice. At first, I did not realize where I was. They took care of me and told me that I would have a very pleasant experience that they would arrange for me. They told me that I would be kind of parachuted into a different world and when I got there, everything would be all right for me.

I was not frightened at all. I felt secure and trusted these nice caretakers. I did not know until I got to the new world that I traveled there in a tunnel of light. It was instantaneous. I immediately arrived where I am now.

They took me to a place which was called a Recovery Center. I do not know why because I did not have anything from which to recover. I felt great, better than ever. But when they asked about my life, I could not remember exactly. I remembered bits and pieces but could not get it all together. They explained that I needed to be there as I recovered from my mind not working right for all those years. My mind felt perfectly fine, but I had to admit that my memories were disjointed.

While I was there, I had many visitors. These visits were part of my therapy. People I had known, especially relatives, came to help me remember the times we shared. I love people, so this was great for me. There they were again as if it was yesterday and we were having fun together. What a pleasant way to remember, with people that I care about. All of these people I knew when we were all alive. What a kick! Everybody looked young again. We were telling each other how good-looking we are now and laughing.

This process is how I prepared for my life review. I needed to remember some of the people and experiences before I reviewed my whole life. It would have been overwhelming to see it all when I first arrived. I really needed to reconstruct parts of it myself, or I would not have been able to comprehend all that I was shown.

As I watched my life review, I became filled with regret. I was so proud of my achievements that I overlooked my failures. Things look different now than they did then. My self-appraisal has flipped. I would congratulate myself because I was socially prominent, knew many people, and had high-level positions during my career. I thought I was leading a very successful life.

Now I see that was only half of the story. I was neglectful to my wife and children. I was overly demanding and impersonal in my relationships with them. I treated them without sensitivity. I had no idea how I affected them. I put myself first and set out to satisfy all my desires, and I had many of them.

I guess I did not understand relationships. Anyway, after I reconciled my former views of myself with what I now know to be true, I felt peaceful. I did achieve many of my life objectives. I saw the list I made before I began my last lifetime and was pleased that I overcame my former tendency to be lazy and not participate in group activities. I think I overemphasized this part too much. I do not want to dwell on what I did wrong, but I do regret my extreme self-centeredness. I have a lot to work on next time.

Now you are up-to-date. I will be released from the Recovery Center shortly. After that, I plan to study music. I have always wanted to understand more about music, especially composing. I am a beginner, but I want to learn. Maybe I will get to be a musician next time.

Thank you for recording what I had to say. I wish I could apologize to my wife and sons and others I took more from than I gave back. People were good to me. I wish I could ask forgiveness from everyone I let down. I plan to be a better human being when I come back.

Another time I asked my guidance about the husband of a relative who died from Alzheimer's disease. They gave this report. After his death, he was transported to a Recovery Center and will remain there until he recovers from the effects of Alzheimer's disease. People with Alzheimer's and other forms of memory loss and dementia are carefully transported at the moment of their death into a Recovery Center where they will remain until they regain their ability to think, reason, and remember. Those abilities return slowly, at a measured pace, while angelic caregivers comfort and entertain them.

The Recovery Centers are places to relax and comfortably adjust to improving conditions, and people stay there only for the required time. Most of them recover and are ready to continue enjoying themselves, as all the newcomers do, after a brief stay. Their full memory and mind functions could be restored immediately. However, they enjoy the slower pace and being with other people that are having similar experiences. They like to joke about what happened to them. The awfulness that they experienced becomes a subject of some clever inside jokes that they enjoy telling. All of them recover their complete ability to function normally.

I was reassured by learning what happens to people who die while suffering severe memory loss and especially enjoyed receiving Jeff's personal message. I have been concerned about what happens to Alzheimer's patients and others with severe memory loss after they die. It is reassuring that those who pass while suffering from any form of dementia are gently ministered to and given what they need to have their memories restored. Knowing that Alzheimer's patients comprehend far more than we might suspect is enlightening and something to keep in mind. I can better understand and relate to people with this illness because of Jeff's explanation.

Gavin

Gavin was a dear friend of one of my sisters. When Gavin was diagnosed with cancer, those who knew him were shocked. Gavin was an active and athletic person living a full and contributing life, and it just did not seem right that he should have to deal with this diagnosis. Gavin held onto life as long as he could, determined to squeeze every bit of joy and delight from his remaining time here. After Gavin passed, one of my siblings contacted me and asked me to ensure that Gavin made it up okay.

As I suspected, Gavin sailed right up into the higher dimensions after passing from his body. By that time, he was ready to go. Gavin was soft-spoken when he was alive, and he still was when the angels brought him to me to have a conversation. His voice was so soft that I had to keep asking him to speak louder. Gavin took a few minutes to become comfortable before he was ready to dictate a message for me to pass on to his wife.

Gavin's Message to His Wife, Barbara

Barbara, I want to apologize to you for making you exhausted. I should have let go of my body a long time before I did. I used my strong will to hang onto the semblance of being okay and pushed to do as much as I could so I could savor every minute of life that I had left. I did not consider your needs, as I should have. It was all about me stuffing what was left of my time on Earth with as many vacations as we could take. I hardly noticed as I ran you ragged from one trip to the next. I was like a glutton for wonderful life experiences, as if my death was going to be the end of everything.

Nothing could have been further than the truth, and now I regret holding on as long as I could to my diseased body. I truly regret squeezing every last second of life out of me. If I had been willing, I could have escaped the hardship I forced on you as I struggled to keep living another day. You were kind, supportive, and patient, which I really appreciated. I did not think that I could do anything about my situation when all along I was making it harder on you, as well as myself. Do not do what I did. Do not stretch out the inevitable when there is nothing positive to gain.

Barbara, I want to thank you for the life we shared together. You were an ideal partner, beloved wife, and mother to our children. You were not pushy or insensitive, ever. Always there by my side, allowing me the freedom to set the direction for our lives. The girls have a perfect role model in you. You set the tone for our family life, and we made beautiful music together.

I wish we could start over and live our life together again. If that were possible, I would first promise you that I would release from my body without hanging on when it was time for me to leave. I did not realize that people tend to stay in their bodies until they are willing to give them up.

If a person has their mind made up to pass out of their body, they actually can. Most people that try to release from their body leave out one required step. Here is the secret in case you want to know. You must feel at peace within yourself, and with every person you have interacted with during your entire life. Carry no grudges, no delusions about yourself and your behavior, no longing for more of anything, and render complete forgiveness to yourself for your detrimental actions and shortcomings. Then dismiss all judgments you have placed upon other people's impact upon you, and you will have prepared yourself to gently release from your body, especially if you are close to the endpoint of its usefulness.

I knew my body had passed the endpoint of its usefulness, but I was determined to keep pushing on. Then I dragged you all over, vacation after vacation. I could see your exhaustion, but I pressed on, not allowing myself to give up. I kept myself going as long as I could. I apologize to you for ignoring your well-being as I madly soaked in every ounce of aliveness that I could draw into myself.

When my body finally gave out, I still did not want to release from it. Oh, was I stupid. The moment I finally let go, I was surrounded by lady angels who were laughing at me. Here I was prepared for the worst, and I had the best right in front of me. If you have never flown with angels surrounding you, you have a treat in store for you when you die. I do not know much about what other people experienced when they died, but my experience was delightful beyond description.

Barbara, thank you for being my sweet, devoted, loving wife. I love you with all my heart. You have been my steady rock, true blue in every way. Always supportive and thinking about how you can help other people. I am sorry to say that I ran you ragged and thought more about my determination to do all that I could squeeze into my limited time remaining than I thought about what was good for you. In the end, it was still all about me. I regret my single-minded focus on myself.

To my loving daughters: thank you for enriching my life. All three of you I hold in my heart and will forever. I will watch over you from my new home in the heavens and will love you every day of your lives. I advise you to strive mightily to express your talents and your loving nature. Each of you is a treasure beyond what you currently recognize within yourself. Give yourself recognition and approval, and then stretch in every direction to ennoble yourself by expressing the beauty and goodness that each of you has.

I included Gavin's message to Barbara because of its significance for all of us. His message provides a lesson about not hanging onto life and refusing to release from our body. After we die, a new beginning appears, which requires no sacrifice from those who love us. When we disengage from our bodily imprisonment, our physical suffering ends, and we remove a burden from those who have seen us through our hardship. Dying is not like jumping off a cliff. Dying is being reborn into vastly improved circumstances.

CHAPTER FIFTEEN

MESSAGES FROM PEOPLE WHO I KNEW WELL

Several of my relatives have passed into the afterlife, and it has been a special joy for me to have the ability to communicate with them. My father, mother, sister, three aunts, and brother-in-law are among those who reached back to communicate with me after they died. Although a few of their recorded conversations appear in this book, I excluded many others because they were too numerous. There were days when I chatted with them for hours, sometimes in the middle of the night. Most of those conversations were engaging for me but would not have had a lot to offer people who did not know them personally.

I went through my notes and carefully chose those I considered the most meaningful conversations to highlight. Within this chapter are several that are thought-provoking. Before I began my commitment to working with deceased people, I used to think that people were pretty much the same. Now I know that each of us is markedly unique and that even from the exterior, when we seem to be a lot like other people, each of us is endowed with wonderful traits that set us apart from others.

My Mother, Dea

Although I was somewhat prepared when our mother passed, it hit me like a ton of bricks. When she died, an angel passed from this Earth. There were six of us, who called her Mom, and every one of us adored her. She was as loving and gracious as a mother could be. We each felt that she loved us the most. She had a way of communicating her love and affection that deeply resonated within all of us.

When we were growing up, Mom had her special way of reinforcing our self-esteem. She would often repeat loving phrases to us. "You can do whatever you want to do." "Put your mind on what you want to accomplish and then go and do it." "God helps them that help themselves." "You are as smart as anyone else." "You are as good as anyone else." These sayings and many others were Mom's way of building our self-esteem when we were young. We did not think about it at the time, but after she died, we realized the powerful impact her endearing support had on our self-concepts. For several years after her passing, every one of the six of us continued to hear her loving, encouraging voice echoing through our minds as if she were still physically present speaking to us.

Her death was a blow to our whole family. I was saddened to lose her, but at the same time, I was happy for her. Her health had been failing due to congestive heart failure, and I was relieved that she would not have to keep struggling with physical deterioration. None of us felt ready to let go of her, but, along with our sense of loss, we were filled with tremendous love for her and gratitude that she was our mother.

The day that Mom died, I received the news at six o'clock in the morning. My head was reeling with the blow of losing her. Immediately, I started sending her telepathic messages telling her how much I loved her and how grateful I was for all that she did for us for those many years. I poured out my heart to her and thanked her.

Her funeral was to take place two days later on Wednesday morning in Littleton, Colorado. Since we lived in Sugar Land, Texas, I arranged to fly to Denver the following day. Early that evening, when I was in my bedroom packing my clothes for the morning flight, I began to hear Mother's voice. It was soft and sweet. She kept repeating, "Kay-bug, Kay-bug. You are my Kay-bug." There was no doubt in my mind; this was my mother's voice calling me by the pet name she and Dad gave me when I was a very young child. I heard that name all the time until I was about five years old, and since then, I had forgotten about it. Mom's voice got louder as she began speaking to me.

Mom: Kay-bug, Kay-bug. I love you, my Kay-bug. I love you, my Kay-bug. I will always love you, and you will always be my Kay-bug.

Kay: Mom, you are here. It is really you!

Mom: They said I would be able to talk to you, that you would hear me. I am so happy to be up here. So very happy to be here. I will miss everyone. I will especially miss seeing our grandchildren growing up. I love everyone in our family and especially the children. I love reading to them and being around them. I always say that children keep us young. Now I will be watching them from above. I will not forget about them or any of the rest of my family. I will still be with all of you even though we are apart.

Tell everyone not to grieve for me. Be happy for me because I am so happy. I know that now I am where I belong. I am overjoyed.

Kay: I am happy for you, Mom. I love you very, very much. Thank you for all you did for all of us.

Mom: It was a wonderful life!

After I heard her words, all my sadness disappeared, and I was floating on a cloud of euphoria. I was overjoyed with all my heart that she was where she was and that I was fortunate to have her communicate with me. Before my mother's death, I had not received a personal message from a deceased person. How fitting it was that my beloved mother was the first to reach back from the heavens to tell me what she wanted to say in words that I could hear. After this, my mother came to me many more times; among the most notable was Mother's Day, several weeks after her passing.

Mom: Kay, I prepared a message for our whole family, and I want you to be sure that they all receive it.

Our Mother's Message to Our Whole Family

I know that many of you are feeling my loss greatly. I understand how it feels to separate from someone you love. I do not make light of these feelings, but from my perspective, I am enjoying my new situation.

Here is how it works for me. I am capable of understanding the thoughts and feelings of my family. In the beginning, I stayed very close. I could feel the anguish and see the tears. I was still among you. Now, I am becoming less concerned about my family. I have had wonderful, enlightening experiences since my death. I know so much more now that I cannot tell you. It would spoil your own journey when you transfer to where I am.

However, I can share a few secrets with you. Death can be a glorious experience as it was for me. I came here instantly without feeling pain, only wonderment. I was surprised at the reception I received. There was such a celebration. I was welcomed with an outpouring of love and affection. Everyone here knew I was coming and was on hand to greet me. I looked back and saw my family devastated. That made me sad, but I was more at home, more comfortable.

I knew I belonged not back on Earth but in my heavenly home. You will understand my feelings after your arrival here. No one would choose to go back to continue experiencing their physical life before death. They would only reluctantly return if they had to because they had not finished their assignment. I had finished, so I could stay.

After the initial welcoming, I was left alone to remember why I had come to Earth. I remembered my desire to teach love to others. I had that as my main objective. There were other objectives too. I wanted to know what it meant to be in love with life, to embrace not only oneself but also the moon and stars and life in all forms. I had the opportunity to notice the joy in the little things that we so often disregard. My goal was to live a simple life rich in detail and experience.

Looking back, I am satisfied. My life was wonderful. The main ingredient was love in many forms. I enriched my soul by living my life.

My next step is to begin another type of existence. Instead of being with my Earth family, I will create a family from among those individuals here who need the benefit of what I learned. These people do not understand how to relate on Earth. They are fine here, but they are lonely and isolated when they go back to Earth because they do not love freely. I will teach them my techniques to help them to have spontaneous love even when they have left this heavenly atmosphere. Therefore, I will have an even bigger family than before. I will do my best to help them understand the process of being a loving person living upon the Earth.

Because of the assignment that I have agreed to undertake, I will be leaving you to accept and love each other. Please take what I offer you and apply it directly in your lives.

Do not be harsh with one another.

Love all, always.

Be forgiving.

Accept love for yourself. Do not push it away.

Be aware of your impact on others.

Extend yourself lovingly, not out of duty.

Take others under your wing but do not suffocate them.

Help but do not control.

Give others the freedom to be different.

Cherish each other.

As I depart to begin my next assignment, I leave you with my enduring love. You can still reach me, but I will not be following family life. It is time for me to step back from my beloved family. Many angels watch over you. You are cared for and safe. I will be with each of you as you reenter your heavenly home. We will be together again.

As you read my mother's words, you receive a glimpse of her wise and loving nature. She was a role model for all of her children and her grandchildren. She was the teacher with a gentle nature who had insight and the instincts to exemplify what she wanted us to learn. Every family member holds our mother in the highest esteem and with the greatest respect. I wish she could have been the mother to everyone on Earth because if she were, Earth still would not be a perfect place to live, but it would be a lot closer than it is now.

Aunt Sis

Aunt Sis was always special to me because she was my godmother, and she gave me a lot of her time and attention when I was very young. Aunt Sis helped care for me when I was two to four years old. Dad served in the military during World War II, so Mom and I lived with Dad's parents and their daughter Dorothy who I always called Aunt Sis. She cared for me as if I were a life-sized doll. Aunt Sis fussed over me and pampered me. I loved it when she sprayed a bit of her perfume on my neck. I would always ask her for some of her *poof poof*. We always put some on before we went for our walks.

I remember seeing her in her wedding gown as she posed for wedding pictures with her handsome groom by her side. I was about five years old at the time. The two of them went on to share a lifetime of commitment to each other and their seven children, my beloved cousins.

When Aunt Sis died, it was merciful, for she had been blind, mostly deaf, and very frail for many years. About a month before she died, we shared an extended telephone conversation. She filled me with delight as she recounted family stories from the past. Many I had not heard before.

She told me the story of distant relatives, two brothers who did not get along with each other. One brother and his wife got so angry with the other brother and his wife that they burned down their farmhouse. The culprits never had to account for their wrongdoing, even though it was common knowledge that they were the guilty ones. When Aunt Sis mentioned familiar family members who had been dead for a long time, I could still see them in my mind's eye looking as they did when I was a child. Her body may have been giving out on her, but her mind and her memory were sharp as ever.

I was very relieved for her when our cousins called to tell us that their mother passed. I knew Aunt Sis would already be in the heavens, that she would not have had any trouble going up. When I asked my angels how Aunt Sis was doing, they brought her to me, and it sure was fun to be reunited. Her voice and inflections were the same as always. It was as if we were enjoying another delightful telephone conversation. One of our conversations was not out of the ordinary except for one subject that Aunt Sis brought up.

Aunt Sis: I never dreamed that heaven would be so much like Earth. I did not know what to think, really. I assumed heaven was a holy place, which I guess it is, just not as I expected it to be.

I thought heaven would be different for people of different religions. I thought Catholics would be in one area, Hindus in another, Muslims in another, that kind of thing. I thought we would be grouped according to our religion.

Kay: And that is not the case?

Aunt Sis: I was surprised that there is no religious separation, and everyone gets along great.

Kay: Can you tell to which religion people formerly belonged?

Aunt Sis: Not really, unless you ask them, or they choose to dress like an authority in their religion. Some newcomers do that.

One Hindu man wears a turban. I think that is what it is called. I have been watching him. He moves around like everyone else. He just has that distinguishing characteristic.

Kay: Maybe he is not even Hindu. I think there may be other religions in which the men wear turbans.

Aunt Sis: I did not ask him, so I do not know. I expected that the followers of Jesus Christ would stay together, and we would be a big group. I have actually seen Him. He did not speak to me, but I have seen him stop and talk to other people, even that man I told you about that wears the turban. They are good friends. I could tell because they embraced each other and were smiling a lot.

I am amazed that religion does not seem to matter as I thought it would. There is a casual acceptance of everyone else, and no one has a bone to pick with anyone. The holy people have a glow around them. You can tell who the holiest ones are. Jesus is glowing brightly, and the man with the turban has a glow. I have looked at myself. I do not think I am glowing. Most of us are not.

This part of our conversation demonstrates that religious divisions like we have on Earth do not exist within the heavens. The indicator of one's spiritual progress seems to be the glow that is apparent around angels and other personages. I remember seeing radiant glows depicted around the heads of saints on the religious holy cards when I was a child and in some books that depict saints and angels. I knew that the glow was a sign of their holiness, but it never occurred to me that this glow is an actuality in the heavenly realms. From what Aunt Sis reported, most of the people do not have a glow. The glow must arise as individuals advance in their spiritual development.

Don and Stephanie

Don and Stephanie met when she was in her early twenties. He was a few years older than she was. There was a strong attraction between them, and they fell in love. They were dating each other exclusively when something happened, which she must have felt was a violation of their commitment to each other, so she booted him out of her life. She would not reconsider, and at that time, Don said to Stephanie, "Steph, you are making a big mistake."

Neither of them had any idea that their paths would cross again, but over twenty years later, that is exactly what happened. Stephanie flew to Minneapolis to attend a conference, and while she was there, she ran into Don, who happened to be attending the same conference. They were both delighted to see each other and hear what the other had been doing since their breakup. Don was still living in Denver, but Stephanie had moved to California. Stephanie had not married while Don had been married and since divorced. They both still felt a strong attraction to each other and decided to give their relationship another go.

This time they had a whirlwind romance. They flew between Denver and San Diego for their dates, and they took fabulous vacations together. Their favorite place was Paris. Don spoke fluent French and loved everything about France, so he and Stephanie took yearly trips to France. They traveled the French countryside and took a barge trip down the Midi Canal. There were trips to Italy and Christmas in Montreal. They were at the Eiffel Tower to welcome the year 2000. Don and Stephanie were living a storybook romance.

After several years, they decided to be together with a commitment to be married. At that point, Don decided to retire, but Stephanie was still working, so Don sold his house in Denver and moved to the San Diego area to be with her. Not long after this, one evening, Mike and I had dinner with them in San Diego. That night Don and Stephanie were not their usual jovial selves. Don had been to the doctor for some tests, and he had just received the results, which indicated that Don had fluid on one lung. Over the next several weeks, Don underwent diagnostic procedures, which indicated that he had lung cancer.

Despite the cancer diagnosis, they both remained positive, very positive. They knew they wanted to be together, and when Don proposed to Stephanie, she accepted. Their wedding was an exceptional occasion. Since Don had been in the Navy, he was entitled to have the ceremony at the Naval Base in San Diego. Don and Stephanie were married in an intimate outdoor ceremony at the Naval Base overlooking the water. Stephanie found her true love, and so did Don.

They had a few vibrant and meaningful years together before cancer took Don's life. Stephanie was by his side throughout the difficult years with an upbeat, encouraging presence. They both kept their sense of humor and determination to fight the illness. Stephanie was strong, considerate, patient, and loving with Don. She stood by him with inner strength second to none, although she must have felt like crumbling inside.

After Don died, he came to me in spirit and asked me to record two messages for Stephanie. I do not think Don knew that I did this work when he was alive, but he sure found out quickly after he died. He was eager to communicate with her. I always liked Don a lot. He was a fellow Capricorn, and I think we may have felt very relaxed and comfortable with each other because of that. He used to call me Special Kay, which delighted me.

Don's First Message

Don: Hi Kay. I see you sitting in your chair. I am going to talk for a while. I have some things to tell Stephanie and you. Was I ever wrong about what it would be like to die. I expected to see my dead friends again, but I did not expect them to look so good. They had a big party for me, and I almost did not recognize some of them. Several of them looked like they were 20 years old, just kids. They made fun of me because I was having trouble figuring out who some of them were. We laughed a lot and teased each other.

I saw your sister, Louise. She looks good. She is still telling people what to do. I think she likes to be in charge. She greeted me warmly and laughed about my good looks. Until she did that, I did not realize that I lost my distinguished gentleman looks. I am better looking now than I was when I first met Stephanie.

Dying turns back the clock to when you were the healthiest and most attractive, so nobody here looks old or sick.

Now I am rejuvenated, and I feel like a kid again. I used to think that dying was a serious occurrence, but it is the most fun I ever had. Everyone I know, who had already died, greeted me as soon as I finished going through the tunnel. The tunnel is like a speed transportation system. I guess I am in heaven because it feels different than I am used to feeling. Here everything is relaxed, with no hurry, no deadlines. There is a lot to do but no sense of urgency to do anything.

I feel like I died a year ago because so much has happened since I found myself outside of my body trying to hold Stephanie's hand. I was there, and then in an instant, I effortlessly moved into the tunnel. It was very peaceful in the tunnel. I was not afraid at all. I felt like I was floating on a pillow of white fluffy clouds. I was excited that I still had my senses. I could see, hear, feel, and touch. My body felt weightless and without pain. I felt more alive in that tunnel than I ever did when I was alive on Earth. I was as excited as a child looking at a Christmas tree with stacks of presents under it.

My life with Stephanie was precious. My love for her grew like a volcano overflowing with powerful red-hot feelings of awe, affection, and wonder that she, who is so devoted, and spunky and tender, and good-hearted, could love me so completely. I felt the greatest love of my life from Stephanie. Her love for me was the greatest gift I received during my entire life.

I want Stephanie to know that I can see her spectacular kind heart, her loving nature, and her tough determination to help me until the end. As I think about her, in my mind, she is my dear, devoted wife, my best friend, my lover, my confidant, and the most valuable person I have known. Her value is much greater than I recognized when we were married. I loved her then, but it was with a superficiality that was all I understood. She taught me what matters most and how to love with all my heart.

Stephanie showed me what love truly is. It is not the superficial posturing meant to impress. In addition, it is not throwing around your weight to make yourself seem more important and your wife seem less important. I competed with Stephanie to control our marriage, not realizing that I was acting shallowly.

When I got sick, I learned what love really is. I learned what is most important about loving someone. She showed me what it feels like to be loved and supported, accepted, and aided even when I had little to give in return. Stephanie's love for me was not superficial; it was without limit, without restriction, without withholding. She gave me her time, attention, and deepest devotion. I learned from Stephanie what I was not able to learn in any other way. From her, I learned to love with all my heart.

Stephanie, I will not abandon you. You may not see me, but I will always remain close to you. I want you to have fun and to enjoy your life. I wish we could have had more time with each other, but I am thankful for the time we had. Because of you, now I know how to love with all my heart. Thank you for taking care of me and for staying with me until the end.

That is it for now, Special Kay. I am sure I will have more to say later.

Kay: That is fine with me, Don.

Don's Second Message

Don: I want Stephanie to know how much I appreciate everything she did for me, and I do not only mean when I was sick. She gave me a good life. We had a lot of fun, and we liked to laugh at anything we could twist around to be funny. We liked to see the funny side of life.

She always treated me with respect. When she was unhappy with me, she did her best to work things out between us. She put her relationship with me above her other relationships. She was always eager to please me. She has no idea how much I value our time together. It was the highlight of my life. I never expected to have such an incredible experience with Stephanie.

I was used to discounting my marriage partner and doing things to undermine the marriage. When I did this to Stephanie, she called me on it. She did not let me get away with my problematic behavior. She was willing to make changes within herself, which helped me to start acting more positively. She could have made everything worse, but she was able to turn around a tough situation, which I created, and made everything better. My behavior put a strain on our relationship. Her behavior helped me to become more honest with myself.

I love and appreciate Stephanie for her care of me when I was sick. She nursed me and kept a positive attitude. I knew I could depend on her to make decisions for me when I could not think clearly. She will always have my deepest gratitude for her treatment of me as I became completely dependent on her. I know I did not deserve to have such wonderful, dedicated, considerate care because I could not have done that for someone else.

Stephanie is the love of my life. She is the love of my heart. She is the one who stuck by me when I was challenging to deal with and when I needed everything from her. She gave me what I was unable to gain for myself. She gave me her tender devotion and her true and honest unconditional love.

From where I am now, I cannot believe how thoughtless and self-centered I was for almost my whole life. I just did not understand what was important. I thought I was superior to most other people. I took all my good fortune for granted and did not bother to notice my shortcomings.

I thought I was God's gift to the female race, and I am sorry to say that I mistreated women by acting condescendingly and being overbearing. It did not occur to me to consider my impact on them when I was misbehaving. In my mind, I was more important than other people were.

Stephanie handled me better than anyone else did. She called me on some of my wrong actions, but she was still patient with me. I thought she was too demanding until I learned that she was far more loving and compassionate than I was. I learned the hard way, by becoming sick and dependent, how important it is to receive patient and compassionate treatment.

If she had treated me when I was sick the way I was used to treating others, I would have felt humiliated and worthless. If she had looked down on me or discounted my feelings, I would have shriveled up inside. Instead, she gave me something to look forward to every day – her smiling face, her tender care, her concern for my well-being. Toward the end, I felt helpless and unable to do anything for myself, but I felt like I was a better person because my heart was filled with love and gratitude. That felt good to me. I guess that was the payoff for going through cancer and dying.

I hope this does not sound morbid. I do not mean for it to sound morbid. I just want to express what I have come to understand so Stephanie can know what a profound and life-altering impact she has made on me. We had a great time together. I would go through getting sick again if we could start over with each other. I would pay any price to be with Stephanie again, live with her, take care of her, put my arms around her, and love her with all my heart.

Thanks, Kay, for writing this down for me. I cannot believe how lucky I am to be able to communicate with Stephanie and you. I know this takes a lot of time, but it is a miracle that you can do this for me. Well, Special Kay, this is the last time that I will be talking to you. Thank you again for giving this to Stephanie.

Don's messages were comforting to Stephanie. Theirs is a love story of great proportion and profound significance. Loving with all your heart brings out the best in us and is the greatest gift we can give anyone, especially those who confront severe health problems. Loving with all your heart brings the comfort of togetherness, which can strengthen the relationship and the will to overcome the obstacle at hand. I do not think Don would have lived as long as he did if he did not have Stephanie next to him, encouraging him, laughing with him, and loving him from the depths of her soul.

Aunt Mary

As I assembled material for this book, my husband's Aunt Mary delighted me with a visit. Aunt Mary had been deceased for a long time without my hearing from her. I adored Aunt Mary from the minute I met her. She came to our wedding, which is when my mother and I both fell in love with her. Aunt Mary was a college professor who was not afraid to speak up and give her opinions. She acted out of concern for all people. Aunt Mary was an absolute delight, and she was always up for having adventures.

After Aunt Mary retired from teaching at the University of Nebraska for thirty-five years, she set out to see the world. Afghanistan was one of her first stops. She was enthralled with the people of Afghanistan, and when invited to stay at the American Embassy, she declined. She much preferred to stay with the Afghan people so she could be close to them.

Even though she was in her seventies by then, she slept in a tent, had to boil the bananas before eating them, and loved every minute of it. When she returned from her trip, she captivated us with stories about the lovely people that she met while she was there. Aunt Mary had an ever-expanding heart that always had room in it for people of all cultures.

One year when I invited her to come to our house for Christmas, she happily declined our invitation. The Chinese government had just opened the Great Wall of China to foreign visitors, so she decided to spend the holidays in China. Aunt Mary had great respect for people she met from places all around the world. She felt privileged to become acquainted with as many of them as she could.

When I heard from my guidance that Aunt Mary would visit me from the afterlife, I eagerly looked forward to hearing what she would say.

Aunt Mary: Hi, Kay, this is Aunt Mary.

Kay: Aunt Mary, I did not expect this. I feel your energy, your glorious energy. You sparkle, Aunt Mary. Your energy is sparkling. You must have come from the very high dimensions.

Aunt Mary: I am enveloping you in my love. I feel great love for you as you do for me. We had a lot of fun together. I always looked forward to your visits with the children. I did not have children of my own until you and Mike brought the boys along. What beautiful people they both are today. You did an excellent job of raising them.

I have completed studying and teaching in the Earth environment. No one enjoyed teaching more than I did. What I learned early in my teaching career is the harder you try, the better you can do. I applied this to myself and worked to instill this principle in my students. Nearly everyone who gave his or her all managed to excel. I made learning fun and gave them a consistent appreciation for their notable accomplishments.

Kay: Aunt Mary, you had teaching in your blood, didn't you? When our boys were young, you used these same techniques on them, which made them try harder and be pleased with their accomplishments. Mark and Kirk loved you dearly. All four of us immensely enjoyed our visits with you. On our way to see you, we would talk about where you were going to take us. Mark and Kirk, and for that matter Mike and I, always wanted to go to the Natural History Museum to see the dinosaurs, and of course, to the ice cream shop that was near the university campus. You were a gracious and delightfully lively great aunt.

Aunt Mary: I am concerned about something now, and that is my reason for this visit. I no longer incarnate on Earth. I finished learning my lessons there a long time ago. Although I passed all the requirements to be exempt from having to return to refine my attitudes and behaviors, I returned repeatedly. I dearly love people, and I want to help however I can.

Do you realize how dangerous it is to live on Earth? There is so much discord and disrespect between people, and there seems to be a split.

Kay: Aunt Mary, what do you mean when you say a split?

Aunt Mary: I am referring to people's intentions. Most people want to live peaceful, enjoyable lives. Other people, mainly these are men, women do not do this as much, want to grab power and impose their will and their personal standards on other people. They act aggressively and with self-appointed righteousness.

The Earth is full of power grabbers. These people have low self-esteem and, to convince themselves that they are somebody, they push themselves forward until they get to the top. In the most extreme examples, wars result. Look at history for confirmation, particularly Hitler's actions, when he got into power and decided to use his authority to annihilate a whole class of people.

Over the years, the good people advance themselves in their perceptions and their behaviors. They are the ones who are making progress. There are other people, who just exist, and do not go out of their way to be better or worse than when they started. They do not advance civilization, but neither do they necessarily cause it to decline.

Then there are those who are a cause for concern. These people do not act in a civilized manner. In fact, these people undermine civilization. I call them the power grabbers. Their intentions are to promote themselves and their particular cause. Instead of acting responsibly and rationally while honoring the rights of all people, they mow down whoever stands in their way.

Such people should not have followers. No one should support their causes, physically or financially. Supporting people such as these puts the stain of collusion and responsibility for the harm done upon those who act against common decency.

All around the world, power abusers promote themselves and their causes, which are against humanity's safety and well-being. People, who encourage actions that are detrimental to segments of society or individual groups or persons, should be severed from any sort of sponsorship. On Earth, many people do not act with purity of intentions. Underlying most decisions that people make is self-consideration: how does this advance my own objectives?

Many people have the ability and determination to make decisions that advance the good of all. Promoting the good of all should take precedence over satisfying one's ego-need to become a big shot to wield power for financial self-gain or for any other reason, including overcoming feelings of weakness or inferiority. If people had pure intentions, better decisions would be forthcoming, and the world would thrive. People must act with logic, reason, and compassion instead of dominating to boost personal egos, which are not strong enough to work for the good of all.

Perception makes all the difference. Perceiving all people as equals regardless of bank accounts or other distinguishing possessions is the first step. If everyone got on the bandwagon of accepting all people, including themselves, as worthwhile, innately worthwhile, without having to prove anything to anyone, everyone on Earth would respect each other. That is all it takes, accepting the actual reality, which often does not exist in people's minds. Equality of all people is the divine standard that is missing on Earth.

Changes need to occur. There is not much time to continue with the distorted thinking and acting prevalent all over the Earth. Humanity needs to grow up, behave responsibly, and reap the rewards of safety and enjoyment of life for every person regardless of what country they live in or which religion they practice. Everyone has a heart and a brain. It is time for everyone to open their hearts, connect their hearts with their brains, and use their connected hearts and brains to create loving, caring societies worldwide.

Kay: Thank you, Aunt Mary; this is wonderful advice.

Aunt Mary: I would like you to share my comments with other people.

Kay: I will be happy to. Thank you for this education you have presented. I love you dearly, Aunt Mary, with all my heart.

Aunt Mary: Ditto.

As I thought about what Aunt Mary said, I felt that she pretty well summed up what is going on throughout the world today. It seems that power-grabbing people push mightily to get into power and then wield that power and position to control and dominate to their advantage without responsibly acting for the good of all. Those in positions of authority are responsible for acting constructively as a concerned father or mother would act toward all of their beloved children.

Most power-grabbers do not care about the harm they bring to other people. They are self-promoting and can be ruthless in their actions. When placed in positions of authority, even good-hearted people can become less ethical in favor of enjoying the high that comes with a powerful position. If individuals held no potential for gain from their leadership status, they would be more likely to act as positive forces for the common good. Positions of leadership are not intended to profit individuals. Leadership positions exist to create orderly, well-functioning societies and governments.

If dedication to serving all people's well-being were a hard and fast preliminary requirement for those in leadership positions, the world would not be as it too often is – destructive for specific segments who experience abuse or are discounted by those who have power over them. Those, who ascend to power and then abuse their power, undermine society. They impede other people's ability to live peaceful lives. Those that are in a position of power have an obligation to uplift and protect their entire constituency.

Scott Richards, M.D.

I was about thirty-three years old when Mike, I, and our two sons moved to the Houston area from Cleveland, Ohio. Life changed for us as Mike's company reassigned him to the home office of Jefferson Chemical Company. We loved living in Aurora, Ohio, with our many friends who enjoyed socializing as much as we did. We were sorry to leave our friends in Ohio but eager to move to a warmer climate.

Mike had already been scouting the Houston area for possible places for us to live, so by the time I could go to Houston to house shop, he had already picked out the area where he wanted to live. As soon as I saw Sugar Creek in Sugar Land in the southwest Houston area, I was in complete agreement. It was easy to understand why Mike wanted to live there. The builders arranged their new homes around the twenty-seven holes of the Sugar Creek Golf Course.

Mike loved golf and joined the country club before we signed the purchase agreement for our home. Mike had played golf in college, and in all honesty, he would rather play golf than do anything else. Mike quickly met fellow golfers from the country club, and he had his favorites. Among them was Dr. Scott Richards. Scott was one of the dearest men on Earth, and he loved the game of golf but did not have the natural ability that Mike had. Scott and his wife Mary were close to a generation older than we were, but that did not prevent us from becoming good friends who enjoyed many wonderful times together.

Many years later, our hearts broke when it became apparent that Scott had developed Alzheimer's disease. He still played golf for a while, but there came a time when he had to give this up. It was heartbreaking to know that Scott and Mary were bearing this burden.

After Scott passed from his physical body, he visited me. I suspect that some angels put him up to it. From out of the blue came the announcement that Scott Richards wanted to communicate with me.

Scott: Kay, can you actually hear me?

Kay: Yes, Scott. I hear you very clearly and nice and loud too, I might add.

Scott: Then I will be gosh darned.

Kay: You did not expect me to be able to hear you?

Scott: I just did not believe that this was possible. I did not recognize the two angels who asked me if I would be willing to talk to you down there on Earth.

Kay: It looks like you agreed. Scott, you always had a tender sweetness about you. You are one of the most caring people I have ever known.

Scott: I set out to respect and care for women in particular. That is why I became a gynecologist. In my practice, I made it a point to treat every female patient of mine as if she were royalty. Several royal families from the Middle East and other foreign countries brought their female relatives to me to care for them. Some of the daughters were already in this country attending college. Others flew in with their mothers to my Houston office for treatment. Kay, I remember telling you when you came in for your first appointment that I made it a point to treat every patient of mine as if she were the Queen of England who would give birth to the heir to the throne.

Kay: Yes, Scott, I do remember you saying that, and I was impressed. That strong statement explains what kind of doctor you were. I did not know you well when I came in for that first appointment, and I was nervous, but I remember feeling completely comfortable with having you as my doctor from that day on. Scott, many years have gone by since that day, and I can honestly say that you are certainly one of the most wonderful people I have ever met.

Scott: Do you know about my childhood?

Kay: I remember hearing that you peddled flowers on the streets of Houston when you were a child, even when you were only six or seven years old. You sold flowers on the streets because you and your mother were destitute. From what I heard, you were as poor as a person could be. Scott, you must have had a guardian angel looking after you.

Scott: You are so right, Kay. There was a Catholic school near where I sold flowers. The nuns took me into their school and gave me an education I would not have otherwise received. I was a good student, and I loved learning. That became my world. The thrill of learning gave meaning to my life and the experience of personal achievement. The nuns were supportive. They recognized that I had a good mind and was willing to work hard.

I went through college on scholarships. I never had any spending money, but I got the most out of my education. That was my ticket to being able to continue on to medical school. I always wanted to be well-dressed. I will never forget how great it felt to start earning money and be able to buy nice clothes.

Kay: Scott, yours is a rags-to-riches story. Look at what you went on to accomplish. The little boy who sold flowers to help support himself and his mother became a pioneer in women's health care in Houston. People recognized you for your sensitivity to women's needs and your creativity in pioneering less invasive surgical procedures.

Scott, on behalf of women everywhere, I thank you for caring so much about our well-being and feelings and for designing less invasive treatments. I did not want to go to you as my gynecologist at first. Since I knew you socially, I thought it would be uncomfortable. Your sensitivity and kindness calmed my anxiety and placed you on a very high pedestal as far as I was concerned.

Scott, there is something that has bothered me for a long time, and I would like to talk to you about this. I was heartbroken when I heard that you had Alzheimer's disease. You were one of the most loving and giving people on Earth, and it just did not seem right that you, of all people, would have to suffer from Alzheimer's disease. It does not seem like a just world when a person who has contributed mightily to other people's welfare has to go through such misery.

Scott: Thank you, Kay, for asking me this question. I am sure Mary wondered the same thing. My wonderful wife Mary was ever by my side, keeping me on the right track.

My work schedule put a great many demands on her, and she almost singlehanded raised our children because I was working all the time. We traveled a lot when we became friends with you and Mike, but our children were grown by then. When they were young, she did it all. In a way, it was almost as if she had another child in me. I was always so playful and loved to be with people and have a good time, but I was not around much when the kids were young. Those were the most demanding years of my practice.

Alzheimer's disease came on slowly, and I did not catch on for a while, but then there was no denying what was going on. Mary probably caught on before I did, but she did not say anything. We took every day as it came, and she took excellent care of me. Her nurses' instincts took over, and she cared for me as a precious patient. Faithful and loyal to the end. Mary was my rock even in our younger years when she kept our household running smoothly, was a great mother to our children, and saw to it that they got everything they needed. She also was our social director, and she kept me at the center of her focus.

As I slipped deeper into Alzheimer's disease, Mary did more and more for me. She was not easy on me. Mary made me perform whatever I could do, never pampering me. She met my needs while making me reach to do as much as I could for myself. How grateful I am that I married Mary. She directed the household and our social lives, and I had the better end of the deal except for when Alzheimer's set in.

Kay: Scott, I was broken-hearted when I heard that you had Alzheimer's disease. My heart ached for you and Mary, your children, and your grandchildren. I kept asking myself why such a tenderhearted person as you, who had lovingly helped so many people, deserved to suffer from the debilitation of Alzheimer's disease. It seemed so unjust.

Scott: I thought long and hard about the same thing when I received the diagnosis. I did not comprehend until I passed the boundary between life and death and faced the reality of my desire to remain alive, even when my time had come to go. In plain English, I did not want to leave my body and the good life I had been living. I could have abandoned my body swiftly had I not wanted to hang onto my life. My impulse was to remain as long as possible even though I knew what was coming.

Kay: One day, when I first started going to you as my gynecologist, I had an appointment for a check-up. While waiting in one of your offices, I overheard your conversation with a husband and wife in the next room. In a most gentle and considerate manner, you informed them that the wife had Alzheimer's disease. You were very sensitive and caring as you helped them to understand what she was going to need. You helped them face a grim reality with sensitivity and compassion.

Many years later, when I learned that you were diagnosed with Alzheimer's disease, I was deeply saddened. It did not seem fair that such a good person who had contributed mightily to the well-being of other people would have to suffer in such a way.

Scott: That is also what I thought when I was diagnosed. I was upset that I had that dreadful illness. I made it worse by delaying the inevitable.

Kay: What do you mean?

Scott: Had I been open to flying off to heaven, I would not have had to suffer from Alzheimer's disease. There are many ways to give up the body when one's life has been fulfilled. Mine certainly was, but I was not ready to give up my body. I fought against giving up my body.

Kay: Will you explain more?

Scott: When life has been good, one tends to want to hang on. No one likes to leave the party early. In addition, when one is afraid to die, they do their best to hang on as long as they can. People with Alzheimer's disease usually, but not always, fall into one of these two categories. Hanging on to what one knows and is comfortable for them is typical of successful people or frightened people. When it is time to cash in one's chips, many people do not want to leave the party.

People who hold on to life more lightly and are not afraid to move on to the afterlife rarely suffer from Alzheimer's disease. Honestly, I would recommend that people get used to the idea of dying way before it becomes apparent that their time to depart is upon them. There is no difference between being alive and miserable and leaving one's body as soon as the call goes out for that person's return to the afterlife, except for one's comfort and well-being. Those that hold onto life without a death grip and are ready to go whenever they are called to return will suffer less in the end.

A speedy exit beats a long-drawn-out time of great suffering usually accompanied by fear of what lies ahead. I did not fear what would lie ahead. I just did not want to leave. In retrospect, I wish I had allowed myself enough time to say goodbye to the life I had led along with the wonderful people with whom I enjoyed it and then made a speedy exit. That would have been better for me and for all those who loved me and took care of me, especially my wife.

Not wanting to let go creates a barrier to leaving and a barrier to continuing to lead a productive and happy life. A strong desire to remain alive at all costs is detrimental to the last period of one's life. It makes the extended life filled with misery for oneself and often for the loved ones who shoulder the burden of one's care.

I recommend that all people be willing to release from the life they are living at any given time when their time is up. Holding that thought in one's mind will give one permission to leave as soon as they receive the call to return. Each person is alive on Earth for a different reason. All have objectives to meet, and when those objectives have been satisfied, they may be free to return to the afterlife.

It is very liberating to take this step. No one should stay too long at a party. When it is over, it is over and time to leave. We give ourselves life objectives before we are born, and when we complete the job, it is time to go home.

Kay, the main reason people extend their lives is that they are afraid of what happens after they die. You would be amazed at the high percentage of people who think they only have one opportunity to be alive. That belief is the leading cause of people hanging on for dear life to a life that is no longer necessary for them to endure. People need to know that everyone has a great place to live after they pass from their physical body, and there is no reason to delay one's transfer there when their lives show definite signs of having reached their natural conclusion.

Had I understood this myself when I was alive, I would have bid all those dear to me a blessed goodbye. I would have declared my great love and affection for them. I would have celebrated our relationship and all the great times we shared, the fun we had, and our efforts to help others. I would have regarded my life as a treasure I was given, and then I would have been ready to say goodbye and tell God to come and get me. I would have released myself from wanting or needing anything in the physical world as I waited for my transportation to the afterlife. I would be ready and waiting for the angels to come and take me home.

Kay, I know that you are writing a book to help people understand more about life and death. I want you to include our communication. I want to participate with you in helping people to understand what is darn difficult to figure out when you are alive on Earth without having inside information.

To the readers of your book, I want to say that there is a lot more for you to experience than what you are experiencing now. Do not think for a minute that this life is the only one that you will have. We come and go. We live our lives. Then we pass out of our bodies to enjoy an even better existence. We go on doing something else until we go back to Earth or other places.

There are all kinds of possible next steps when we are planning what to do next. It is all about learning, learning to be better people, and proving that we can do it by living on Earth and demonstrating the goodness within ourselves. That sums it up. That is what life is all about for everyone.

Kay: Scott, I cannot thank you enough. What you said will help people understand what life is all about. Thank you for visiting me today. I want you to know that I will always hold you tenderly within my heart.

We should pay attention to Scott's words of advice. He clearly stated the reason for our being alive on Earth. If we take what Scott said about Alzheimer's disease to heart, we might be able to ensure that we avoid entanglement in years of suffering, which we could have avoided. I love how Scott put it, "When the party is over, it is time to go home!"

CHAPTER SIXTEEN

A SPIRITUAL EDUCATION

My sister Louise and I were born thirteen months apart. I was the first to arrive, and then came Louise. During our early years, we dressed alike, and every day we played with each other exclusively. Into adulthood, we kept our closeness. When I entered a room where Louise was, my heart instinctively reached out for hers, and hers reached out for mine. It always felt right when we were together.

When Louise was four years old, one of our relatives asked her what she wanted to be when she grew up. I looked on as four-year-old Louise, with her doll tucked under her arm, confidently responded, "I am going to be a nurse." She had a clear path to her heart's desire for how she wanted to spend her life, and she did not waver from this determination.

After graduating from high school, Louise enrolled in nurses training and became a registered nurse. Louise was a take-charge kind of person. Within Fort Logan Mental Hospital's adolescent units, she found her occupational home. Several years later, Louise married her sweetheart, Tom. Louise's joy was complete when she had two beautiful children, Ben and Emily, who she adored and always held dear to her heart.

Louise was in her fifties when doctors diagnosed Louise as having breast cancer. The first round of treatments appeared to be successful, and Louise resumed her active life. A few years later, the malignancy flared up again. She put up the best fight she could with solid resolve, but she could not beat it in the end. When she passed, our family was heartsick. Even though we knew by then that this was coming, our hearts felt a tremendous sense of loss.

Our entire family gathered to be with Louise the day she passed. By late morning most of the family was already there and, as we waited for the rest to arrive, we encircled her hospital bed and sang Louise's favorite songs and other family favorites. When our brother Steve started singing "The Bear Went Over the Mountain," some of us moaned, and Louise's heart monitor indicated that she did not like it either. After the last family members arrived, the doctor took our precious Louise off life support. That was about two o'clock in the afternoon.

That night about 10 P.M., I heard Louise's cheerful voice as I was getting ready for bed.

Louise: Hey, Toots.

Kay: What?

Louise: Kay-bug!

Kay: Louise!

Louise: I am free of that awful body. I am glad to give it up. Next time I am going to be choosier – no myriad of health problems. Next time I am going to be glamorous, but I am in no hurry to come back. Tomorrow I will tell you what happened. Tonight you must sleep. I just wanted you to know that I am fine, and I appreciate everyone coming to say goodbye. Tomorrow I will tell you what happened to me.

Early the following day, Louise continued our conversation. As soon as I entered the white light, I became aware of the many mistakes I made during my lifetime. I could see how frightened I was inside, how I took over telling others what to do because I did not think things would come out right unless they were done my way. Why is it so hard to understand what we are doing wrong when we are doing it?

Now I understand myself better, but I wish I would have understood when I was physically alive. I recommend a trip through the white light before we die, maybe about the age of 21 before we get into too much trouble.

After the experience in the white light, I was alone with both Jesus and Mary. They hugged me and kissed me. Jesus kissed me on the top of my head, and Mother Mary kissed me on my right cheek. It made me cry with happiness. They told me how much they loved me and let me see my whole life review. It was wonderful. I saw all the fun we had, the trips we took, the parties. I saw us as children with Mom and Dad. I saw all the love and attention that we got as children and how that formed our lives.

I saw all the nasty things I did, and it was wonderful. I sure had a good time even when I was nasty. I also saw all the beneficial things I did, how I helped people and how I did too much so I could take charge. I could see it all, my faults and my strengths. I love myself, all of me. I wish I could have done better, but I think I did pretty well. I was with people that I loved, and they loved me.

I was born into a joyful family who knew how to relax and have fun and who got a kick out of being with each other. My life quickened when I met Tom, and we had our children. My dreams came true with them. My life held mainly good times, which I appreciate. I suffered a lot towards the end, but the rest of my life was busy doing things, meeting people, stirring up a little trouble.

I want everyone to know that I realize I could have been easier to deal with at times. I am sorry if I created hurt feelings. I did not get the trip through the white light until after I died. I could have used it earlier. I want everyone to know how much I love each one, and this love feels even stronger now. I can see how lucky I am that I had all of you in my life.

Dying does not separate. It educates and refines. Now I am more aware and more accepting of myself. I am still connected to all my loved ones. My heart is directly connected to every loved one I left behind.

Will we see each other again? Just as Mom was there for me, we will both be there when each one of our family members pass. However, you may not recognize me. I am the young skinny one.

I was thrilled to receive Louise's message. It was such a relief to hear her being delightfully happy and upbeat. Never would I have expected to receive such a cheerful message from Louise the day after she died. Then the next day, she returned to continue describing what happened to her.

Louise: Hi, Kay. I have some more information for you. This experience has shown me how little I knew about what life is all about. I thought that heaven was far away and you had to do certain things to get there. What I found out was that we never really leave heaven to live our lives on Earth. We only think we do.

If I understood better, I would have realized that I did not have to prove anything to God. I came to Earth to prove to myself that I could handle a different set of circumstances. It is like flying blind to have the Earth experience. We are born, and we live our lives without knowing what the ground rules are. We satisfy ourselves, we do what we want, and we try to please God.

We do not understand that God is part of who we are, and we have our lives to bring this out into the open. It is challenging to realize this about ourselves and act in wholesome, godlike ways to overcome the shortcomings that keep us from recognizing ourselves as living parts of God. I certainly did not feel that God was inside of me, a part of me. I thought I had to follow the rules and go to church to be close to God. God is everywhere, in everyone. God looks human, but humans rarely look like God.

It is like flying blind. We do not really know what we are doing. That is what makes it so hard. We cannot see what we have inside of us. We cannot detect all of our innate goodness or recognize the opportunities we have to develop ourselves. We entangle ourselves in what irritates us, causes us displeasure, and leads us to strike back at others. We think that we are right even when we hurt others, or we push ourselves as having all the answers for other people's lives. There is a desperate need for some people to have things their way, influence others, and think they are right – to insist upon it and force others to follow their way. This need comes from insecurity, poor self-esteem, and not realizing that God is within.

As soon as I got into the light, I could see myself. I was no longer flying blind. I could see how critical I was, how I had to have things my way, and how weak and insecure I felt even though I came on strong. I did not know that God was not sitting in heaven far away and that God was within me. If I had been able to discern that, I would not have been insecure and so human.

I wanted you to know this and share this with those who will not be upset with my words. Once you step into the light, it is easy to be aware of the truth. What you cannot figure out while you are alive just comes to you. You finally know, and it feels good. It makes you happy and relaxed. There are no more fears, no anguish, no need to have things your way because God's way feels good. It is right. It is within you already, and now you know it.

Human beings are all parts of God, with no exceptions. God is alive upon the Earth in every person. Now I know this. Please do not grieve for me. I am fine. Please share your God-within freely. Do not stay in the dark as I was.

This message is the best I can do to give you the benefit of what I learned by stepping into the white light.

Kay: Thank you, Louise. I sure love you.

Louise: I love you too, Kay.

Louise returned several times over the years, and each time we had an enjoyable visit. We usually talked about family matters such as weddings, children being born, and what was happening to individual family members. Over time, the visits tapered off, and there were long periods when there was no contact. During 2014 however, Louise returned on two memorable occasions and gave me a delightful surprise. She came to tell me about two experiences she had that relate to the topic of religion.

Louise: Hi, Kay-bug. I asked permission to come and talk to you again.

Kay: This is great, Louise! How are you?

Louise: I have had a ball since I got here. You would not believe how spectacularly beautiful everything is. All of our senses are heightened. The sounds that we hear and the sights that we see are heavenly. By this, I mean that every view is spectacularly magnificent, and the sounds are different from what you hear on Earth. The sounds are melodies. The birds chirp, and it sounds like a bird symphony – so sweet and beautiful. I stop whatever else I am doing and become delighted and enthralled by their sounds.

Earth is beautiful, but wait until you get here. Everything is sparkling with luminescence, so flowers radiate light. Even rocks radiate light. We look like we radiate light too. To some extent, we all do, but certain people radiate a lot of light. Luminescent light reflects everywhere, and the different planets have the same thing too. We have millions of planets. I do not know how many. Some are relatively close to where we are, and we travel to them at will. It is easy to get there. First, you have to know where you are going. Then you direct your will to be there. At least, that is how it works where I am.

Some people live on certain other planets that we cannot access. We would not do well there. Those planets remain reserved for elevated beings, people from Earth, and other locations who have advanced themselves by developing outstanding spiritual traits within themselves. Those planets exist in much higher vibrational frequencies, which the people where I am could not tolerate. To be comfortable, we need to be where we are. Although the vibrational frequencies where I am are much higher than on Earth, they are not nearly at the high end of the range.

Only people who managed to elevate their frequencies to an exceptionally high level when they were on Earth can keep raising their vibrations when they get here. It is more natural for them to keep elevating their vibrations, whereas almost all of us where I am, stay at the level that is the least elevated of all the higher dimensions. It is comfortable for us to be here but not at the higher levels.

Kay: Louise, who do you know that stays in those higher dimensions? Do you have any examples?

Louise: I can identify many people that leave the higher dimensional planets to come here. These people have a recognizable glow around them. As we walk around where I am, most people either do not have a glow or are just beginning to get one. I do not have one yet, but Mom does. She had one as soon as she got here.

Famous people of different religions on Earth have expansive glows. Mother Theresa glows brightly. I see her sometimes, and she does not stay at the place where I am now. She visits here and returns to more elevated dimensional levels when she leaves. I do not really know where her home base is. Jesus is here a lot. He likes to welcome new arrivals, and it means a lot to all of us when he welcomes us individually.

I hope you do not think that only Catholic religious figures are here because I mentioned Jesus and Mother Theresa. That would be a mistake. Buddha visits. I have seen him many times. Gurus from India greet their followers when they arrive up here. I do not know for sure, but it seems that they welcome every one of their followers because I see them in the receiving area more often than I see any other religion's personages. There are holy people from the Islamic faith and Chinese holy people, and others who look like they represent all the world's religions.

There is no arguing between them. All of the holy people have the expanded halo kind of glow around them, verifying their spiritual advancement. I would not expect to reside where they do. They are more accomplished than the rest of us, who are based where I am.

Kay: Louise, thank you. I find this very interesting. What about God. Have you seen God or know anything about what He is like?

Louise: That is what I wanted to know when I got here. I asked many people who did not know the answer, which was confusing because I expected to see God in heaven. I am obviously in heaven. It is so much nicer here than on Earth. You would not believe how much better, but God does not seem to be here. I have not seen any evidence of God. I have asked other people too if they have seen God, and so far, no one has seen Him themselves. I do have a friend up here, though, that says he knows about God.

Kay: Tell me, what does he say?

Louise: He explained that God is different from what we might expect. He said that God is what we see in the radiant glow that emanates from people that carry a very high vibration within them, like the religious personages I mentioned. They have God within them. They have God's presence working through them. He said that God is not one person, but God is within every person, even those of us that do not have a glow. He said that the more godlike we become, the more we will build our radiant glow.

He went on to say that these glows do not happen because of what we believe to be true. The glows come from all the good we do when we are physically alive. The glow indicates that we are allowing God to work through us. Instead of thinking about what we want for ourselves, we think primarily of what we can do to help other people.

My friend says he knows this because the historical figure Abraham explained this to him. My friend was Jewish when he was alive, and when he got here, he asked everyone where Abraham was because he wanted to talk to him. I guess my friend asked someone who had contacts because after a while, Abraham sought him out, and they had a series of visits. Abraham explained many things. Do you want to hear about it?

Kay: I sure do, Louise. Please continue.

Louise: Abraham told my friend that almost everyone on Earth thinks that God is separate and apart from him or her, so they go looking for God, wanting to be special in God's eyes. They follow religions hoping that this will gain God's favor and that God will notice them and let them go to heaven. Then when they get here, it is so lovely that obviously, they have arrived in heaven. However, it is confusing because everyone else is here too, even people from different religions or no religion. Moreover, not only that, but they cannot find God.

If they were to stop and ask any of the saints or founders of the world's religions where God is, they would receive the same answer. God is within you and every other person as well. No one is without God. No one can be without God. God gives life to all people and animals, trees, flowers, and in fact, to all of creation. Creation does not exist without God. Therefore, the answer to where God is, is that God is throughout the planets and universes and within you and me. All of us, all of this is part of God. Does this make sense to you? This is what Abraham told my friend.

Kay: What did your friend say?

Louise: My friend told Abraham that now everything finally made sense to him and thanked him for his explanation. Abraham said that he would continue to explain more after my friend had the opportunity to think over what he learned. My friend was delighted when he told me about this, and he invited me to be there for Abraham's return visit. I saw him myself. What a wise man and so non-assuming. You should have seen the radiant glow around him as he talked to us. He became more and more radiant, it seemed, with every question we asked.

I wanted to know why we could not tell that we had God within us, why we could not feel this for ourselves. Abraham said that we do, but we do not think that is what we are feeling. He said that God is radiating through us when we feel pure love in our hearts, but the love has to be pure, selfless love. Not many people know how to do this yet, evidently, because Abraham said that a large number of people are not able to love selflessly, compassionately, and generously, even to the people they know and like, for instance, their family members. Abraham said that this is the best place to start for most people because it is unusual for people on Earth to love everyone. People usually reserve their affection for those with whom they share a respectful connection.

Then, I asked if it was even possible for us to love people we did not like or those who hurt us. After that, he asked me a question, "You were raised Catholic, were you not? What better role model could you have than Jesus? If he could do it, so can you. The same potential is within you to manifest pure, divine love, which is God's presence."

Then my friend asked Abraham why God was not a person, as we learned to believe. Abraham answered by saying something surprising after what we had just heard. He said that God has a human-like presence. God thinks, feels emotions, and is active. He does not appear as a distinct individual because He is comprised of all of His creation. Even so, He relates to all of us individually. Abraham said that God is knowable to us personally, and He wants to make His presence known, but it is up to each of us to go to him and make His acquaintance.

So then I asked, "How are we supposed to do this when we do not know how to contact Him?" To this, Abraham replied, "Aha, now you are asking the most important question of all. God is hidden within your heart. It is up to you to make his personal acquaintance. He will talk to you if you keep telling him that you know He is there with you. You have to earn his attention. You have to reach out to Him every day for months or years, and with a pure, innocent heart and mind, and invite him to have a personal relationship with you. Do not give up. He does not reveal His presence to curiosity seekers.

"This is all you need to do. Eventually, your love and persistence will pay off, and you will begin to feel His presence tingling within you. God's vibration is so high that not many people can detect it, but as you go searching for Him within yourself, your vibration will rise until you begin to feel His presence. Try it. It works.

"Everyone on Earth can feel God's presence inside of themselves but not if they are dishonest or hurtful. If people want to feel God's presence, they have to behave like God. They need to act out of love and consideration for all people. God's presence expands in those people who work for the good of all humanity with a pure heart. This is the best way to become close to God and know him individually."

Kay, my head was reeling after he said this. Why did we not learn this as children? Everybody needs to know this.

Kay: Louise, I agree with you, but we cannot teach what we do not know. I am wondering how we were supposed to know. How were we supposed to learn what other people did not know?

Louise: My friend asked Abraham the same question. He answered that God sent many messengers to teach his children, but the people disregarded the messengers, or after their deaths, other people polluted the original teachings. He said that on Earth, there is a focus on personal advancement and some people felt entitled to twist the pure initial teachings to suit their objectives – their personal objectives that had nothing to do with what God's true messengers taught.

Abraham said that it is difficult to act for the good of all without taking personal advantage of the situations that arise on Earth. He said that people needlessly create conflict on Earth and point the finger of blame at the other party to shield themselves from disclosure that they were truly responsible. He said that there are too many shenanigans on Earth, which cloud people's perceptions and create needless conflict. Abraham also said that is why people have to live lifetime after lifetime until they finally perceive that it is only acceptable to live a life of high integrity. That is what we need to do to remain in heaven and not have to keep going back for another incarnation.

Kay: Louise, you sure hit the jackpot when your friend told you about Abraham and invited you to meet him.

Louise: I am going to change myself when I am born again on Earth. I am forming my to-do list based on what Abraham said. I wish I had received his wisdom when I was growing up last time. I do not know, though. I had a hard head, and I liked to stir up trouble. Mom used to tell me that I had to learn things the hard way. I do not like admitting it, but she was right. Nevertheless, I am going to do my best to change my old ways.

I have been afraid to go back and live another lifetime because I can see myself making the same mistakes. I will prepare myself ahead of time now that I know the point of living on Earth. I am going to find God's presence within me and become His best friend.

After a few weeks went by, Louise returned to pay me another visit.

Louise: Hi, Kay, I am back.

Kay: Louise, how wonderful. This is a treat for me.

Louise: I am so excited. I want to tell you what happened.

Kay: Tell me. This sounds like it is going to be very interesting.

Louise: Do you remember my friend that I told you about? The one who took me to visit Abraham?

Kay: Yes. Go on.

Louise: I was visiting with him after our last conversation, and he told me that I could probably talk to whomever I wanted, even if the person was someone very important.

Kay: Like Abraham?

Louise: Yes. That is to whom he was referring. He said that if I did what he did – just keep asking how to find whomever I wanted to speak with – that it might work out for me as it did for him with Abraham.

Kay: So, did you follow his suggestion?

Louise: I took a while to decide whom I really wanted to contact and what I would ask. I kept coming back to the idea of meeting with the Big Three all at once.

Kay: Who are the Big Three?

Louise: Muhammed, Jesus, and Krishna.

Kay: Louise, I am speechless. How did you ever think of trying to contact all three of them? Did it work?

Louise: I told my friend about my plan, and he thought it was a great idea. He encouraged me and mentioned to Abraham what I wanted to do. Abraham laughed when he heard about my idea, but without telling my friend and me what he was up to, convinced all three of them to meet with me. Do you want to know what they said?

Kay: I sure do. Tell me.

Louise: The three of them are very friendly toward each other. They get along great and laugh a lot. They were very curious why I wanted to meet all three of them at the same time.

Kay: What was your answer?

Louise: I wanted to know which religion is the best one.

Kay: Hmm. What did they say?

Louise: They said that they were trying to educate their followers to learn what they had discovered for themselves. They emphasized that each of them had pure, loving hearts, but many of the people they taught had difficulty understanding the tenets they were presenting. Some understood but only partly, while some misinterpreted the teachings. Others forgot them as soon as they departed from their presence. People also adjusted what they said to blend in with their personal points of view.

There were no newspapers back then to distribute their direct teachings, word for word. Over time, people who did not come into direct contact with these spiritual leaders came to accept, as fact, tenets that had been distorted. Confusion occurred even though there were devoted followers who did their best to remember the original teachings. Over time, what people came to accept was a mix of authentic teachings and misrepresentations.

They also said that the purpose of religions is to turn people's lives into worthwhile experiences. Religions tell people that there is more to being alive than satisfying their ability to get whatever they can for themselves. Religions introduce the concept of God as the Creator. Religions also teach the need to do things right, follow the rules, and strive to be pleasing to God.

These uplifting concepts came through all of the world's great religions in their pure form, and many people have applied them beneficially within their lives. Numerous distortions led to conflicts that turned some religious groups against others. Human behavior, especially the need to feel superior and to dominate, splintered the original teachings, which came from Divine Loving Intelligence working through those few people, with the capacity to internalize the Loving Intelligence within themselves, and the capability of teaching those who were willing to learn. Those willing to learn went on to teach others. Generation after generation, the teachings were disseminated throughout different areas of the world during different times.

Some who hold to the proper form of the original teachings are still at work today on Earth. These people uphold the highest principles of being kind, loving, working for the good of all, and knowing deep within their hearts that God created humanity in His image. Others hold to distorted, self-serving versions of the original teachings and use these to provoke conflict. They stand behind the concept of God to justify their dishonorable actions when their primary purpose is to gain control and dominate for personal power. This occurs regularly. The pure intentions of religion are obfuscated by evil actions, which disregard people's well-being. Self-gain is the primary undermining factor that has sullied the inherent purity of some of the world's religions.

Kay: Wow. Louise, they said all that?

Louise: They all agreed.

Kay: Did they say anything else?

Louise: They talked about how discouraging it is to watch what happens on Earth when people use the concept of God, which only a few truly understand, to justify hurtful behavior towards other people.

Kay: Anything else?

Louise: They said that the hurtful ones will feel repulsed and contrite when they get up here where we are. That was their last statement. They thanked me for asking them such an interesting question before they left.

Kay: Louise, whatever gave you the idea to ask that question?

Louise: Up here, we know what is happening on Earth. It is sickening how many people target and even kill other people, and sometimes it has to do with religious differences. Up here, everyone gets along and does not care what other people's religions were when they were alive. It does not matter.

Kay: Louise, thank you for telling me about this visit. I love receiving inside information from elevated sources. Being in the higher dimensions sure provides a clearer perspective.

When Louise came to revisit me, she topped off her prior visits with two of the most beneficial communications I have received. These messages answered, simply and understandably, questions that I had in my mind for years. There is a need for this kind of explicit instruction to enlighten us all.

CHAPTER SEVENTEEN
MY FATHER'S EDUCATION

I do not know which symbol best personifies my father - a rosary or a bottle of Jack Daniels. Dad built up a persona of someone who loved nothing better than a shot of "Jack," and to hear him talk you would think that he drank a lot. He would allow himself only one shot of Jack Daniels, which he truly relished, but at family parties, he spoke as if he could not put the bottle down. He entertained the family with his ongoing shtick about his Jack Daniels. Despite his antics, dad was a moderate person. He did not over imbibe either food or alcohol; however, candy and ice cream were different. In many ways, Dad was a big kid who liked to have a good time, but he was also a mighty prayer warrior.

Dad's favorite spot in the house was his recliner. He liked to station himself there and pray for people. Dad sat in his recliner half the day, praying because the list of people he prayed for was very long. Dad prayed for everyone that he knew who needed divine intervention. He was on the job to help them. It could be sick people, those who died, or even those who had a house to sell or a job to find. The sick people remained on Dad's prayer list until they recovered, and if by chance they died, they retained their spot on Dad's list. As a result, dad had an ever-expanding prayer list. Helping people by praying for them was Dad's primary dedication in life during his later years.

One day I happened to sit in Dad's recliner, which turned out to be a delightful experience for me. That recliner was humming with divine energy. All of Dad's prayers had created a blessed feeling in and around his recliner. My body was tingling all over, and I was thrilled to recognize that I was sensing the same high vibrations that I feel when the angels and I communicate. How lovely, I thought, that Dad was creating heaven on Earth in his living room through his prayers.

Dad passed at age ninety-three after years of what I would refer to as service to humanity. He was profoundly religious and strong in his faith, but about two years before he died, he started referring to the fiery chasm. The fiery chasm is something he remembered hearing a clergyman talk about when he was in first grade. Dad remembered the clergyman say that if you were not a good person after you died, you would not be able to cross the fiery chasm to get to heaven.

I think Dad may have been evaluating his life at that point and severely focusing on some past behaviors that he regretted. He must have been harshly judging himself, or this reference to a fiery chasm would not have popped back into his mind with as much impact as it had. My siblings and I were incredulous. Dad was compassionately praying for people many hours each day, and he was worrying that he might not qualify to get into heaven!

The night before Dad died, as his attendant was preparing him for bed, the attendant said, "Have a good night's sleep, Steve." Dad answered, "Oh, I will because the Angel of Mercy is with me." Dad gently passed early the following morning.

On May 16, 2012, a few days after Dad passed, a voice talking to me woke me up. It was precisely 6 AM, which was fitting because Dad always was an early riser. I had been hoping that Dad would come back to communicate with me. I was sound asleep when I became aware of the sound of his voice. At first, I was not sure who it was because I was still half-asleep.

Dad's voice: I love you. I love you. I love you.

Kay: Who is this?

Dad: Your father. My life now is different than I thought it would be. Sorry to wake you up, Kay.

Kay: That is all right, Dad. How is it different?

Dad: It is like another world. I feel like I live in a better place, but it is full of people.

Kay: What do you mean it is full of people?

Dad: It is like where you are. People are coming and going doing all kinds of interesting things. I thought it would be different, that people would be praising God, and angels and saints would be everywhere.

When I left my body, I could not believe what it looked like without me in it. I heard you repeatedly saying, "I am so happy for you, Dad." I was still there. Your deceased mother was right there holding my hand when I left my body. She looked beautiful, radiant, and very happy. I was bewildered. I was standing next to my body, looking at it. Dea explained that I was so used to my body being part of me that I instinctively wanted to stay with it.

I had all kinds of feelings about my body – mainly wonder when I thought about how I looked when I was a child playing with my sister, and how my body looked lying there in the nursing home bed, and all that happened to me in my life. Dea held my hand, and we left together after I said my goodbyes to those who came to view my body. You were the most excited for me.

I got scared even though Dea told me that everything was going to be wonderful. I could not stop thinking about all my sins. There is a lot I have not told you about, Kay, and I do not want to say to you. I lived through some rough experiences. Times were tough, and I felt entitled to express myself without caring what I did to other people.

I did not learn to behave as well as I should have from my parents. My mother was confusing; she loved us but acted disturbingly. She had a way of humiliating my brother and me. We both grew up angry and took our anger out on others. I am sorry for what I did that hurt other people. Mother Mary helped me understand that I was not entirely to blame, that my attitude would have been exemplary had my mother been sensitive and kind to my brother and me. That made me feel better. Before she said that, I did not think that I deserved to live in heaven. Mother Mary helped me to understand why I did what I did and to forgive myself.

Kay: Have you seen your parents?

Dad: Yes, for a short time. They look wonderful. You would never recognize them. So young. So happy. You become washed clean of past offenses by understanding and accepting responsibility for what you did that caused harm to other people. There are refinement lessons for those that need them. I was told that a series of teachers would help me better understand myself, as I was and as I have the capacity to be next time.

I love being here. It is not what I expected, but I am very comfortable and joyously happy. I thought people would be living in a church-like place, spending their time going to Mass with angels and saints. However, it is different. People are doing all kinds of things and going places – very active – lots to do and see. I feel like I have been here before. There is such familiarity.

There is no time here. You do not have to sleep or eat, but you do not get tired or hungry. So, I am going to explore other worlds. Earth is not the only one. Other places are nothing like where I am now. I am still getting used to being here. I could stay here forever.

I have been with my brother. It is fun to know him in heaven. We are both different without living in the confines of our life experiences. Here we are unlimited. We are expanding our perceptions and understandings. There is so much available to us now. We both feel like we are better people than we were before we arrived. It is easy to be a good person when you are in heaven.

Kay: You have not said how your body feels.

Dad: It feels exactly like I was hoping it would. My body feels light and airy, and I feel better than I ever did before I arrived. You could not hurt yourself even if you tried. I am a spirit now, but I feel like I did before.

Kay: What do you mean?

Dad: I feel like I am in a physical body, although it is not physical. The sensations are similar. My body feels like it did before I was 20 years old. Nothing hurts or is sore. I can do everything I did then and even more. My body feels like it did when I was 20 years old. For example, I would like to play baseball now. I could hit that ball a mile.

Kay: So, you do not need a walker in heaven?

Dad: I had such a strong identification with my physical body but not anymore. I do not even need to walk. I can navigate to where I want to go by thinking. Over here, thoughts create whatever you are thinking about. I have my own navigation system in my mind. I can find anyone by thinking about him or her.

The days and weeks before I died, I did not talk about what I was experiencing. I could feel your mother and Louise close to me. I knew they were with me. I knew it, and I did not. It was as if a deeper part of me knew, but consciously I did not. Only as death came real close was I consciously aware. The few days before I died, I was consciously aware that they were with me all the time. They were not the only ones. Different angels would come too. They would talk to me and tell me how happy I was going to be.

I wanted to go with them the first time an angel appeared, but I also did not want to leave. I was afraid that I would not be acceptable. I hung on as long as I could, but I spent more time with them each day, and it felt so wonderful. I wanted to sleep all the time so I could be with Dea, Louise, and the different angels.

When the Angel of Mercy came and told me I would receive forgiveness, I decided to let go of being in my body. Then I was not afraid anymore. I did not have to cling to being in my body, so I relaxed and released my spirit.

Oh, glorious relief! I could not believe the instantaneous rush of health, wellness, strength, intelligence, and the feeling of lightness. Your mother and Louise were smiling at me. They held my hands and squeezed them, and I felt their love pouring into me. I knew then that nothing could get me back into my body, that I was safe from it. Then I started looking at it lying there, not moving anymore and I felt compelled to stay with it. I knew that some of you would be coming because I heard the conversation about notifying the family. I was curious about how they would react.

Louise left, and Dea promised to stay as long as I felt I needed her. So, we were both there looking at my body and talking about our lives together. That was a special experience for the two of us.

When I arrived in heaven, I was told that deceased family and friends had gathered to greet me, but I could not face them until I confessed my sins. Mother Mary was kind. She listened as I unloaded. I told her all my regrettable actions – mistakes that I made out of ignorance and lack of consideration for those I hurt. I was hard on myself. I had to be. I did not want to receive something that I did not deserve.

She helped me feel better about myself. Then I could go to the celebration. All my old friends looked like kids again. Then I noticed that I did too. I had been concentrating so hard on my sins that I overlooked how much I had changed. I felt like a kid again. We were all laughing and saying how good it is to be here, how lucky we are and how we would never leave. Even some of the Chicago gangsters are here. I recognize them. They do not look any different from anybody else.

Kay: What do you mean?

Dad: Everybody here is happy, calm, and certainly non-violent. They fit right in.

The next thing I want to tell you about is the options I have been given. I could choose to return to Earth to continue being with our family. I am still considering this possibility, but right now, I am inclined to stay put. Why would I want to leave when I just got here?

The next option is to study with a friend of yours, Archangel Zadkiel. He offered to take me as one of his trainees. He has a beginner group, and that is where I belong. Other options include traveling or taking classes. They offer courses in anything you can imagine. I could study mathematics, medicine, or music, for example. I could travel to other regions that provide spectacular beauty different from where I am now. There are endless possibilities, and I am just learning about some of them.

I do not have to decide until I am comfortable making the decision. I do not think I will delay, though. I feel myself wanting to be with Archangel Zadkiel. He is brilliant, gentle, and endlessly patient. I could not choose another option until I study with him.

When I got to the point of not being able to take care of myself, I realized how much it means for someone to help another with kindness and sensitivity. It means so much when someone helps you and is sensitive to how you feel. When you are old and cannot take care of yourself, it is a hopeless feeling. Little by little, I gave up everything I had. What hurt the most was leaving St. Elizabeth's Assisted Living. I think I would have lived longer if I had stayed there. When I left, I decided that I did not care to continue the struggle. It was too much effort.

Looking back, I realize what a gift it was to become so debilitated. Had I not gone through what I did, I would have missed the biggest lesson of my life. What I finally learned is what it means to love someone truly. Loving is giving with respect and tenderness, and it has to do with being there for someone in the way that they need you to be there for them. How many times I said, "I love you," when I did not really know what it meant. Now I know.

There are other lessons. A big one for me is to balance work and family and not to think that I am more important than my wife and children. My parents were not good role models. At least my children had an excellent role model in their mother. Dea modeled to me what it means to be a supportive spouse. She was kind and encouraging to all of you children and me. Unfortunately, I did not pay enough attention to her because my single-minded focus was on my job and what I felt that I needed to do.

Life lessons are tough to swallow when they interfere with your plans. It is easier to keep doing what you want to do while ignoring what you are supposed to be doing. I know that the way I was did not make for good, healthy relationships with my children when they were young. Fortunately, all of my children overlooked my negligence and included me in their lives. For this, I reaped rewards that I honestly did not deserve.

Everyone is entitled to be in this beautiful place after dying, but we all must take full responsibility for what we did during our lifetimes. My life review was fascinating; I saw my actions, my motivations, and my self-deceptions. Boy, was I inaccurate. I had applauded what turned out to be defects in my behavior. I did not hold myself accountable for anything I did wrong until I was an old man. Then I was harsh with myself, but I did not even think about most of my shortcomings. I was blind before I lost my vision. I sure did not see myself accurately. I would have brutalized myself even more than I did if I had seen the whole picture.

I do not mean to keep talking about what I did wrong. It just came as such a surprise to me. I do not know who will read these notes you are taking. Still, if I could say one thing to them, it would be this: look deeper into what effect your behavior has on others and do not feel justified by your position, authority, or beliefs to impose unkind or unsympathetic behavior upon anyone. That is my message, and it is worth considering as the highest priority in everyone's life.

Kay: Thank you, Dad.

Dad: There is another subject if you have time.

Kay: Sure do.

Dad: Our family is truly remarkable because the strong bond of love within our family stretches and bends however it needs to for the bond of love to remain unbroken. With such a big family and some with powerful personalities, the bond of love has to have a lot of stretch in it sometimes. Our family's commitment to getting along with each other, making allowances for others' preferences, and treasuring every family member is solid. This commitment gives me joy, happiness, and a sense of accomplishment if I contributed.

I heard from Dad frequently right after he died but less often as time went by. I experienced this same pattern with my mother, Dea, and my sister, Louise. When I received these messages, I was truly present with each of them again. What a thrill it was to connect with my dear deceased family members and hear about their experiences!

When Dad first arrived in the higher dimensions, he told me that he would stay there for as long as he could, and there was no hurry to return. Then early in 2014, he announced that he was getting ready to come back for another incarnation. I was stunned to hear him say this. So, I recorded the rest of this conversation.

Kay: Seems so soon to come back.

Dad: I have a lot to learn. I am not afraid. I just hope I do better this time. I've had enough of being hardheaded, strong-willed, and thinking I was right when I was not.

We still had occasional conversations until May of 2014, when Dad came to me for the last time.

Dad: I will not be able to come to you again. I am starting to fade.

Kay: What do you mean?

Dad: I feel the pull to be with my new mother and my dad-to-be. I like him a lot, and he is very nice to my mother. She treats him well too. I am glad to see that.

Kay: So your attention is staying focused on them.

Dad: Yes and no. It is just that I feel compelled to stay with them even though I still want to do other things.

Kay: Dad, it sounds to me that you are forming a strong attachment with them.

Dad: I am happy with who my new parents are. I think my parents will treat me more gently this time. I am hoping to learn better behavior from the time I start. That is the best benefit a child can receive, along with being loved and given candy and ice cream.

Kay: Dad, you are too cute!

Dad: I mean it. Candy and ice cream are an essential part of childhood. Okay, Kay-bug, this might be our last time to talk like this. I will come back to visit you if I can, but it will not be long before I am wetting my pants and crying for ice cream. Of course, they will think I am just hungry, but I will be trying to tell them that I want ice cream.

I wish you could hold me as a baby and tell me to remember what I learned when I was in heaven. I am afraid I will forget.

As Dad started to speak again, his words became faint and inaudible. Then they stopped. That was my last message from my father, who taught me things about the afterlife that I would not have learned from any other source.

Did you notice that the person headed back for another go-round on Earth knows who their parents will be? There does not seem to be randomness involved but deliberate planning. In Dad's case and other instances when I communicated with people who were about to be reborn, I found the same pattern. There is an acclimation period, during which the person returning for their next lifetime shadows their parents-to-be.

In one instance, a very precious and loving person I had known before she died told me that she had been observing the husband and wife who would be her new parents. She, too, was very pleased with who her parents were going to be. She spoke with me a few days before she slipped into the infant body that her parents had produced, and then she appeared as their newborn baby. I want to tell you the best part of this story. Before this beautiful child was reborn, archangels surrounded her. They continuously stayed with her as she was preparing to be reborn because they loved her so much.

Sometimes newborn babies are returnees, rejoining the families they left behind when they died. These turnarounds are not unusual. When there are close ties of a beneficial nature, there is the possibility that a deceased person will be reborn into the same family that mourned their passing not long before. We might be surprised if we knew the number of people who discard their worn-out bodies and turn right around and are reborn. Each of us will have the opportunity to decide when we are ready to tackle another lifetime. No one has to come back until they are ready, and some folks do not want to delay.

Sometimes when relationships are especially warm and loving, two or possibly more people reincarnate close to the same time as each other so they can be together again. I am aware of two deceased siblings who coordinated to come back as sister and brother into a warm, loving family. I would expect that Anton and Marni will be together again, sharing another lifetime. As we saw in Chapter 9, he is deceased, and she is still going strong here on Earth and not ready to leave yet. However, the bond of love between them is so powerful that I would not be surprised if they chose to share another lifetime.

Now that I have a clearer picture of what goes on behind the scenes when people leave the elevated dimensions to come back for another lifetime, I have even more questions in my mind. None of the people who told me about preparing to be reborn said anything about being in the womb. However, they did say that they went back and forth between what they were typically engaged in doing within the higher dimensions and drawing close to their parents-to-be in the physical world, observing them as they prepared for the baby's arrival. This period of going back and forth is when they seemed to be bonding with their new parents. Only when birth was near did I lose contact with those who were returning to be reborn.

This observation brings up the question of when an individual's physical life begins. Is it at the point of conception or when the baby takes its first breath? I have memories of being born. I remember traveling through the birth canal, landing at the base of the canal, and calling back to those I left behind "I made it. I am okay." I remember being placed in my mother's arms for the first time and being enveloped in the power of her love for me. However, I do not have any remembrance of developing as a fetus.

There is a point when physical life ends, and that is when a person has taken their last breath. There is a moment when the physical life begins, and that is when the baby takes its first breath. This does not imply that the child and the parent's relationship is nonexistent until the child is born. On the contrary, the child is far more aware of the parent's feelings and desires than the parents could be of the incoming child's. This is an important point to bring up.

When a child is born, he or she already knows if they are wanted. They know how their parents feel about having them, and they are psychologically marred when they are an unwanted child. Any child brought into our physical world deserves two but requires at least one parent who loves them deeply and is devoted to their well-being.

Some newly deceased people refer to being transported into the elevated realms by traveling through the tunnel of light. Angels ministering to the newly deceased person tuck him or her into what appears to be a person-sized spacecraft, which seems to move at incredible speeds. The deceased person has the experience of zooming through space at warp speed wrapped in a cocoon of effervescent light, peace, and joy.

Afterward, the person assumes that they were transported to a different region of creation and are puzzled when the same angels who initiated this journey-like event greet them. The travelers mistakenly perceive that they covered a vast expanse of distance almost instantaneously, making it impossible for those angels who initiated their transfer to have already arrived at their destination before they did. Delightfully, for many people, the first sight they see when they arrive in the elevated realms is the smiling faces of their helper angels who arranged for them to have the tunnel of light experience.

By undergoing the experience of traveling through the tunnel of light, newly deceased people become acclimated to the greatly heightened vibrational rates within the elevated spheres of existence. This procedure delivers enhanced frequencies to those who would not be able to adapt to the vibrations of the elevated spheres without assistance. Those newly deceased people who naturally carry high vibrations within them do not require this step. For most of us, when we depart from the earthly plane, we still carry the lower Earth vibrations within our spirit bodies even when we have been living exemplary lives. Only those who have maintained deep spiritual connectivity to the Earth, or people upon the Earth, or their concept of a benign all-encompassing God will instantaneously ascend into the heavenly spheres without requiring assistance.

The difference between here, where we are, and the elevated realms of existence is a difference in vibrational frequency. We live in the third dimension, characterized by low vibrational activity such as conflicts, hoarding, and dishonesty. After dying, many people are incapable of transferring directly from the lower vibrational atmosphere, where they have been living, into the high vibrational upper realms without some form of assistance. In these instances, angelic beings step in to assist the newly deceased. They utilize the tunnel of light, which is a tool that adapts the newcomer's energetic vibrational frequency to the elevated levels, which are required to have consciousness within the higher spheres of existence.

Changing your energetic vibrational frequency may be less challenging to understand if you are familiar with meditating. When in deep meditation, one loses consciousness of one's body and has the experience of floating upward into increasingly more refined vibrational levels. The person who is experiencing deep meditation is somewhat like a person undergoing the effects of the tunnel of light.

The meditating person instills within them self the ability to traverse the range of vibrational frequencies that deceased people travel when they experience being in the tunnel of light. The main difference between deep meditation and the experience of going through the tunnel of light is that the traveler in the tunnel of light no longer has a physical body. They go up even higher into the elevated spheres. In contrast, the person engaged in deep mediation will come back into full-body consciousness and continue living upon our lower vibrational planet Earth.

All existence is vibrational in nature, from the low vibrations of the In-between that entrap people who do not have a clear direction of where to go after they die, up to the most elevated dimensions where the great world servers such as Buddha, Krishna, Jesus and Muhammed reside. Each of us is on our way to becoming qualified to ascend to the highest spheres after we die and remain there as a permanent resident. It may not look like it, but every one of us has the potential to become a permanent resident of the most elevated spheres of existence.

CHAPTER EIGHTEEN

IN CONCLUSION

Now is the best time to sift through your beliefs regarding what happens after a person dies. Whatever comes next will be a function of one's convictions. You are most likely to create that which you anticipate. If you believe in a continuance of life in a higher dimension of existence and reach for it, you will be setting yourself up for the best outcome after dying. If you dismiss the existence of a desirable afterlife or decide that you would not qualify to be included if there is one, you will be shutting a door that needs to remain open. If you do not put up roadblocks, you will create an ideal experience for yourself after passing from your physical body.

The golden moment of opportunity exists right after a person dies when their escort, consisting of already departed loved ones or angelic beings, is there to assist them. This extraordinary assistance is automatic for everyone. Keep this in mind, and I suggest that you practice a preparation drill.

Picture yourself in various death scenarios, and be sure to include those, which would jolt you the most. For example, imagine finding yourself separated from your physical body because of a fatal car accident, which you did not see coming. You were driving along. Everything was normal. Then in a split second, you experience floating above the scene, looking down at your lifeless body.

If this happens to you, keep yourself from falling into a frantic state of mind, and scan the area around you. Specifically, be looking for angelic assistance and do not hesitate to call out to angelic beings while expecting an immediate response. The urgent command, "Angels, help me!" is highly effective. The main point is to take your mind off whatever caused you to separate from your physical body and turn your attention to your most beneficial next step.

Remain calm and alert. Notice what is going on around you. When you are relaxed and alert, you are far more likely to perceive your best path forward. In every case, your best path going forward is available to you; however, you must completely disconnect from the past. If you want to make forward progress, look ahead and not behind.

When this initial opportunity to connect with angelic support is not actualized, deceased people slip into the dream-like state of the In-between and begin to lead a confused existence. They do not know where they are or how they got there. They do not know what to do next. For many people, this is their disturbing new reality. However, even when this happens, they do not have to remain there. The In-between is not a permanent residence.

Angels have brought a vast number of people to me from the In-between when the people could not detect the presence of the angels, who delivered them to where I was. Because of this, we know that these helper angels have the ability to maneuver and assist those deceased people who have not sunk too far down and are still able to respond to the angels' influence. Therefore, do not underestimate the value of praying for deceased family members and friends. Praying for departed loved ones may be all that one needs to do to bring them to the attention of angels, who can then devise ways of helping them.

I learned this lesson first hand when my friend Ray cornered me before church one Sunday morning and insisted that I read a specific book he had in his truck. He would not take no for an answer, so after the service, I reluctantly followed him out to the parking lot to retrieve his book, which I did not want to read. Just as Ray handed me the book, a small newspaper clipping Ray had tucked inside fell to the ground.

I bent down to pick it up and, as I touched the newspaper clipping, I became engulfed in a heavenly beam of light. The angels that I work with sent me a clear signal. They put me on notice that there was a job for us to do. When I handed the clipping back to Ray, I asked him what it was. He looked lovingly at the picture on the newspaper clipping and said that this was his nephew's obituary. Ray explained that his nephew died a year earlier, and since then, Ray had kept his nephew's obituary in that book.

This clipping explained why Ray insisted that I read his book. It had nothing to do with the book itself. Ray must have been divinely inspired to deliver that obituary into my hands. I eagerly accepted Ray's book with the obituary tucked back inside and went directly home. As I began to call on my angels, I glanced at his nephew's picture. The photo could have been the boy's high school graduation picture. It was chilling to see this smiling, cheerful-looking teenager and know that he died a year ago. No mention of the cause of his death was in the accompanying article.

As you might suspect, the angels I work with had no difficulty locating Ray's nephew and taking him up into the heavens. At that time, I did not tell many people about my collaboration with angels, and I hesitated to reveal this to Ray. Since most people do not believe that what I do is possible, I risk being considered delusional and then shunned, which has happened to me in the past.

I weighed what was going through my mind against the importance of Ray having the peace of mind that would come to him by knowing that his nephew was in a good place. Then, I got my courage up and dialed his phone number. When Ray answered, I joyfully reported that although his nephew died the previous year, it was on Saint Patrick's Day of the current year that his nephew went into the higher dimensions. Ray was greatly relieved and delighted with this news.

To me, it was evident that Ray's insistence that I read his book, which happened to contain the obituary of his nephew, was an angelic maneuver, and so was the obituary flying out and landing on the ground right by my feet. Ray loved his nephew dearly, and knowing Ray, I am sure he prayed for his nephew frequently. Ray put his nephew on the angelic radar screens that all of us can access. Praying for deceased loved ones and those you may not even know personally has the potential to connect them with loving angelic assistance.

Each of us can develop a relationship with the many angels who are available to interact with us. You might be surprised at how easily this can occur. It all begins when you hold this intention within your heart and mind and then follow specific instructions. However, there is a caveat for you to follow. If you go into this exercise with anything other than a pure heart and an open mind, you are unlikely to meet with success.

Before going to sleep at night, get comfortable and be sure to quiet your mind. Do not think about anything bothersome or the random things that happened during the day. Instead, remain peaceful and only think how nice it would be to feel that angels are with you. Then completely clear your thoughts and within your mind direct the following message to the angelic realm: "Angels, may I feel your presence?" Then utilize your sensing ability to detect the light tingling sensation that indicates the angels' presence.

Sometimes their response is immediate, and sometimes it is somewhat delayed. If these instructions do not work the first time, you may have to take another pass at quieting your mind. Unfortunately, adults do not typically carry the naturally high vibrations of innocent young children. Our minds become troubled with life's responsibilities and problems. It is challenging for us to contact angelic beings when we are mentally unsettled, so the first step, quieting your mind, is most important. After letting go of the lingering thoughts of the day, relax your body and gently direct your focus solely upon reaching the angelic realm.

Remember to remain relaxed and receptive and do not think, "I'll bet this will not work for me." Keep going through this same exercise every night until you get the payoff. You will find no more pleasant way to fall asleep than sensing the presence of one or more angels. The comfort and gentle exhilaration you feel are likely to give you the best night's rest you have had for a long time.

Communicating with angels before going to sleep at night and receiving the payoff of their gentle presence will put you on their radar screens. If you would like to deepen your relationship with them, I recommend the following technique. After clearing your mind and becoming peaceful inside, initiate slow deep breathing with the intention of raising your vibration.

When doing this, it helps to take deep breaths inhaling through your nose and then slowly exhaling through your mouth. While maintaining this breathing pattern, as you inhale, pull your mind upward and mentally repeat, "I raise my vibration. I raise my vibration" time after time. For me, my head in particular, but my whole body as well, fills with a delightful light, effervescent sensation. When you feel that sensation, you are ready to communicate with angelic beings. Use mental telepathy to connect with them. Be certain that you do not direct your transmission into space without a destination.

When you communicate with angelic beings, hold the intention of sending your mental transmission directly to them. Remember that angels like to send their energetic patterns as a greeting, so stay relaxed and have your sensors alert to detect their signature greeting. Each of the angels has a particular energetic pattern, but all have the effect of creating a warm, loving sensation within your body. You will make many angels dance with delight when you directly reach out to them and then detect their energetic presence responding to you.

The angelic kingdom and our world are interspersed. Angels are here to help us, but we do not utilize their presence as we could when we are unaware of their availability. In most of our minds, if we picture angels at all, we imagine them as being far away from us. However, they are reachable, and the more adept we become at connecting with them, the more they will respond to us and contribute when we need them.

I suggest that we practice communicating with angelic beings now, establishing a spot on their radar screens for ourselves. Then, when we call out to them in our time of need, they will perceive our communication and assist us. Do not think that you need to wait until you die to get to know angels personally.

Every one of us can make ourselves available to work cooperatively with the angelic realm. Having a loving heart and being willing to pitch in when needed gives the angels a contact they can utilize in the physical world. Angels receive many pleas for assistance, and often they need physical hands to manifest the contributions they are maneuvering to deliver to people in need. I have a real-life example of this type of angelic partnership to share with you.

During a certain period in my life, I attended a bible study class at a charismatic church in Houston. One particular day when our small group was meeting, we received a notification that a homeless couple who had been living in a truck had come to the church that morning seeking assistance. The wife was pregnant and was due to deliver her baby in two weeks. The office staff was trying to find them housing, and they asked our study group to provide some supplies for the baby.

There were six or seven of us attending that class, and we each contributed some money. Then, the question came up about who would do the shopping for the baby. Simultaneously, four of those in attendance turned and looked directly at me and said, "Kay, you do it." I was shocked because I am not much of a shopper, and I had my children many years before and did not know where to begin. The situation was desperate because the family's need was great, and we only had thirty-seven dollars with which to work.

Reluctantly, I agreed to do the shopping, and off I went in a cold sweat to see what I could accomplish. I was not comfortable taking this assignment, and with such a great need and with so little money, I hardly knew where to begin. When I got to a store in my neighborhood, I went to the section that displayed diapers. I thought that would be a good place to start, but I stood there confused about which ones to buy when I noticed a young mother in the same area. I told her about the woman who was about to deliver her baby without having any of the necessities and asked her opinion on which diapers to buy.

This young mother was truly wonderful. After she gave me a few diaper recommendations, she invited me to come to her home, which was about a half of a mile away, to see what she could give to the homeless parents-to-be. It turned out that this kind woman's youngest child just moved out of the baby bed because he had outgrown it. So, she offered the baby bed, a stroller, a high chair, bundles of baby clothes, and toys.

I was stunned and in a state of utter joy. Was this a coincidence? I do not think it was. As I see it, the angelic kingdom must have been conspiring with my fellow bible study students to get me to do the shopping for the new baby. Then the angels maneuvered the generous-spirited young mother to the diaper department exactly when I got there and probably set up the whole interchange between the two of us. To me, this was a magical moment in time when I was part of an angelic effort to aid the desperate parents-to-be.

When you are openhearted and willing to assist other people, you put yourself on the angelic radar screens, and then angels can figure out how to put you to work. It requires flexibility on your part to accept what they put in front of you, which may not make sense to you at the time. It takes trust, faith, and a willingness to step forward to aid another, especially when you feel inadequate. The more sure you are that you are not acting from an ego motivation but a genuine selfless desire to help, the more likely the angelic kingdom will recruit you to be their partner.

Angels would like to reach out to all of us, so do not put up a hindrance such as believing that you are too old or too sophisticated to relate with them. Children indeed have a natural closeness with angels because children are innocents. Angels are most attracted to those with pure intentions and helping hands. Keep this in mind. Like any friendship, the more you nurture it, the stronger it becomes. It is wonderful to develop a long-term working relationship with angels. They always appreciate helping hands in the physical world to advance their ability to assist people.

By establishing a commitment to do whatever I could to help humanity and not defining what this could look like, I was open to going in my particular direction. As a result, collaborating with angels has become a central part of my life. I am thankful that I did not close the door of opportunity when it opened to me. Without a doubt, if we manage to keep an open mind and are willing to interact with angels, our lives will expand in ways we may never have envisioned.

Our willingness to help others opens doors that usually remain closed. When these doors open, there can be interplay between people on Earth and those blessed beings who navigate without a physical body in their efforts to elevate conditions upon Earth. We can keep this door tightly sealed within ourselves by being unwilling to accept the existence of angels or by believing that they are not accessible to us. However, we can swing this door wide open by setting aside the barriers that prohibit open-mindedness and mask our innate inner knowing that there is more to our existence than what we can physically detect or than science can explain.

An ongoing concern of mine is people who kill themselves. After separating from their bodies, many regret their decision and become distressed that there is no way for them to reverse the events. They remain confined in their spirit bodies, not knowing what to do next, often staying close to their loved ones who are still alive. In their grief, their relatives and friends rarely detect the presence of the person who killed themself.

Loved ones take the brunt of enormous psychological damage caused by the person who committed suicide. Yet, if they are willing, their loved ones can give the person who committed suicide a tremendous gift. Although it will take a determined act of selfless love, there is a critically important role for those closest to the deceased person to play during the time immediately following the suicide.

Although one's heart may feel shattered by the action of the loved one who committed suicide, and one feels angry, abandoned, and disregarded by them, those closest to the deceased have an opportunity to give them a precious going away gift. This gift takes tremendous emotional control. Despite a broken heart, those that the deceased are most likely to be staying close to, such as immediate family members, can verbally talk to the deceased person extending them forgiveness, comfort, and direction. I do not suggest employing mental telepathy. Those who committed suicide are usually at such a low vibrational level, before and shortly after they died, that they would not perceive your mental communications, so you need to speak aloud.

The deceased person in these instances needs to hear three things from those who are dearest to them. They need to hear that you still love them and that you forgive them. They also need to hear that they have a better place to be than remaining among those who are still alive. Set them free to travel on to the higher dimensions by explaining that there are divine companions present to assist them and, if they relax and focus on seeing them, their escort will come into view.

I recommend that you raise your frequency before beginning to perform this act of service. If you elevate your frequency, you may be able to detect your deceased loved one's presence near you. I also suggest that you go through this act of deep caring numerous times to raise your chance of having the deceased person be within range to detect your contact. Many deceased people attend their funerals, so that would be an ideal time to reach out to them.

I realize that following these instructions will be heart-wrenching for the loved one who is desperately trying to understand what made the person who committed suicide take this action. However, with an aching heart and yet a firm resolve to control one's grief and anger, the loved one can give the person who committed suicide this most precious last gift – directions on how to find their way into the elevated realms. In addition, by extending love and forgiveness, the loved one's burden lightens, and they have the satisfaction that they selflessly served their dear friend or relative this one last time.

Even though you are probably well-prepared by now, I still would like to emphasize that in *all instances,* the proper path to take after dying is to immediately connect with your escort and ascend with them into the higher dimensions. You must release even those you felt responsible for when you were alive. No longer can you care for them but be consoled that you will not be turning your back on them either. You will be able to check on them after you have established the heavenly vibrations within yourself.

With these higher vibrations seated within, you can travel back and forth between the higher dimensions and Earth. People within the heavenly realms often talk about checking on their loved ones who are still alive, so we know that loving connections endure. People who have transferred to the higher dimensions still hold their loved ones within their hearts.

Sometimes a family member or close friend may detect the presence of a deceased loved one who did not successfully transfer into the heavens. When this occurs, it may have unintended negative repercussions, as in the following instance. Immediately after I relayed to my friend Ray that his nephew ascended into the heavens on St. Patrick's Day, he told me that he knew of a person who was in a terrible predicament since her son died. Ray said that her son had been in the military when he lost his life, and since his funeral, she and her teenage daughter had been noticing telltale signs that his spirit was in the house with them. Ray wanted to give her my phone number, and I agreed.

She called me within ten minutes and told me the rest of the story. After the military funeral, she and her daughter started to detect her son's presence within their house. They would often catch fleeting glimpses of her son when they looked into their full-length mirror in the bedroom. They were both deeply unsettled by what was going on.

The mother started crying as she told me the most chilling part of the story. Since they began to see her son's spirit reflected in the mirror, her daughter began to talk about committing suicide. Her daughter felt compelled to be with her brother and talked openly about going where he was to be with him. This mother's heart was convulsing with fear. Losing her son and her daughter would be unbearable for her. I told the mother I would check on her son immediately and then call her back.

When my angels found her deceased son and brought him to me, he confirmed that he had been trying to attract their attention. He said that he did not want to frighten them and that he just wanted to be reassuring. He was upset that his sister was thinking about killing herself, and he desperately wanted to talk to her. The angels waited as he told me what he wanted to say. I recorded his words to relay to his sister.

In his message, he told her that she was not supposed to die and he did not need her to be there with him. He said that it was too soon for her to be where he was, and she had many things to do before she finished living her life. Then he described how happy he is to be going with the angels.

After he departed with his angelic escort, I called his mother on the phone. She cried when I told her what happened. I read her the message that her son dictated for his sister, and the mother was very relieved. When I saw Ray at church the following week, I asked him if he knew how the family was doing. He happily reported that things seemed to be okay now. The daughter had stopped talking about committing suicide, and neither the mother nor the daughter had seen or felt the young man's presence with them again.

This story holds a warning about the newly deceased trying to make contact with grieving loved ones. They are rarely successful and, as in this instance, instead of having a comforting effect, another tragedy nearly resulted. When the deceased remain attached to their loved ones, they are limited to observing as their loved ones live their physical lives without providing any benefit to them.

From their intention to watch over and aid their still-living loved ones, an ever-increasing problem arises for the deceased person. With their strong focus on those they left behind, they miss perceiving the angels who come to retrieve them. The deceased obscure their angelic connections by remaining solely focused on people who remain physically alive.

There is an appropriate time to return to Earth to visit loved ones. However, the right time only occurs after the deceased person has settled into the higher realms and learned the ropes. With the heavenly vibrations seated into them when they arrived in the higher dimensions, they are free to come and go and then have the ability to check on those who were closest to them when they were alive. Sometimes the deceased fashion signals of their presence to delight and reassure a loved one with whom they were very close.

After my sister, Louise, died and about two weeks had gone by, the toaster in my kitchen started to pop up at random times. I would stare at the toaster and mentally ask, Louise, is that you? I received no reply until one day, right after the toaster again popped up, I heard Louise laughing. She teasingly declared, "I am just showing you that I am here!"

After my mother died, the ceiling fan in my father's living room began to turn on by itself in the evening, usually around 8:30. When this happened, he would smile, feeling reassured that his wife, Dea, had returned to say hello to him. There must be many treasured after-death reassurances, which come in very imaginative forms to console grieving loved ones.

Another time I attended the funeral of a friend of mine. Cynthia had two children, a son and a daughter. During the reception held at her home following the service, Cynthia talked through me to her college-age son. She told him how proud she was of him and gave him many endearing statements of encouragement. He was spellbound and glowed as I delivered her words to him. I thought he would think I was crazy for saying these personal things to him, but he took in every word from his mother that came through my mouth as if she were standing in front of him instead of me. It appeared that he needed to hear precisely what she was saying to him.

Afterward, I thought about how Cynthia must have regretted not saying these things to her son when she was still alive. The urgency with which she took over my ability to communicate verbally indicated that she was desperate to tell her son how she truly felt about him. Cynthia was not a demonstrative person, and after she died, she most likely regretted that she was not a lovingly expressive mother. I suggest that you express the love that is truly in your heart to those closest to you, even if this may be difficult for you to do.

Another instance of a deceased person attending her own funeral happened during my mother's funeral. Several weeks after my mother's funeral, my father quietly divulged that he saw Mom during her funeral service, and she looked like she did when she was about twenty years old. She sat at the end of her casket, facing the people in the church with her legs crossed, kicking her feet up like a young girl. He said that she looked very interested to see who had come to her funeral service and that she remained there the whole time. These instances are gifts given to dear ones to ease their sorrow.

I owe a big thank you to my many angelic partners. Together we have enjoyed the thrill of finding displaced deceased people and assisting them to their proper destination. Sometimes this has been hard work, as when the clearing of the In-between was taking place or when the people that we were trying to help attacked me.

I have endured many assaults from deceased people who were of evil intent. Having violence thrust upon oneself from disembodied beings is an awful feeling. Even though I contacted my angelic protectors to come to my rescue, I suffered hours, nights, and sometimes days of agonizing torment at the hands of vicious deceased entities who were hell-bent on causing me as much harm as they could.

I do not recommend that anyone attempt to try their hand at moving discarnate entities into the higher dimensions. Certain deceased people are not ordinary people. There is evilness that lies within certain deceased people residing in the In-between. Although this evilness usually ignores regular people, it would be foolhardy to do anything to attract their attention.

Examples of evil deceased people interfering in living people's lives appear in Chapter Seven. Evil deceased people who do not transition into the higher levels after passing from their physical body can delight in causing a severely adverse effect in the lives of vulnerable people on Earth. Do not leave yourself open to entanglements with those treacherous beings.

I would like everyone to know that multitudes of angels are on the job to assist us in our time of need and support our evolutionary progress. Part of humanity's progress is to realize that we have powers inherent within us that we typically do not access, such as the ability to detect the presence of angelic beings. So, reach for the angels, determined to become close to them. Angels are here to help all of us, and they do not choose only certain ones to receive the benefit of their attention. Unequivocally, the angels support humanity and reach out to those with good intentions to develop personal relationships and aid them.

We have isolated ourselves from angelic companionship by not allowing ourselves to entertain the possibility that they are available and willing to interact with us. A new world of delight awaits us when we raise our vibrations and invite angelic beings to visit us. It is a glorious experience to detect their effervescent tingling presence within us. If you are looking for a new best friend, I suggest that you use your innate ability to become acquainted with any one of the wondrously supportive angelic beings.

Angels are a class of creation that models noble behavior. They are available to assist anyone in need without judgment or desire for personal enrichment. They do not judge or condemn or shy away from anyone that needs their support. When we evolve ourselves to an advanced enough level that we no longer have to return here to Earth to refine our behavior, we will be much as they are. We will be expressing the same noble attributes that they display.

I consider all of us as angels in the making. As of now, we may not feel like an angel or act like an angel, but we all can become as they are. To accomplish this, we must instill the desire to act selflessly, watching over and protecting those we share our lives with, those we know, and those we do not know personally. We can be as loving and helpful as heavenly angels are even though we are still angels-in-training.

Our deceased teachers give us the formula for an ideal existence when describing the heavens where they now reside. We might want to ask ourselves where we would be more satisfied to be, here on Earth as it is now, or here on Earth if it were more like the heavens are described. We can modify our attitudes and behaviors here on Earth to match how we will be when we are vacationing between lives in the divine atmosphere of the elevated dimensions. We can create heaven on Earth for all of us.

If you value what you learned, please submit a review at Goodreads.com

DIVINE RESOURCES FOR ALL

The best way to live is to keep in mind what you are here to accomplish. Go beyond the typical aspirations. Think about the last day of your life and where you are going afterward. Also, consider how you will feel about the choices and decisions that molded your life. *What It Is Like to Die and What Comes After* has prepared you to move into the higher dimensions after your death, no matter the circumstances. This book's companion, *God Talks to All of Us,* enlightens you on how to live your best life.

To discover more about available resources on how to evolve, now and after death, visit **DivineResourcesForAll.com**.

SHARE YOUR THOUGHTS AND HELP OTHERS DISCOVER THE INSIGHTS IN THIS BOOK

If you gained value and enjoyed *What It Is Like to Die and What Comes After*, we would love you to pop online and leave a review on Amazon or Goodreads. Reviews help other people find and enjoy independent books.

For Amazon in the USA:
1. Scan the QR code to go straight to the review page for *What It Is Like to Die and What Comes After*

2. Enter your star rating and review
   Note: Amazon requires you to spend at least $50 per year to be able to leave a review

For Amazon in other countries:
1. Search *"What It Is Like to Die and What Comes After"* in the search bar
2. Click on the book page
3. Scroll down to where it says Customer Reviews
4. Click on Write a Customer Review
   Note: You'll need to be logged in to your Amazon account

For Goodreads:

1. Scan the QR code below or search *"What It Is Like to Die and What Comes After"* in the search bar
2. Click on the book page that comes up under the search bar
3. Click on the box under the cover image and change to Read
4. A pop-up box will appear for you to leave a review
5. Once you've typed in your review and left a star rating, click save.

Kay would love to hear how this book has impacted you. To share your story, please do get in touch via DivineResourcesForAll.com.

God Talks to All of Us is a powerful narrative direct from God clarifying why you are alive on Earth. This book empowers you to work towards the betterment of yourself and the protection of our planet.

This book is presented by Kay Mielenz, author of *What It Is Like to Die and What Comes After*.

Kay Mielenz developed an urgent desire to understand the significance of life. To her, it did not make sense if life had no purpose other than experiencing one's youth, middle age, old age, and then dying. One day, while meditating, she experienced a powerful presence blanketing her with extraordinarily high vibrations. Then she heard God speaking to her for the first time. His divine voice said, "I am Creator God, and I am going to dictate My communication to humanity for you to record and distribute. I want to speak to all of My children so they will understand My true nature."

This booklet contains selected excerpts from *God Talks to All of Us* to support your daily endeavor to evolve your attitudes and behaviors. Keep in mind that even with a firm desire to advance your personal traits, your path will bring both successes and failures. Be patient with yourself and remain dedicated. Enjoy your feelings of well-being as they multiply.

You can find these books on Amazon, from DivineResourcesForAll.com and in all good bookstores.

Made in the USA
Columbia, SC
31 October 2021